SOURCES OF NATIONAL INSTITUTIONAL COMPETITIVENESS

Sources of National Institutional Competitiveness

Sensemaking in Institutional Change

Edited by
SUSANA BORRÁS
and
LEONARD SEABROOKE

OXFORD
UNIVERSITY PRESS

OXFORD
UNIVERSITY PRESS

Great Clarendon Street, Oxford, OX2 6DP,
United Kingdom

Oxford University Press is a department of the University of Oxford.
It furthers the University's objective of excellence in research, scholarship,
and education by publishing worldwide. Oxford is a registered trade mark of
Oxford University Press in the UK and in certain other countries

First Edition published in 2015
Impression: 2

Published in the United States of America by Oxford University Press
198 Madison Avenue, New York, NY 10016, United States of America

British Library Cataloguing in Publication Data
Data available

Library of Congress Control Number: 2014941214

ISBN 978-0-19-967874-7

Printed and Bound by
CPI Group (UK) Ltd, Croydon, CR0 4YY

Acknowledgments

The Sources of National Institutional Competitiveness project, known to all involved as SONIC, emerged as a collective expression of the type of research being conducted at the International Center for Business and Politics (now the Department of Business and Politics) at the Copenhagen Business School (CBS). The aim of the project, generously supported by CBS's World Class Research Environments scheme for 2008–14, was to advance new research that crossed over between comparative political economy, institutional theory, and organizational sociology. This aim reflects the strengths of scholars in the center, who frequently combined insights from these fields. Led by Ove Pedersen and Peer Hull Kristensen, the SONIC project began to explain new terrain, investigating comparative cases in different areas of regulation and business.

Over the years of the project SONIC team members discussed a common theoretical stance at length, seeking one that would permit cross-fertilization across scholarly fields, as well as provoking all involved to reflect on their case material. The discovery that sensemaking processes were common across all the cases investigated was, in itself, a clear case of sensemaking at work. Drawing on work in organization studies and institutional theory, Susana Borrás and Len Seabrooke refined a sensemaking framework for SONIC and the team discussed abstraction and replication, and retrospective and prospective cases of sensemaking as identified in their research. Our thanks go to the SONIC team and to Vivien Schmidt for their input in the project over the years. Our gratitude also goes to the research assistants who worked on SONIC, especially Adam Baden and Rune Riisbjerg Thomsen, for their excellent work. Thanks also to the early career scholars who attended the SONIC YOUTH conference in late 2013, where the next generation of scholarship fusing organization studies, institutional theory, and comparative political economy is emerging. Last but not least, our special thanks go to David Musson, Clare Kennedy, and those at Oxford University Press for their encouragement of this project and their patience in awaiting its delivery.

Susana Borrás and Leonard Seabrooke

Frederiksberg, Denmark

Acknowledgements

Contents

List of Figures and Tables

FIGURES

TABLES

List of Figures and Tables

FIGURES

List of Abbreviations

ACAS	Advisory Conciliation and Arbitration Service
AE	Arbejderbevægelsens Erhvervsråd
ANVAR	Agence nationale de valorisation de la recherche
BDPME	Banque du développement des petites et moyennes entreprises
CBO	Congressional Budget Office
CEA	President's Council of Economic Advisers
CIFRE	Conventions industrielles de formation par la recherche
CME	Coordinated Market Economy
CNC	Computer Numerical Control
CNRS	Centre national de la recherche scientifique
CRITT	Centres régionaux d'innovation et de transfert de technologique
CRS	Congressional Research Service
DA	Dansk Arbejdsgiverforening
DEG	Digital Era Governance
DI	Dansk Industri
DØR	Danish Economic Council
EBISS	Effective Behavioral and Instructional Support Systems
EPL	Employment protection legislation
ERAC	(formerly CREST) European Research Area Committee
EU	European Union
GAO	Government Accountability Office
GDP	Gross domestic product
GTS	Godkendte Teknologiske Serviceinstitutter
HQ	Headquarters
HR	Human resources
ICT	Information and communication technologies
IPR	Intellectual property rights
KBE	Knowledge-based economy
LME	Liberal Market Economy
LO	Landsorganisationen Danmark
NEC	National Economic Council

List of Abbreviations

NPG	New public governance
NPM	New public management
OECD	Organisation for Economic Co-operation and Development
OMB	Office of Management and Budget
OMC	Open method of coordination
PRES	Pôles de recherché et d'enseignement supérieur
PVM	Public value management
SME	Small and medium-sized enterprises
SNRI	Stratégie nationale de recherche et d'innovation
SSP	Social systems of production
UN	United Nations
VoC	Varieties of Capitalism

List of Contributors

SUSANA BORRÁS is Professor in Governance and Innovation and the Head of the Department of Business and Politics at the CBS. Her other books include *The Innovation Policy of the European Union* (2003), *Innovation Policies in Europe and the US* (2003, co-editor with Peter Biegelbauer), *Cluster Policies in Europe* (2008, with Dimitrios Tsagdis), and *The Politics of the Lisbon Agenda* (2012, co-editor with Claudio Radaelli).

LEONARD SEABROOKE is Professor in International Political Economy and Economic Sociology in the Department of Business and Politics at the CBS. His other publications include *US Power in International Finance* (2001), *The Social Sources of Financial Power* (2006), *Global Standards of Market Civilization* (2006, co-editor with Brett Bowden), *Everyday Politics of the World Economy* (2007, co-editor with John M. Hobson), and *The Politics of Housing Booms and Busts* (2009, co-editor with Herman Schwartz).

SØREN KAJ ANDERSEN is the Director of the Research Centre for Labour Market and Organisation Studies (FAOS) at the University of Copenhagen. He is an expert on comparative studies of labour market regulation and has published in the *European Journal of Industrial Relations,* among many others.

ROBERT BOYER is an economist at the Centre for Economic Research and its Applications (CEPREMAP), the Director of Research at the National Centre for Scientific Research (CNRS), and Professor at the School of Advanced Studies in Social Sciences (EHESS). His works in English include *The Regulation School* (1990), *States Against Markets* (1996, co-editor with Daniel Drache), *Contemporary Capitalism* (1997, co-editor with J. Rogers Hollingsworth), *The Productive Models* (2002, with Michel Freyssenet), *Japanese Capitalism in Crisis* (2000, co-editor with Toshio Yamada), *Regulation Theory* (2005, co-editor with Yves Saillard), and *Diversity and Transformations of Asian Capitalisms* (2011, co-editor with Hiroyasu Uemura and Akinori Isogai).

JOHN L. CAMPBELL is Class of 1925 Professor in the Department of Sociology at Dartmouth College. He is also Professor of Political Economy in the Department of Business and Politics at the CBS. His works include *Collapse of an Industry* (1988), *Governance of the American Economy* (1991, with Leon Lindberg and Rogers Hollingsworth), *Legacies of Change* (1997, with Ove K. Pedersen), *The Rise of Neoliberalism and Institutional Analysis* (2001, co-editor with Ove K. Pedersen), *Institutional Change and Globalization* (2004), *National Identity*

List of Contributors

and the Varieties of Capitalism (2006, co-editor with John A. Hall and Ove K. Pedersen), *Oxford Handbook in Comparative Institutional Analysis* (2010, co-editor with Glenn Morgan, Ove K. Pedersen, and Richard Whitley), and *The National Origins of Policy Ideas* (2014, with Ove K. Pedersen).

CARSTEN GREVE is Professor of Public Management and Public Governance in the Department of Business and Politics at the CBS. His works include *The Challenge of Public-Private Partnerships* (2005, co-editor with Graeme Hodge), *International Handbook on Public-Private Partnerships* (2010, co-editor with Graeme Hodge and Anthony Boardman), *Reformanalyse* (2012), and *Rethinking Public-Private Partnerships* (2013, co-editor with Graeme Hodge).

PEER HULL KRISTENSEN is Professor of the Sociology of the Firm and Work Organization in the Department for Business and Politics at the CBS. His works include *The Changing European Firm* (1995, with Richard Whitley), *Governance at Work* (1997), *The Multinational Corporation* (2001, co-editor with Glenn Morgan and Richard Whitley), *Local Players in Global Games* (2005, with Jonathan Zeitlin) and *Nordic Capitalisms and Globalization* (2011, co-editor with Kari Lilja).

OVE K. PEDERSEN is Professor of Comparative Political Economy in the Department of Business and Politics at the CBS. His works in English include *The Politics of Flexibility* (1991, co-editor with Bob Jessop, Hans Kastendiek, and Klaus Nielsen), *Evolution of Interest Representation and Development of the Labour Market in Post-Socialist Countries* (1995, co-editor with Jerzy Hausner and Karsten Ronni), *Legacies of Change* (1997, with John L. Campbell), *The Rise of Neoliberalism and Institutional Analysis* (2001, co-editor with John L. Campbell), *Europeanization and the Transnational State* (2004, co-editor with Per Lægreid and Bengt Jacobsson), *National Identity and the Varieties of Capitalism* (2006, co-editor with John L. Campbell and John A. Hall), *Oxford Handbook in Comparative Institutional Analysis* (2010, co-editor with Glenn Morgan, John L. Campbell, and Richard Whitley), *The Role of Legends in Nation Building* (2013, with John A. Hall and Ove Korsgaard), and *The National Origins of Policy Ideas* (2014, with John L. Campbell).

VIVIEN A. SCHMIDT is Jean Monnet Professor of European Integration and Director of the Center for the Study of Europe at Boston University. Her works include *Democratizing France* (1990), *From State to Market?* (1996), *Welfare and Work in the Open Economy Vol I & II* (2000, co-editor with Fritz W. Scharpf), *The Futures of European Capitalism* (2002), *Policy Change and Discourse in Europe* (2005, co-editor with Claudio Radaelli), *Democracy in Europe* (2006), *Debating Political Identity and Legitimacy in the European Union* (2011, co-editor with Furio Cerutti and Sonia Lucarelli), and *Resilient Liberalism in Europe's Political Economy* (2013, co-editor with Mark Thatcher).

1

Sources of National Institutional Competitiveness

Sensemaking in Institutional Change

Susana Borrás and Leonard Seabrooke

1.1 INTRODUCTION

In contemporary capitalist economies, organizations are embedded in a multiplicity of contexts defined by complex sets of institutions. Actors in these organizations are required to navigate formal and informal institutional arrangements that shape specific environments. They are also required to note the way in which institutions operate, interact with each other, and are utilized. On top of institutional assemblages lie large socioeconomic problems that must be addressed, such as rapid changes associated with economic globalization, ageing societies, and tightening fiscal purses. The ways in which those economies adapt and change their institutions largely depend on how those issues are perceived and acted upon. This is so because national governments, firms, public organizations, civil society organizations, interest groups, households, individuals, and other key socioeconomic actors, are all constantly interacting with their socioeconomic realities. And in so doing, they are regularly confronted with how to formulate and address current and future problems in a way that improves their individual economic performance and the economic performance of their socioeconomic context (national economy, local community, etc.).

Our book argues that sensemaking is a crucial process in the construction of decisions that inform institutional change, and reflect and transform related socioeconomic discourses. We start from the observation that, in order for organizations to adapt to challenges, those who populate them are required to engage in sensemaking processes (Weick, 1995, 2009). Organizations aim to achieve socioeconomic success primarily by capturing local information and knowledge, and utilizing it to their comparative advantage when fulfilling their role and purpose. Looking within their organizational environments and across these institutional landscapes, actors must make sense of their situation, and locate the past and the future. It is in sensemaking processes where narratives about expectations and belonging are formed by those looking back. Those looking forward use sensemaking processes to establish the grounds from which to provide solutions to problems and find the appropriate knowledge.

From this perspective we understand *institutional competitiveness* through the lens of sensemaking processes; through agents' articulation of narratives and strategies to generate socioeconomic success within their national/local/community economic framework (Campbell & Pedersen, 2007). Processes to improve institutional competitiveness are best understood in a comparative context (either within a peer group, within a national state or local economic system, internationally, and globally) mainly because they invoke institutional configurations in a given economy as a means to fulfilling an organization's goals. The pursuit of these goals occurs through sensemaking processes that are triggered by the relationship between unexpected challenges and existing identities, and institutional configurations (Weber & Glynn, 2006).

We locate our interest in the relationship between sensemaking and institutional competiveness alongside the work on "comparative capitalisms." In the fields of comparative political economy, organizational sociology, innovation studies, public management, and comparative politics there are a range of answers on why national systems differ. We need only look at the various works that provide overviews of institutional change to comprehend not only Varieties of Capitalism (VoC) (cf. Campbell & Pedersen, 2001; Crouch, 2005), but varieties in how we examine differences. From the range of literature on "Varieties of Capitalism" (Hall & Soskice, 2001), national business systems (Morgan, Whitley, & Moen, 2005), and the earlier work on "social systems of production" (Hollingsworth & Boyer, 1997), it is clear that how institutions are aligned in national frameworks is an increasingly important factor in determining national and international economic performance. Variations in the alignment of institutions provide the content for explaining institutional competitiveness. This important work has provided us with typologies with which to identify variation, and has delineated the relationship between finance, production, and education (primarily through vocational training). This work has also been criticized for being too static in its depictions of how institutions are aligned within countries (Blyth, 2003), and for failing to appreciate rapid changes attributable to changing logics among the broader population, such as the relationship between financialization and housing prices in the most recent financial crisis (Schwartz & Seabrooke, 2008; Heyes, Lewis, & Clark, 2012).

Institutionalist approaches have carefully examined forms and processes of institutional change (Peters, 2005), with some of this work suggesting that path dependence can have particularly strong effects. For these scholars change typically occurs during periods of crisis where the institutional equilibrium has been temporarily punctured and interest groups have scrambled to defend their interests through the formation of coalitions (Gourevitch & Shinn, 2005). Dissatisfaction with these approaches (most eloquently critiqued in Crouch, 2005), has sent many scholars off into a search for "agency" and the drivers of change (Mahoney & Thelen, 2010; Moschella & Tsingou, 2013), and into an integration of discourse in institutional change (Seabrooke, 2007a; Schmidt, 2010). Likewise, in some ways, some scholars associated with work on national business systems were looking for agents through their emphasis on innovation and experimentalism at the firm level (Whitley & Kristensen, 1996).

One particularly interesting departure from the comparative capitalisms framework was made by Pepper D. Culpepper (2003) with his focus on *reason* rather than *deliberation* within national economic systems. For Culpepper, the world of VoC depicted by Peter Hall and David Soskice (2001) painted a system in which the actors knew their interests and all the learning that needed to be done had been done. But in cases where the actors are uncertain and trying to transform their system, they must engage reasoning rather than deliberation in order to learn. Culpepper used reason to skate between the "rationalist" and "constructivist" worlds, whereby the former stress fixed interests and structural forces, while the latter emphasize how agents can construct change (e.g. Sabel, 1994). We take heart from Culpepper's intervention because it acknowledges the uncertainty and ambiguity in which agents operate, and because it asks us to focus on the process by which actors make sense of how the institutions in their economy are seen to be aligned (or not) (Seabrooke, 2007b). We do, however, consider "reason" to be too loaded a term for the process of absorbing, processing, and articulating information about how institutions should change; especially since it suggests a link to cognition that places the individual at the forefront when we really want to understand the inter-subjective process of generating change (cf. North, 2005). We focus on the agents' sensemaking, as an inter-subjective process linked to identity, normative propositions, and strategic interaction.

Sensemaking is defined here as the reflexive process through which the agents of change give meaning to past experience, and provide a plausible narrative on what should happen to their organizations and their institutional environment. As stated by Karl Weick, sensemaking provides the "feedstock for institutionalization" and institutional change (Weick, 1995: 35). It is also a source of variance across different national systems since sensemaking is informed by the social cues provided by identities and existing institutions, including feedback processes that place limits on institutional change

(Weber & Glynn, 2006). Our emphasis on sensemaking includes reflection on the need for institutional change to combat problems and to improve institutional competitiveness. In short, we suggest that sensemaking is a key source of change in national institutional competitiveness, and that an analytical focus on sensemaking among actors allows us to distinguish not only VoC transformation, but also the drivers behind socioeconomic regeneration. Sensemaking is important in providing a narrative to continuity, reasons for institutional change, rallying points to generate consensus, and justifications to those who are affected by institutional transformation. Sensemaking directs our attention to the agents' constitution and co-creation of changes to institutional environments, as well as agents' reflection and interpretation of organizational goals and practices. This view on the sources of institutional competitiveness directs us to examining how:

1. **Sensemaking conforms to specific identities,** in which actors are able to locate meaning and attribute ways to move forward that incorporate "local" needs, be they national, sub-national, or regional.

2. **Sensemaking invokes normative propositions,** that reasons provided for institutional change align with, or are derived from, values shared by the community of interest to be plausible.

3. **Sensemaking involves strategy** and the use of ambiguity as actors mobilize support for their plans, including the construction and co-creation of ideas and concepts, such as competitiveness.

Sensemaking breaks with the institutional equilibrium model often assumed in comparative capitalisms literature—that institutional arrangements are stable until broken by exogenous crises. By contrast, the sensemaking approach permits an understanding of how institutions are configured, including in relation to other national institutions, in periods of normality where ambiguity is still present. As such, a focus on sensemaking assists in providing an endogenous explanation of institutional change—an aim similar to those working from a discursive institutionalist approach (Schmidt, 2010).

1.2 CROSS-NATIONAL VARIATION AND CHANGE

As Reinhard Bendix (1984) once stated, we cannot help but think comparatively. In political economy, organizational sociology, and policy studies, comparative work on why different national systems differ has produced a range of explanations and typologies. In historical sociology, work on "state capacity" sought to differentiate the sources on why some states were able to compete economically and military, while others were not (Mann, 1986; Skocpol, 1979). These studies focused, in particular, on how states responded to external pressures to compete and to what extent they responded by isolating or embedding themselves in their societies. Some societies were able to improve their state capacity by providing greater representation to the broader population—who in turn bought into the fiscal system (Hobson, 1997)—or contributing to deepening pools of capital (Seabrooke, 2001), while others stressed how "governed interdependence" between the state and business interests permitted improved strategy on boosting a country's competitiveness in the world economy (Weiss, 1998).

At the domestic level, work by J. Rogers Hollingsworth and Robert Boyer (1996; 1997), and others (Berger & Dore, 1996), emphasized that in the face of external constraints, and in contrast to theories of convergence, there was actually a great deal of divergence in "social systems of production" (SSP). This work on variation typically located the source of variations in institutional coordination at the regional and national levels, with an implicit stress on trust relationships. Other work emphasizes how capitalist practices were changing in organizational form, if little in substance, providing variation at the national level (Kitschelt et al., 1999).

Famously, Peter Hall and David Soskice (2001) transformed their earlier work, with a good dose of inspiration from both the SSP literature and microeconomic theory, into "Varieties of Capitalism"—an approach that now dominates the field and also university and business school teaching on why different national economic systems vary. Hall and Soskice sought to provide a theory of the firm, but really provided a new separation of two ideal types based on the American and German experience: liberal and coordinated market economies, respectively. Their aim was to discuss institutional complementarity and why different systems exhibited variation in how firms were financed, their management structure, the employer–employee relations, and inter-firm relationships. There are good reasons why this approach has become dominant in the field, since the ideal types facilitate comparisons, including the location of systems that are more "hybrids" rather than the liberal or coordinated market economy types (Campbell & Pedersen, 2007).

This scholarship strongly echoed work on "national trajectories" of industrial development (Zysman, 1994), where path dependence is especially strong (cf. Crouch & Farrell, 2004; Pollitt & Bouckaert, 2011). The VoC "school" has been criticized for presenting many economic systems—and the institutional arrangements within them—in a way that is "same as it never was" (Blyth, 2003). Seabrooke (2006), for example, has pointed out that the role of state intervention in the US case is very strong in financial markets, especially those linked to housing, which does not fit with the Liberal Market Economy (LME) conception. Others have pointed out that the German system, the ideal-typical Coordinated Market Economy (CME) is changing in ways that we associate with the American system more than German or European values (Höpner & Schäfer, 2010).

One of the central tenets of this literature is that Varieties of Capitalism are based on distinct forms of national institutional complementarities. Wolfgang Streeck has argued that, since the national context is simultaneously a platform for power games with a distinct constellation of interests, national systems are always under an endogenous pressure to disorganize by exhausting different pre-existing institutional complementarities (Streeck, 2009). From this viewpoint Varieties of Capitalism are intrinsically unstable, as there is an unequal distribution of power and some actors in the system make strategic use of institutions in a way that distorts the institutions' initial purposes. This is not the outcome of a designed plan by a specific class or political coalition. Rather, organizing and disorganizing processes unfold in each institutional sector for distinct historical reasons as the constellation of actors develop novel conflicts and contradictions, partly as an outcome of the way the institutions affect behavior of actors. Disorganization in one sector can have spillover effects on others, leading either to a virtuous process of reinforcement of institutional complementarities, or to a vicious circle of disorganization undermining pre-existing institutional complementarities. Along similar lines, James Mahoney and Kathleen Thelen (2009) address the issue of the implicit ambiguity of institutional contexts, which provide different levels of discretion in rule enforcement. For them, agents of change make the most of these differences, performing roles as subversive agents, parasitic symbionts, insurrectionaries, or opportunists. Studying different forms of gradual change, Mahoney and Thelen are skeptical of the structural approach to continuity in work on Varieties of Capitalism.

Scholars such as Colin Crouch (2005) have also criticized the VoC school for relying too heavily on the notion of path dependence and not permitting an understanding of institutional change in which ideational and discursive factors matter. The standard perspective here is that institutions establish a "system of ideas and standards which is comprehensive" (Hall, 1993: 277). Interest groups and coalitions plug into the institutions and the ideas they represent, and provide stability until a major crisis occurs and provides a period of great uncertainty in which institutions can be fundamentally realigned and represent different ideas (Blyth, 2002). The "switch" between ideas is not explained other than by the presence of the institutions and how they complement each other. Critics, like Crouch and others, suggest that this literature has a tough time explaining institutional change and transformation beyond which coalition is endowed with more resources during a period of crisis and fighting (Seabrooke, 2007a). The sequence of change follows the dominant interests that are presumed to be path dependent (Pierson, 2004). A further problem is that all information necessary for transforming the system is presumed to be available within the system, which harks back to Culpepper's earlier point about deliberation versus reason. Given these weaknesses, while there has been a great deal written on Varieties of Capitalism, our understanding of institutional change and the sources of national institutional competitiveness needs greater conceptual development. Some of this has taken place through the work on ideas and ideational change, which we turn to next.

1.3 CONSTRUCTING INSTITUTIONAL CHANGE

Scholars working on ideas and institutional change have stressed how some actors can use ideas to change how we see institutions' functions, their purpose, and the ideas they embody. These scholars typically see a false separation between "ideas" and "interests," since an interest is also a social construction and contains an idea about what is desired (Campbell, 2002). Scholars working in welfare studies have long considered these issues based on questions such as, "if Swedes are so wealthy, why does only half the population own property?" (Kemeny, 1980), with the answer that different ideas and interests about paying taxes are a reflection of the "welfare trade-off" in different societies (Castles, 1998), including the development of a "varieties of residential capitalism" approach to provide one set of answers to such questions (Schwartz & Seabrooke, 2008; 2009). In general, those considering how interests are constructed have drawn heavily from organizational institutionalism within sociology, particularly the notion that institutions create logics of appropriateness that condition actors' behavior (DiMaggio & Powell, 1991). The discussion of how ideas and norms affect institutional change has been an issue of much discussion in the last two decades. Recent approaches have broken from early constructivist literature. This comes from a shared frustration that previous constructivist scholars left largely unresolved the central issue of why and how ideas matter for institutional change (cf. Jacobsen, 1995). The unresolved issue was whether ideas provide a useful supplement to interest-based explanations, or whether ideas can matter in their own right as a key explanatory variable.

Approaches from constructivists in the field of political economy see actors carrying ideas into their battles over institutional change from a socially constructed rather than merely instrumental basis. Seen this way, ideas are not merely selected on the basis of self-interest, but, instead, ideas are those essential factors building causal stories that can cut across class and consumption boundaries to create new collectivities. In his study of the construction of the contemporary Swedish model of capitalism, Blyth (2002) suggests that in a context of great economic uncertainly such as the Great Depression, the Swedish Social Democratic Party successfully managed to put forward Keynesian ideas based on the need to provide universal protection to individuals (regardless of their class) against the excesses of market forces. The Social Democratic Party was able to build a new political consensus across the aisle, which was simultaneously redistributive and pro-market. One of the crucial aspects of comparative political economy has been to examine how institutional change takes place in periods of uncertainty. This is so because high levels of uncertainty generate "highly fluid conceptions of interest" in which actors are required to bring new ideas and normative commitments able to deal with new problems (McNamara, 1998: 7; Parsons, 2003: 8–9). In other words, uncertainty creates an open space for reinterpretation of the nature of problems and of possible solutions, searching for new angles and considerations about how the economy should work. Such environments compel actors to resort to "repertoires of action that resonate with their core identities" and transform their conceptions of self and others' interest (Blyth, 2002: 267). The stability of a broad political consensus based on a set of institutionally maintained ideas disappears as soon as a profound socioeconomic crisis generates a high degree of uncertainty to the actors. The window of opportunity generated by this uncertainty can be grabbed by ideational entrepreneurs putting forward some specific options that fit with their normative commitments. A new consensus is formed after some ideational struggles, after which a new consensus is built up and legitimizes a concrete option. This process is essentially characterized by an ideational punctuated equilibrium.

There are two main problems with this account. The first is that if ideas are embodied in individual persons, then change is only subject to them. Allocating too many explanatory factors to those "great individuals" and their normative master frames is problematic because, taken to the extreme, it means that institutional change only happens under very extreme conditions (namely, a high level of uncertainty and the presence of entrepreneurs as great individuals), and the rest is just mere continuity based on "logic of appropriateness." This seems to be too narrow an account of institutional change, especially when the emphasis on the construction of consensus for institutional change comes back to ideas being a property of great men or women (Seabrooke, 2007a). The second problem involves a conception of power beyond ideational power. It is commonly argued that those producing "master frames" require political and material resources behind them (Parsons, 2003: 19, 32), and the strategic and tactical element of sensemaking should not be clouded by an overemphasis on ideas. We suggest that the relationship between ideas and behavior, and sensemaking and actions is a useful way of considering differences among approaches. It is also suggested that sensemaking is an important process driving the construction of discourses, and we see a fruitful relationship between work on sensemaking and institutional change, and discursive institutionalism (Schmidt, 2010). Like work by Vivien Schmidt and others, we suggest that discourses cannot be understood as free-floating, and both sensemaking and discursive institutionalism have a strong interest in process rather than content-oriented accounts of institutional change.

1.4 SENSEMAKING AND INSTITUTIONAL CHANGE

We suggest that sensemaking is a key process in institutional change that has been under-theorized (Weick, 1995; 2009). We start by acknowledging that uncertainty is not a situation that happens sporadically and in times of major socioeconomic turmoil, but is essentially a permanent condition embedded in the intrinsic, ambiguous nature of institutions and of the political support behind the specific institutional arrangements through time. We also acknowledge that, while ideational entrepreneurs are important, they do not hold the monopoly of making sense of the economy and of institutions (including the rules these institutions define). Importantly, the work on sensemaking places emphasis on the relations among those involved rather than on the attributes of the dominant actor (Weick, 2009: 10). As such, the relationships involved in sensemaking, including the role of identities and what cues are taken to guide behavior and to view the institutional context is more important than the assumed attributes of the actor (Czarniawska, 2008). In principle, all organizations in a system are agents of change in their daily individual sensemaking of the competitiveness of the economy and of the institutional framework in which it is embedded.

Different elements of past experience and data sources can be combined and composed in ways that provide different pictures. Likewise, considerations about the current nature of economic-related problems, and the subsequent needs for future institutional solutions to those alleged problems, are naturally not pre-given by the experience and information as such, nor are they universally shared in a society. Instead, they lay at the very core of social and political debates regarding the past and future direction of the economy.

Since institutional configurations are formed by different types of rules interacting in multiple ways and are subject to some degree of imprecision, we can assume that the organizations and actors operating within those complex institutional configurations will be confronted with inherently unstable and to some extent open-ended forms of interaction. The inherent instability of institutional configurations in a national context means that institutional change might not necessarily always be the outcome of the opportunistic behavior of a handful of powerful actors/agents of change, but most likely the gradual outcome of a collective move of actors who are trying to make sense of those institutions in their attempt to change them (or not change them). Therefore, from our approach, what matters is not the nature of the rule/institution or institutional configuration, but essentially its relation with the agents who engage in sensemaking (Jordana & Levi-Faur, 2004).

In exploring the role of sensemaking in institutional change, we propose an extension of the concept based on an application of James March's arguments concerning learning processes drawn from ambiguity and experience (March,

2010). Following March, "replication learning" involves actions that replicate success with minimal effort to reflect and to provide a causal understanding. For this volume, "replication" refers to modes of making sense of problems and situations by using previous experience on a trial-and-error mode of learning. Contrasting with that, "abstraction," for us, seeks to "understand the causal structure of the events of experience and to derive action implications from that understanding" (March, 2010: 15). As with the work of March, the sensemaking approach emphasizes the role that intellect plays in the agents' process of articulating courses for institutional change in environments that are intrinsically ambiguous and uncertain. We therefore consider that abstraction and replication in how experience is considered constitutes a fundamental aspect in sensemaking processes of agents. Complementing this, we see that there is another aspect that is relevant in these processes. This aspect has to do with the time-perspective of sensemaking. While the sociological literature of sensemaking typically focuses solely on the creation of narratives in a retrospective manner, we suggest that sensemaking can be either mainly retrospective (responding to current problems and issues, and looking at the past for cues in this regard), or it can be mainly prospective (defining courses of action that define, advance, and prevent future issues and problems).

Table 1.1 provides the range of ideal types of sensemaking processes found in this volume according to these two aspects. We differentiate between retrospective and prospective modes of sensemaking, as well as abstraction and replication. We suggest that these four ideal types of sensemaking explain much of what is going on with institutional change and provide a different take on constructivist and rationalist insights.

Moving clockwise around Table 1.1, a retrospective abstraction-based form of sensemaking can be seen in the creation of narratives of causes and causal analysis. Causal analysis seeks to identify the key drivers of change and identify patterns of behavior. This retrospective activity is common in different policy organizations, here including think tanks, which are charged with the task of understanding why particular events took place. *Causal analysis creates a narrative based on the study of previous patterns of behavior and of the inferences that can be drawn from them.* Some of these policy organizations engaging in this abstraction-based retrospective work insulate themselves and their scientific knowledge from political pressure by increasing sharing data and statistics on institutional change. This is the case of think

Table 1.1 Four ideal types of sensemaking processes

	Retrospective	Prospective
Abstraction	Causal analysis	Search systems
Replication	Belonging	Expectations

tanks, which seek to insulate the role of abstraction from direct political pressures and from the "spin" that appeals to less reflective expectations and belonging (see Campbell and Pedersen in this volume).

Moving to the top right-hand corner, prospective abstraction-based sensemaking can be seen as the process of sensemaking based on the use of explicit future-oriented search systems. *Search systems work by creating an analytical framework that identifies and organizes important information in a future-oriented manner in order to help address organizational and institutional forward-looking uncertainties.* One example of search systems is when firms constantly update their benchmarks and actively seek to organize data on how to position themselves in future market and technology contexts (see Kristensen in this volume). Another example of sensemaking processes based in search systems is the "open method of coordination"—a benchmark-based policy coordination mechanism across countries put up by the European Union (EU). This open method is not aimed at negotiating solutions to negative policy externalities in Europe, but to stimulate national reforms by identifying challenges ahead through the use of benchmarks and other search tools (see Borrás in this volume). In these cases the creation of search systems for forward-looking and analysis-based knowledge is the key way of handling institutional change.

Prospective replication-based sensemaking can be understood as expectations. *Expectations are judgments about how life and work conditions will change based on projections from current experiences.* Narratives of prudence in crisis provide one example, as can be seen in the current debates about austerity. Prospective replication-based sensemaking informs what institutions should be defended or changed according to expected trade-offs (see Seabrooke in this volume) and estimations of how trends will proceed based on current activity. Prior to the most recent crisis, for example, changes in housing markets in many liberal economies were fuelled by expectations of future profits from increased housing prices (Schwartz & Seabrooke, 2008). These expectations rapidly changed how homeowners and investors behaved in these markets, including what would now be identified as irrational behavior, out of sync with economic rationales and social norms. The imagined institutional order during this change in liberal markets was to shift away from rationalizing credit and property growth as natural and necessary phenomena to supporting notions of living within one's means (see Stanley, 2014). Such sensemaking does not reflect systematic study, as with abstraction, but instinct about what to expect and what institutional order to imagine and support (see Andersen and Boyer in this volume).

Finally, retrospective replication-based sensemaking can be understood as often grounded in belonging. Here *belonging refers to the creation of narratives to explain what happened in terms of cues and stories from embedded identities and social norms.* Sensemaking processes seek to explain and attribute meaning to phenomena from cues given by identity traits. Holding onto a sense of belonging during processes of institutional change may provide greater grounds for path dependence than historic pacts from interest groups (Campbell & Hall, 2009). During a period of institutional change sensemaking may focus on belonging to slow and manage reforms (see Greve in this volume). Identities provide cues for sensemaking and establish boundaries on which institutional orders can be imagined, and sensemaking through the lens of belonging establishes these boundaries. This view differs from path-dependence explanations often found in work on institutional change because the actors involved need not remain constant. Trade unions making sense of their situation in the 1970s and 1990s may invoke historic pacts at some points to justify their stance, but the sensemaking process need not be similar or rely on the same interpretation of the pact. Rather, making sense of belonging provides a narrative while also permitting new discourses on what is appropriate and legitimate to take hold.

We have defined sensemaking as the reflexive and interpretative process through which the agents of change give meaning to past and future events regarding the institutions supporting the performance and competitiveness of their economy. Sensemaking is therefore linked to three essential dimensions of this actor-based process of institutional change: (1) the (re-)definition of the agents' identity and needs from their experience regarding their interactions with the institutional context, (2) the (re-)definition of the values that guide the actors' action and the normativity behind the institutional context, and (3) linked to these two, the process of mobilizing specific forms of transformative action. These three correspond to the above-mentioned aspects of sensemaking, in that they conform to specific identities, invoke normative propositions, and involve strategies. In the following we discuss how these three dimensions are related to institutional competitiveness.

1.5 MAKING SENSE OF WHAT? INSTITUTIONAL COMPETITIVENESS

When studying the dynamics of change in cross-national comparative terms, this book suggests that one crucial factor for understanding different change outcomes has to do with the way in which the agents of change make sense collectively of the institutional competitiveness in a given economy. Since making sense corresponds to an inter-subjective process of agents' collective reflection and interpretation about the performance of the institutions in the economy, it is important to look at the "object" of this inter-subjectivity, namely different views on institutional competitiveness.

The way in which a given set of institutions (institutional configurations/arrangements) is improving (or not) the competitive performance of an economy is an issue of major social and political debate in any society, as it lies at the core of economic policy-making and the institutional configurations shaped by those policies more generally. However, many of the issues associated with the economic performance of institutional configurations are largely embedded in multiple possible explanations, and a certain degree of uncertainty and ambiguity. When economic, social, and political agents engage in sensemaking, and examine the experience and information associated with the past economic performance of institutions, they have to account for divergence in views. This is so because experience and information per se do not provide a single plausible explanation on "what happened" or "what might happen in the future." On the contrary, as several scholars point out, there is a considerable amount of uncertainty and ambiguity in such experience and information (March, 2010).

We wish to be particularly careful when it comes to specifying what we mean by "institutional competitiveness". The notion of "competitiveness" has been widely used among economists and business managers to assess the degree to which a firm is able to keep its competitive position in a market. Since the early 1990s, this notion was also used in the context of an entire national economy. Michael Porter's (1990) *The Competitive Advantage of Nations* was a landmark in this regard (cf. Sum and Jessop, 2013: ch. 7). A large number of comparative indexes and benchmarks have been introduced since, measuring overall performance. Yet, the use of the notion of national competitiveness has not remained uncontested: some scholars insist that competitiveness can only refer to firms, as they are the ones competing with their products in a market. States do not compete on the same terms, but are strongly informed by how their institutions are configured and aligned to complement one another (Pedersen, 2010). The view of the state as a "competition state" is linked to macro-level processes of political globalization, but also essentially to an understanding that views institutions as framing the competitiveness of firms in international markets (Pedersen, 2011).

The remarks above serve to point to one important issue for this book in that the process of institutional change—where institutional configurations are formed and transformed, and where the relative national institutional competitiveness is self-defined—is largely dependent on how firms, organizations, and individual actors interact with this institutional context. This interaction is based on a constant process on the part of the organizations making sense of the value, coherence, and performance of the institutional context in which they are embedded. Actors are making sense of the institutions because institutions tend to be open-ended and imprecise, and because they perceive the performance of these institutions as a crucial variable for their own success and identity.

1.6 THREE KEY DIMENSIONS IN SENSEMAKING

Having identified four ideal types of sensemaking processes, we need now to revert to the starting point of our discussion, the three key dimensions that are essential parts of every process of sensemaking. As mentioned in the first sections of this chapter, during the process of sensemaking, actors deal with three crucial dimensions: they conform to specific identities, they invoke normative propositions, and they define strategies. Conforming to specific identities means that, in the process of sensemaking, actors attribute institutional changes with meanings that reflect a specific understanding of the self. This is most relevant when views on institutional competitiveness are associated with a need for institutional change. The way in which actors make sense of institutional competitiveness is highly related to identity issues. The "Who is 'us'?" question is very central in competitiveness discussions and actors' sensemaking (Strange, 1998).

Second, sensemaking invokes normative propositions (or norms), so that reasons provided for institutional change relate to or are derived from the values shared by the community. Normative propositions are crucial in this process, partly because the cognitive and normative double nature of ideas in institutional change are closely intertwined (Campbell, 2002) and partly because normative propositions and values serve as guiding posts for future action and for actors' choices in situations of uncertainty. When studying the sensemaking process of institutional competitiveness, what is important is the observation that values and norms are associated to overall political views about the purpose of collective institutional contexts.

The third dimension in the process of sensemaking has to do with the strategic interactions of agents for the explicit generation of transformative action, or how agents mobilize support for their plans. This mobilization aspect of sensemaking processes is associated with what Vivien Schmidt (2010) has identified as the coordinative and communicative functions of discourse in institutional change. As already mentioned, sensemaking can involve strategy and the explicit use of ambiguity, as actors aim to mobilize support for their plans, including the construction and co-creation of ideas and concepts. From the angle of national institutional competitiveness, this mobilization entails specific strategies promoting the advance of crucial and broad terms such as "globalization," "competitiveness," or even "knowledge-based economy." This corresponds to an intellectual mobilization around a broadly defined ideational repertoire that becomes subsequently structured around some very specific discourses with a particular meaning. The strategic dimension of this sensemaking process determines the meaning of these broad ideational repertoires, and informs what concrete discourses are produced that guide actions to improve institutional competitiveness (Borrás & Radaelli, 2011).

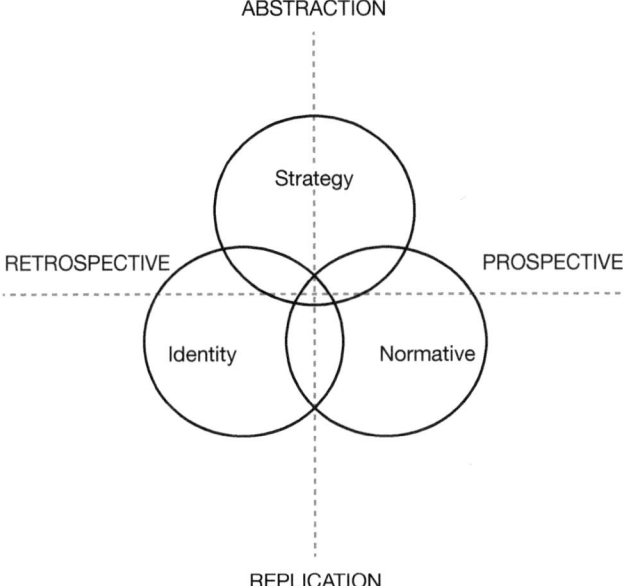

Figure 1.1 The three dimensions of sensemaking

Identity, normative propositions, and strategy are three essential dimensions present in any type of sensemaking process of institutional competitiveness. However, they are not equally relevant for each of the four ideal types of sensemaking processes identified. Figure 1.1 illustrates how we understand the interaction between these three dimensions in all sensemaking and the four ideal types of sensemaking processes presented.

Starting with identity, this dimension is very prominent in the ideal type of sensemaking, which is retrospective and replication-based, namely, what we branded in the sensemaking processes as "belonging." Naturally, identity is present in the other ideal types of sensemaking processes, but in a much less prominent manner. Sensemaking processes of belonging are strongly related to the dimension of identity and self-understanding of the actors involved. This has to do as much with the actor's own individual identity, as to the extrapolation of this identity into the wider community that this individual/ organization believes it belongs to. Hence, we argue that when relevant organizations and actors in a given national/regional/local context make sense of their competitiveness in a retrospective and replication approach, they tend to rely heavily on their own identity definition in order to make sense of what is going on and what needs to be done in terms of institutional change.

Just like identity, the normative dimension is present in all four ideal types of sensemaking processes. However, it is most prominent when sensemaking is based on prospective and replication modes, in what we branded the ideal type of sensemaking as "expectations." This is so because expectations are judgments about life and work conditions, and these judgments are anchored in specific value sets of what is "good" (or not), and on what must be done (or not). This normative dimension is therefore strongly reflected in the actors' sensemaking of institutional competitiveness according to specific value-laden preferences formulated in "possible futures" according to concrete projections in the future.

Last but not least, we see the strategy dimension as being crucial when sensemaking processes are based on abstraction-based learning modes, what we earlier branded as "causal analysis" and "search systems." As already mentioned, we understand strategy as a dimension in which actors making sense of institutional competitiveness and mobilize support for their plans, including the construction and co-creation of ideas and concepts. Naturally, this mobilization happens in all four ideal types of sensemaking processes, but it is particularly salient in those characterized by abstraction because the co-construction of ideas and concepts is heavily dependent on sophisticated analytical tools and instruments.

1.7 THE CHAPTERS OF THIS BOOK

This book explores the themes through a range of cases on the sensemaking process related to institutional competitiveness at national, European, regional, and firm levels.

John L. Campbell and Ove K. Pedersen's chapter explains how national policy research organizations, such as private think tanks and government policy units, make sense of their country's economic situation—and in particular its institutional competitiveness—through data analysis and forecasting. These organizations and the institutions by which they operate constitute what they call a "national knowledge regime." Comparing the US and Danish knowledge regimes, these authors find that abstraction types of sensemaking tend to gain ground in both countries with differing degrees, even if the organization of knowledge regimes is very different (competitive and partisan in the US, whereas collaborative in Denmark). Their study shows as well that, in the case of national knowledge regimes, it is analytically difficult to disentangle the retrospective and prospective sensemaking process in actors, although the emphasis of these think tanks and government policy units is on the retrospective aspect of the national economy's competitiveness.

Peer Hull Kristensen's chapter examines the experimental search for new ways of organizing production at the firm and inter-firm level that was set in motion in the wake of the first oil crisis and has continued up until today. In many ways this experimental search is a break-up from a former production regime of hierarchically integrated mass production towards a disintegrated production regime with open innovation systems and horizontal collaborative ties (within and among) firms. The chapter studies how Danish firms and their constituencies made sense of ongoing transformations and mobilize institutional resources to help them accomplish a tentative outcome. In terms of sensemaking, reflective actors combine a variety of templates (managerial fashions and social ideals) or what Athens (2007) has called "phantom-communities" for navigating through a lasting epoch of volatility. In so doing, the chapter discusses the ongoing search processes in the light of an imagined ideal state of the emerging production regime and asks whether it makes a difference for solving current inconsistencies in liberal, coordinated, or hybrid market economies, as in the case of Denmark.

Looking at EU-level sensemaking processes, Susana Borrás's chapter examines how the EU's Lisbon Strategy generated the abstraction-based sensemaking process among different national policy-makers. The Lisbon Strategy was a political strategy seeking to improve European competitiveness through the mechanism of the so-called "open method of coordination," coordinating national institutional reforms. The chapter compares the reforms undertaken in Denmark, Sweden, France, and Germany in the specific area of innovation and technology policy, and it studies the processes of sensemaking of national policy-makers engaged in this. The chapter finds that the abstraction and prospective sensemaking processes are characterized by giving the participants an overview and by generating networks of influence. It also finds that the ability of these cross-national interactions to exert influence on national-level debates is related to the organization of national public administrations and the timing of political attention at the national level.

Carsten Greve's chapter studies public management reforms in Denmark since 2001, and discusses how key actors have made sense of these reforms. The Danish public sector has been reformed substantially since 2001 through at least eleven public management reforms through themes that include quality, structural changes, and digital era governance changes. The performance of the Danish public sector is widely regarded as being exceptionally high. In the World Bank's "Governance Indicators" project Denmark is ranked as having the most effective public sector in the world. Why and how have recent public management reforms happened in Denmark? What are the dynamics of the reform institutions and processes? An incremental approach allows for more sensemaking by organizational actors and individuals. After examining the different takes at the literature, the chapter investigates the nature of different sector reforms in Denmark since 2001. The findings show a strong path dependency of public management reform which started in the early 1980s, yet key actors have made sense of the new reforms in more sophisticated ways than before, and mainly in terms of efficiency and effectiveness. The sensemaking process reflects a strong connection to conceptions of belonging, with replication reflections on what it means to hold a coherent identity determining much of the activity in the policy space.

Similarly, Søren Kaj Andersen's chapter studies the non-reform of Danish labour policy in relation to the short-term labour schemes, which were introduced in other European countries. In 2008–09, when the financial crisis began to impact on the labour markets, some EU member states introduced some schemes for short-time work. Germany extended the existing short-time work scheme significantly. Predictably, and in line with the liberal policy regime, the UK took no initiatives in this area. More surprisingly, Denmark refrained from a more proactive use of an already existing scheme, and in Sweden—where no such scheme existed—the government rejected the idea of introducing it. This chapter explores the processes of sensemaking in those countries, with particular attention to the Danish policy choice of non-reform. Andersen explores the tensions between interests asserting replication and retrospective sensemaking processes to guide policy reform. Employers' associations, trade unions, and governments are the actors making sense of policy initiatives in this field via their interpretation of organizational needs and interests. Specific policy initiatives on short-time work became part of a larger institutional set-up, which raises the questions of institutional fit of new initiatives and especially how it affects institutional competitiveness.

Leonard Seabrooke's chapter makes a simple point: institutional competitiveness is essentially social and economic replication, and such replication has an intergenerational aspect. His chapter applies a sensemaking framework to intergenerational relations and institutional competitiveness and focuses on the role of housing credit, since this is an issue that brings together and divides societies along generational lines. The chapter provides an exploratory framework for understanding generational change as a source of national institutional competitiveness. The chapter draws upon examples from members of the Organisation for Economic Co-operation and Development (OECD) and has a particular focus on the Australian and Danish experiences, highlighting the role of expectations and the normative and strategic considerations that affect prospective replication-based sensemaking processes from different generations within these countries.

Finally, and at a greater level of aggregation than Seabrooke, Robert Boyer's chapter looks at the process by which welfare became (and still is) a factor of institutional competitiveness in the economies of the Nordic countries. The chapter shows how some national welfare systems display a *specific logic* that makes compatible dynamic economic efficiency and social cohesion. It also shows that this double positive performance can be sustained in the long run. After identifying some common trends that characterize the Nordic model(s), the chapter argues that the reforms of these countries in the 1990s towards a Neo-Schumpeterian welfare regime were based on an abstraction-based sensemaking process that superseded the previous replication-based sensemaking process in the early phases of the emergence of the Nordic model. Boyer identifies a historical movement from institutional configurations based on identities and belonging towards these same institutions being used to create search systems for welfare innovation that combine identity with strategic and normative elements.

Taken together, the chapters of this book provide a rich account of different cases of actors' sensemaking in relevant processes of institutional change related to views on competitiveness. In so doing, these cases offer in-depth accounts of the diversity and variation of actors' sensemaking processes in contexts where competitiveness became a crucial turning point for major organizational reforms and institutional changes. The sensemaking approach taken by this book aims at bringing forward at least three novel contributions to the literature of institutional change. First, sensemaking is an approach that is able to link the intrinsic ambiguity of actors' experience, and of institutional indeterminacy, with processes of identity and normative definition through the strategic mobilization of actors. Second, and related to this, sensemaking is able to give accounts of actors' intended, as well as unintended, changes that are the backbone of the sources of national and regional economies' institutional competitiveness. Last but not least, sensemaking provides the basis for a research design that combines deductive and inductive research strategies. All in all, for these reasons, the agent-based perspective brought forward by this sensemaking approach is a promising venue for our efforts to better understand how countries change their institutions in order to enhance their competitive performance in the world economy.

2

Making Sense of Economic Uncertainty

Knowledge Regimes in the United States and Denmark

John L. Campbell and Ove Kaj Pedersen

2.1 INTRODUCTION

This chapter examines how policy analysts, experts, and others operating in national knowledge regimes in the United States and Denmark made sense of economic uncertainty since the stagflation era of the late 1970s—a period of simultaneously high inflation and low economic growth—and the subsequent advent of globalization.[1] *Knowledge regimes* are fields of policy research organizations, such as think tanks and government research units, and the formal and informal institutions—that is, the rules and norms—that govern them. Policy research organizations produce data, analyses, theories, and policy recommendations and disseminate this information to policy-makers in the hope of influencing their thinking. Knowledge regimes constitute a source of institutional competitiveness insofar as policy-makers use the information they get from policy research organizations to reform political and economic institutions in ways that improve their country's economic performance. Indeed, policy-makers have turned increasingly to policy research organizations over the last thirty years or so for all sorts of inspiration to help them find ways to boost their country's international competitiveness (Pedersen, 2010). As such, knowledge regimes are an important component of any advanced capitalist political economy. And each one tends to have its own unique national character (Campbell & Pedersen, 2014).

Knowledge regimes are particularly important during periods of heightened economic uncertainty when policy-makers need to make sense of unprecedented

---

[1] We use the term "globalization" as shorthand for the increasingly integrated and competitive nature of economic activity among nation-states particularly, but not exclusively, in the advanced capitalist world.

situations. Immediately after the Second World War knowledge regimes in the advanced capitalist countries were staid and sleepy places because most policy research organizations accepted Keynesianism as the appropriate intellectual framework for making sense of their economies (Rich, 2004; Smith, 1991). But Keynesianism was ill-suited to explaining stagflation as well as a variety of other economic problems, including many associated with growing government budget deficits and heightened international competition that cropped up in the 1980s and 1990s. Uncertainty mounted over the causes of and solutions for these problems. As a result, people in both the United States and Denmark began to change their knowledge regimes in ways that they hoped would help them make better sense of these problems. This involved establishing new policy research organizations and reorienting others. One outgrowth of all this was the rise of supply-side economics as a new intellectual framework for making sense of these economic problems. This played out, however, in different ways in the United States and Denmark with the United States succumbing to the supply-side view—especially in its neoliberal form—more than Denmark.

Supply-side economics should not be equated with neoliberalism. Supply-side economics held that stagflation could be resolved and a nation's international economic competitiveness bolstered by better providing the inputs the economy needed, such as a more efficient labor force, more investment capital, better technologies, and improved infrastructure. This could be done in a variety of ways, including relying on the state to provide these inputs. Neoliberalism, however, rejected the statist approach and held that the way to provide such inputs was through cutting taxes for potential investors, reducing government regulations, and limiting government welfare expenditures. In other words, neoliberalism was a particularly conservative version of supply-side thinking that advocated less government intervention into the economy. Of course, both approaches differed considerably from Keynesianism, which emphasized manipulating aggregate demand to manage the economy. But all three approaches were intellectual frameworks with which policy research organizations tried to make sense of economic uncertainty.

It is important to note that sensemaking, as explained in Borrás and Seabrooke in this volume, can take different forms. James March (2010) suggested that there are two forms of sensemaking that people may use when they cope with uncertainty. First is low-intellect or *replication learning* where people make sense of uncertain situations by utilizing already available scripts, cognitive templates, and other ideas that seem to have been useful and appropriate in the past. What he has in mind here is something very similar to what organizational sociologists refer to as "mimetic" and "normative learning" where organizations adapt to environmental uncertainty by either copying what seem to be the practices of successful organizations around them or adopting what seem to be normatively appropriate practices (DiMaggio & Powell, 1983). Second is high-intellect or *abstraction-based learning* where people make sense of uncertain situations by determining what precipitated them in the first place. The important point is that abstraction-based learning involves causal reasoning, such as that based on analytic modeling, whereas replication learning does not.[2] As Borrás and Seabrooke point out in Chapter 1 of this volume, replication and abstraction-based learning can be either *retrospective* or *prospective*—people can try to make sense of either the past or what is likely to happen in the future. This is not inconsistent with March's view. Nor is the notion that sensemaking is often a contested process or that it may involve, in varying degrees, competition, cooperation, and compromise over whose interpretation of the situation is the best or most expedient politically.

What March neglects, however, is how organizational and institutional contexts affect sensemaking. This chapter sheds light on this by focusing on how knowledge regimes facilitate sensemaking. After all, knowledge regimes consist of policy research organizations operating within institutional contexts and trying to make sense of economic uncertainty. They do so retrospectively by interpreting the past in order to predict prospectively the effects that economic policies would likely have. And they can base their retrospective and prospective sensemaking on either scientific empirical analysis of an abstraction-based sort or normative interpretations of a replication sort— that is, political or ideological principles—depending on their type of organization and institutional context.

We will show that how knowledge regimes are organized influences how policy research organizations try to make sense of the world for themselves and then for policy-makers through the analyses and advice these organizations transmit to them. This involves, in varying degrees, retrospective and prospective sensemaking as well as replication and abstraction-based sensemaking. Beginning in the early 1980s the US knowledge regime became more partisan politically, so sensemaking became very competitive and ideologically contentious. Depending on the policy research organization in question, sensemaking involved various combinations of replication- and abstraction-based learning. This resulted in sharply divergent policy analyses and recommendations. This was reflected, for example, in the US Council of Economic Advisors' reports for the president, which flip-flopped back and forth between neoliberalism and other approaches. Meanwhile, the Danish knowledge regime became much less ideologically partisan, so sensemaking became more consensus-oriented and focused on abstraction-based rather than replication-based learning. This resulted in much more stable and consistent policy analyses and proposals, as reflected in the Danish Economic Council's (DØR's)

---

[2] The distinction between low and high intellect learning is reminiscent of the distinction made earlier by March and Olsen (1989) between the logics of appropriate and instrumental behavior, respectively.

reports for the government, which were slow to shift toward supply-side economics and were highly averse to neoliberalism.

Let us clarify two things. Firstly, we are concerned with the *process* rather than the *outcome* of sensemaking, except insofar as reports from the national councils of economic advisors is concerned. These are among the most important analyses and recommendations the US and Danish governments receive every year. And, as we will explain, they are a reflection of each country's sensemaking process. Secondly, we do not claim that knowledge regimes are the sole determinants of sensemaking, policy-making, or institutional competitiveness, which are, of course, influenced as well by a myriad of additional factors.

2.2 DATA, RESEARCH DESIGN, AND METHODS

Our analysis is based primarily on interviews and other documents we collected from a variety of policy research organizations in the United States and Denmark.[3] Within each country we selected four types of research organizations for examination that have been identified by others as the most common in advanced capitalist democracies (e.g. Rich, 2004; Denham & Stone, 2004). First are private academic-style *scholarly* research organizations, sometimes referred to as "universities without students." These are staffed with scholars, professional researchers, and analysts, often with joint university appointments. They produce expert research monographs and journal articles much like those found in academia. They also tend to be politically non-partisan. Second are *advocacy* research organizations. These tend to be more partisan politically and ideologically. They are less concerned with conducting scholarly research than with consuming, packaging, and disseminating the research and theories of others in order to influence the political climate, public debate, and public policy. Third are *party* research organizations. These are closely associated with political parties and provide a source of expert advice and analysis for party leaders. Fourth are *state* research organizations directly affiliated with specific government departments and ministries.[4] Scholarly and state research organizations are more likely to engage in abstraction-based learning, such as through sophisticated econometric analysis and forecasting, than other types of organizations, whose sensemaking tends to be

---

[3] The analysis of the US and Danish cases reported here is part of a much larger study that also includes France and Germany. Detailed discussion of sampling and data analysis methods can be found in Campbell and Pedersen (2014) and Campbell et al. (2013).

[4] Rich (2004: 11) notes that state and scholarly research organizations are often rather similar in terms of the sort of work they do.

based more on ideological and political interpretation—that is, replication learning. All four types, however, engage in retrospective and prospective sensemaking.

We conducted thirty-four interviews in nineteen organizations in the United States during April 2008 and August 2009, and twenty-two interviews in nineteen organizations in Denmark during May and July 2008. Interviews were supplemented with data from organizational annual reports, websites, and secondary literature. The purpose of this part of the data collection was to determine what the topography of the knowledge regimes looked like, and how and why it changed in response to stagflation and globalization. We also examined reports from the President's Council of Economic Advisers (CEA) in the United States and the DØR. Here our purpose was to determine whether the structure and practices of each knowledge regime influenced the sort of ideas that top-level policy-makers received and might use to make sense of their national economic situations. These reports were published in 1987, 1997, and 2007. We examined the reports of the national councils for two reasons. Firstly, of all the policy research organizations we visited these were the closest to power insofar as they reported directly to the heads of the executive branch of the government—the president or prime minister. Secondly, they each prepared analytic and advisory reports about the national economy for the political leadership on a regular basis.

Our analysis covers a fairly long time period—roughly from the early 1980s through the early 2000s. This is necessary in order to capture the important changes in sensemaking structures and practices in these countries. After all, change in fields of organizations is typically slow moving and incremental (Campbell, 2004). The same is often true of shifts in sensemaking frameworks (Skogstad, 2011).

2.3 UNITED STATES: PROLIFERATION AND COMPETITION

The American knowledge regime underwent a period of increasing fragmentation and competition thanks to a proliferation of policy research organizations in civil society beginning in the late 1970s. This precipitated a shift in sense-making approaches that was reflected in reports from the CEA.

2.3.1 Changes in the US Knowledge Regime

The American knowledge regime is marked by a fragmented structure of scholarly, advocacy, and state policy research organizations. Many of these in civil society are engaged in a fiercely competitive struggle to influence policy-makers.

Among the most prominent is a set of scholarly organizations, such as the Brookings Institution, the American Enterprise Institute, and the Hudson Institute, which are financed privately, often by foundations, corporate grants, and individual contributions from wealthy donors, and staffed to a significant degree with formally trained researchers. Closely related to these organizations is another set of private research shops, like the Urban Institute, the RAND Corporation, and others, some of which are for-profit companies and all of which are funded to a much greater extent by government grants and contracts than the rest. In addition, there is a set of prominent government research agencies, which also have research capacities. Some receive their mandates and funding from Congress—such as the Government Accountability Office (GAO), Congressional Budget Office (CBO), Congressional Research Service (CRS), and the Joint Committee on Taxation—while others are located in the executive branch, such as the CEA, the Office of Management and Budget (OMB), and the Department of Treasury. All of these have research, modeling, and forecasting capacities. The Federal Reserve Board, which is independent of both government branches, is another important state policy research organization. The Fed and Treasury have especially impressive analytic capacities. Treasury, for instance, has hundreds of PhD economists on staff.

Many of these organizations were established long before the 1970s, but proliferation on the private side really began in the late 1970s, as conservatives began to build a number of more aggressive advocacy organizations, led by the pioneering Heritage Foundation. Politics were important in spawning proliferation. The initial rise of conservative organizations in the 1970s and 1980s was in part a response to the perception on the right that the liberals had seized control of government in Washington and that conservatives needed to develop a concerted effort to push back against hegemonic liberal ideas. However, proliferation was also driven by concerns among conservatives that these liberal ideas—Keynesianism being notable among them—were out of date and inadequate for making sense of the stagflation and globalization situations (Ricci, 1993). Wealthy conservative benefactors began to offer money to set up policy research organizations that shared their political and ideological views. As a result, a number of conservative research organizations—both scholarly and advocacy—were founded and expanded in the 1970s and 1980s, such as the Cato Institute in 1977 and the National Center for Policy Analysis in 1983.

Liberals responded in kind. Especially after the 1994 election, when the Republicans seized control of the House of Representatives for the first time in a generation; and then after the 2000 election, when George W. Bush won the White House and the Democrats no longer controlled either the House or Senate, liberal Democrats and others on the left recognized that they needed new places to generate and disseminate policy ideas that would counter those being offered by conservatives to understand the nation's economic situation.

Thus, liberals established their own scholarly organizations like the Economic Policy Institute and the Center on Budget and Policy Priorities, as well as advocacy organizations such as the Progressive Policy Institute and in 2003 the Center for American Progress (e.g. Rich, 2004; Ricci, 1993).

An increasingly fragmented and competitive knowledge regime resulted, driven by corporations, philanthropic foundations, and wealthy patrons seeking to finance organizations to make sense of the stagflation crisis and other national economic problems. Their largesse was facilitated by a booming economy in the 1990s and early 2000s that enabled them to invest in new policy research organizations—especially for advocacy work. Much of the money invested was politically colored and inspired by competition between conservatives and liberals to gain advantage in a war of ideas that had broken out in policy-making circles in the late 1970s and 1980s. And insofar as advocacy work was viewed as being increasingly important, organizations such as the Cato Institute, the Heritage Foundation, the Center for American Progress, and the Century Foundation—most funded by corporate or family foundations and wealthy individuals—tended increasingly to direct their publications toward the media and general public rather than just policy-makers. They were also more apt to advocate particular courses of policy action.

The point is twofold. Firstly, private money plays a substantial role in the US knowledge regime, which is why private policy research organizations represent a comparatively large portion of this knowledge regime. In turn, there is much competition among organizations. Some of it is for funding, particularly as the number of policy research organizations has increased and the economy has weakened. There is also competition for staff. But perhaps most importantly, proliferation has increased competition among private policy research organizations seeking to be heard by policy-makers and the public. In other words, proliferation has led to a cacophony of voices competing to be heard. Secondly, the proliferation of advocacy organizations meant that replication learning was becoming more prevalent. Whereas the traditional scholarly organizations engaged in abstraction-based learning through data analysis and forecasting, the new advocacy organizations were often more inclined toward less rigorous analytic work.

Things are rather different insofar as state policy research organizations are concerned. Here there was virtually no proliferation since the 1970s and more of a coordinated division of labor. For instance, the CRS provides information and research to Congress to help policy-makers figure out what to do on an issue. The CBO and OMB estimate how much various policies will cost. And the GAO evaluates how well programs work. Furthermore, the White House's National Economic Council (NEC) and the Domestic Policy Council coordinate policy analysis and advice for the president, and monitor implementation of the president's policy agenda. The NEC is responsible for most economic policy matters. Most members of the cabinet serve as regular attendees at its meetings and representatives from other government agencies also attend frequently, such as the director of the OMB and the chair of the CEA. Most economic policy advice for the president comes from the so-called "troika"—CEA, OMB, and Treasury, with Treasury typically being the most influential member.

Paradoxically, among a few policy research organizations in civil society, a modicum of cooperation and coordination emerged in response to the rapidly escalating partisanship and ideological polarization in national politics, which began to spill over into the knowledge regime. Analysis and policy recommendations from private policy research organizations characterized as either liberal or conservative were increasingly dismissed as people began to assume that their work was politically partisan. Hence, a credibility crisis began to engulf some of the most prominent private policy research organizations. In turn, some of them joined forces to defend their reputations and draw attention to the fact that partisan politics in Washington was making it increasingly difficult for policy-makers to address some of the nation's most pressing economic problems, such as underfunded entitlement programs like Social Security and Medicare. So, for example, the Urban Institute, Brookings Institution, American Enterprise Institute, and a few others started to convene joint conferences and panels. They also collaborated occasionally on research projects all in an effort to create credibility for their work and to enable themselves to be heard above the growing cacophony of voices that proliferation and competition had spawned.

Related to this was a trend among some of these organizations toward elevating the scientific quality of their research. Some private policy research organizations explained to us that their credibility, and therefore their ability to be heard above the fray, depended increasingly on being known for high-quality analysis. Scientific rigor, sophisticated quantitative analysis, forecasting, and econometric modeling became increasingly important for some organizations.[5] In some cases, however, the reverse seemed to be true—that is, politics and ideology trumped research. A few people accused other organizations of slipshod research and tailoring their research conclusions to fit their political agendas. In short, while some organizations depended on their research to defend against attacks of being politically biased, others depended on their research to legitimize their political views.

Overall, then, the American knowledge regime underwent significant changes. It grew more competitive as its private side was populated increasingly by new policy research organizations, many of which were ideologically partisan and

---

[5] We heard this especially from organizations typically characterized as being liberal or progressive, such as the Economic Policy Institute and the Center on Budget and Policy Priorities. We heard this as well at the Heritage Foundation, which pioneered a variety of advocacy tactics. Since our interviews, however, Heritage hired a new president, Jim DeMint, a Tea Party icon who has taken the organization in a much more ideologically partisan advocacy-oriented direction. As a result, a number of its more analytically inclined staff have left.

advocacy-oriented. Importantly, this affected sensemaking in profound ways, as competing ideas were introduced to understand the new and uncertain economic environment. Keynesianism fell into disrepute and was no longer assumed to be the appropriate paradigm for understanding the national economy. Alternative views emerged, many of which favored a supply-side approach involving less government intervention into the economy. We will return to this issue shortly. Insofar as these views were based on political ideology rather than scientific analysis—a phenomenon that some of our interviewees insisted was the case thanks to these organizations being financed by politically partisan benefactors—some sensemaking turned toward the replication learning form described by March. Put differently, making sense of the economic situation entailed applying politically partisan and ideological principles learned previously to current circumstances. However, a counter-vailing trend also emerged where, for some private organizations, rigorous scientific analysis became especially important as it had long been for most state policy research organizations. In this regard, some organizations turned toward abstraction-based learning. As a result, increasing competition within the US knowledge regime also entailed competition between these two different approaches to sensemaking.

2.3.2 Competing Recommendations from the CEA

Some of the developments we have described were reflected in the way the American CEA made sense of the nation's economic situation. The CEA is part of the executive branch. It consists of three economists drawn from universities as well as a staff of about thirty analysts. It produces annual reports for Congress in the name of the president. The president appoints the three council members. Unsurprisingly, then, we found no example of the CEA criticizing the president or his administration. Moreover, the CEA's reports were more political and sometimes ideological in tone than reports from its Danish counterpart. The CEA reports engaged, for instance, in discussions about the appropriate role of the market and government in economic matters. The mixture of political manifesto and analysis is evident in all three reports, especially in 1987 where the first forty-five pages describe the economy's performance, but many of the following pages introduce neoliberal supply-side ideas to highlight ideologically the need for politicians to address distortions of market mechanisms and disincentives for growth.

One of the most striking features of these reports is how the CEA's basic understanding of the economy shifts from one period to another. This certainly parallels shifting control of the White House and how an escalating crisis of partisanship in the knowledge regime influenced the CEA's reports. In other words, the competitive and ideologically partisan nature of the knowledge regime was reflected in how the CEA made sense of the economy. It also echoes a lack of unanimity among American economists over theoretical assumptions as well as the appropriate way to manage the economy. For instance, the 1987 report from the end of the Reagan era subscribed adamantly to the belief in market efficiency. The report touted a whole array of neoliberal ideas, including privatization, fiscal austerity, regulatory reform, tax cuts, liberalization of agricultural prices, and more, with the obvious intention of "rolling back the state" and reducing its intervention in the economy. This was a supply-side approach the objective of which was, "to enhance . . . the productive activities of individuals and businesses."[6] Similarly, the Reagan CEA argued that markets will be more efficient with less government regulation because regulation distorts competition and restricts consumer choices.[7]

But the Clinton administration's CEA took a sharply different approach, where markets and the state were viewed as complementary rather than antithetical to each other. For example, economic regulation was not viewed as being necessarily good or bad, but rather something that should be cost-effective and consistent. So while the emphasis was still on regulatory reform it was more nuanced and stressed the need to "refine the role of government in the U.S. market economy."[8] This combination of enhancing markets through regulatory reform, but assuring "cost-effectiveness across regulations" was framed with the concept of complementarity—that is, the idea that government regulation can facilitate and not hobble market competition.[9] This was the Clinton administration's "Third Way" approach, which navigated between two diametrically opposed world views: one that worried about government failure and another that worried about market failure.[10] According to the 1997 report, "Over the last four years, this administration has promoted a third vision, one that synthesizes and transcends these two polar worldviews."[11]

In 2007 the CEA reversed itself again. During the George W. Bush administration it did not discuss the complementarities between state and market. Nor, however, did it return entirely to the language of the 1987 report, which only emphasized market efficiency. Instead the CEA accepted the possibility, but certainly not the inevitability, of market failures. According to this report, "Economists generally attempt to justify government intervention into private market outcomes by suggesting potential market failures that may exist in the

---

[6] *Annual Report to the President*, 1987, p. 50.

[7] *Annual Report to the President*, 1987.

[8] *Annual Report to the President*, 1997.

[9] *Annual Report to the President*, 1997, p. 189. The notion of complementarity is especially pronounced where the CEA discusses "using public policy to bring competition to regulated industries" and "markets and public policy as complements" (pp. 196–7).

[10] *Annual Report to the President*, 1997.

[11] *Annual Report to the President*, 1997, p. 19. The discussion of complementarity involved a number of public policy issues running over forty-four pages in the report (pp. 190–235).

absence of any government intervention."[12] Nevertheless, the 2007 report did not dwell on this or waste time on ideological arguments justifying the idea of "potential market failures." This was, after all, still an administration bent upon reducing the government's role in the economy.

This sort of competitive and partisan flip-flopping of CEA ideology was matched by CEA policy recommendations. While all three reports were steeped in supply-side thinking, which focused on providing the appropriate inputs for the economy rather than worrying about managing aggregate demand, they differed significantly in how they advised policy-makers to implement a supply-side program. For example, in keeping with a neoliberal approach the 1987 and 2007 reports emphasized that high taxation was a barrier to economic growth and employment because it undermined incentives for investment of all kinds, including human capital. But the 1997 report, which veered away from strict neoliberalism and stressed the complementarity of government and markets, recommended tax reforms mixed with a variety of state financed supply-side labor market policies to improve education, training, and labor market mobility—in part to help guard against inequality and poverty.[13] Moreover, while the 2007 report stressed that improved labor productivity was crucial for improving the nation's economic competitiveness, it recommended that the way to do this was not through government labor market programs, such as those called for in 1997, but in large part by holding down the costs of labor. Also, the 2007 report returned to the theme of the 1987 report in putting tax cuts front and center as the key to improving market efficiency, deepening capital investment, cultivating worker skills, attracting foreign investment, encouraging innovation and entrepreneurialism, and facilitating research and development. In the CEA's words, "The goal of pro-growth tax policy is to reduce tax distortions that hamper economic growth. Most economists agree that lower taxes on capital income stimulate greater investment, resulting in greater economic growth, greater international competitiveness, and higher standards of living."[14]

Despite the fact that there was much flip-flopping in the ideological and philosophical views among the CEA reports, there was also a consistent trend toward more rigorous scientific analysis. As we have explained, the onset of stagflation, globalization and other problems, and increasing political partisanship led some policy research organizations to beef up the scientific rigor of their work. The three CEA reports we analyzed exhibited a tendency for greater emphasis on scientific references, analysis, methods, and the use of databases and models. For example, between 1987 and 2007 we found a dramatic increase in the number of references to scientific journals, academic

---

[12] *Annual Report to the President*, 2007, p. 91.
[13] *Annual Report to the President*, 1997, pp. 33, 41, and 158.
[14] *Annual Report to the President*, 2007.

papers, and reports from other forecasting organizations. We also found an increase in the number of databases the CEA utilized and the introduction of new microeconomic models for measuring the productivity of the American economy. The CEA, for instance, began using a Dynamic Stochastic General Equilibrium model based on rational expectations theory. Finally, the reports relied increasingly on the style of argumentation found in academic journals and papers.

Over all, then, the CEA reports reflected the politically partisan, competitive, and ideologically charged nature of the American knowledge regime of which it was a part. Partisanship and competition in the knowledge regime infected the CEA by virtue of the fact that the composition of the council changed with each administration and, therefore, tended to resemble the ideological color of that administration insofar as its economic assumptions and priorities were concerned. As a result, the CEA reports took on a certain schizophrenic quality. Firstly, there was considerable philosophical and ideological flip-flopping between neoliberal and non-neoliberal supply-side viewpoints. In some cases the CEA viewed government economic intervention with considerable suspicion as a threat to market efficiency and competition. But in other cases it saw the possibilities for such intervention as being complementary to markets and a source of improving competition. Policy recommendations followed this flip-flopping pattern. Tax cuts for the wealthy and potential investors were held in high regard by the two Republican administrations but not Clinton's Democratic administration. So, although all of the reports embraced the supply-side approach to managing the economy, they did so in rather different ways. Secondly, in contrast to this flip-flopping pattern, there were certain important consistencies across the reports. They demonstrated a propensity for ever more scientifically based argument as demonstrated, for instance, through the use of more sophisticated analytic techniques, databases, and the trappings of academic-style argumentation. The blending of science and ideology was another schizophrenic dimension in these reports.

All of this can be viewed as well from the standpoint of sensemaking insofar as the CEA reports exhibit two sensemaking approaches. On the one hand, philosophical and ideological flip-flopping was based on the invocation of deeply held assumptions inherited from the past to help make sense of the current economic situation—assumptions that varied depending on the political character of the administration for whom the CEA worked. This is an example of March's replication learning where scripts, templates, or other ideas learned in the past are used to make sense of the present and forecast the future. However, the rise of more sophisticated scientific analysis represented efforts to better understand the causes underlying the nation's economic situation and thus illustrated the abstraction-based form of sensemaking. The use of both forms of sensemaking—in both retrospective and prospective ways—underscores the schizophrenic nature of the competitive knowledge regime in the US. Things were much different in Denmark.

2.4 DENMARK: COOPERATION AND CONSISTENCY

Denmark's knowledge regime was marked by cooperation rather than competition among policy research organizations. It was also one in which ideology as the bedrock of policy analysis was jettisoned in favor of more analytic and scientific approaches. As such, cooperative abstraction-based learning replaced ideologically competitive replication learning. And the state played an increasingly important role in facilitating all of this.

2.4.1 Changes in the Danish Knowledge Regime

Denmark's knowledge regime is dominated by policy research organizations from the state and the social partners, by which we mean organized business and labor. The most prominent organizations are those from the state and among those the Ministry of Finance is especially important. It houses databases and economic models used in every corner of the knowledge regime. It publishes the most comprehensive forecasts and overviews of the Danish economy. It prepares the medium-term plans for public expenditures and policy reforms, and it organizes the annual state budget. It is also responsible for ensuring the quality of all public regulation and performing cost-benefit analyses of all new policy reforms and laws. As a result, it is also involved in the negotiation and formulation of the yearly law program (*Lovprogram*) in which the government presents its plans for new initiatives, laws, and policies. Moreover, the Ministry publishes a great number of analytical papers, including policy analyses on welfare issues, working papers on methodological issues, and suggestions for reforms of the public sector. Finally, it is involved in ad hoc commissions and committees working under tripartite agreements as well as running hundreds of working groups within and between ministries. The Ministry of Finance is without peer in the Danish knowledge regime.

There are also a number of state and semi-public policy research organizations that do apply research on behalf of the government.[15] Several are integrated with universities or established as independent state research organizations and located in different ministries. For instance, the government

---

[15] By semi-public we mean policy research organizations that are funded and often organized by the state but operate independently from it.

funds the DREAM group and the DØR. It also funds a number of research programs that are outsourced either to universities or state research organizations like the Danish National Center for Social Research and the Danish Institute of Governmental Research, which publish analytical reports, papers in academic journals, and working papers, and also arrange public conferences and hearings. Another way the government participates in the knowledge regime was introduced in 2005 in the form of knowledge councils, which were inspired by examples from England and introduced by the Prime Minister's Office to strengthen the government's role in policy debates as well as facilitate negotiations with political parties, the social partners, and others over important policy matters. First were the Globalization Council, established in 2007, and then the Growth Forum, established in 2009. Both were intended to advise the government on future challenges and include the social partners and others in decisions about which topics to include in future discussions. Both councils had the Premier Minister sitting at the table.

Expert ad hoc commissions are another relatively new way for the government to organize policy research and advising. In the mid-1980s a conservative government decided to dismantle the traditional corporatist tripartite commissions, choosing instead to seek advice from expert commissions (Pedersen, 2011). Tripartite commissions had been organized routinely over the years to do analysis and provide policy advice on a wide range of policy issues. But the turn toward ad hoc commissions of experts meant that the labor, business, and employer associations had to find new ways of influencing policy discussions. Thus, business and labor peak associations, as well as banks and financial institutions, started to build up their own analytical research units in order to complement, if not compete with, the government and its ad hoc commissions in producing economic analysis and forecasts. As a result, today, a more pluralistic system has developed in the sense that the government, semi-public research organizations, interest associations, and financial institutions publish reports, analyses, and blue prints, often providing them to the press for public discussion. However, this is all orchestrated increasingly by the state, principally the Ministry of Finance, so that pluralisation on one side has been matched with centralized coordination on the other. Moreover, as we shall see, this has not led to the sort of partisan competition found in the American knowledge regime.

It is important as well to emphasize the role played by the peak associations in all of this. The Landsorganisationen Danmark (LO), the national labor union confederation, is an important partner in policy negotiations with the government, but is also a lobbying organization. The LO has a research unit whose work it uses during negotiations and lobbies on a variety of policy issues. Another research unit, Arbejderbevægelsens Erhvervsråd (AE), is closely associated with the labor movement, although independent from the LO. Not to be outdone, the Danish employer's confederation, Dansk

Arbejdsgiverforening (DA), has its own scholarly modeling and forecasting operation, but also does advocacy and lobbying work on behalf of its members. The big banks and other organizations, most prominent among them being the Danish industrial association, Dansk Industri (DI), also have sophisticated analytic capacities. But they are also involved in lobbying and advocacy work.

The point is that in Denmark the lines separating state, scholarly, and advocacy policy research organizations are much blurrier than in the US. Blurring things further is the fact that the state began collaborating more with these organizations and that the ideological differences that had previously divided them and mitigated collaboration and cooperation among some of them began to fade away. How this happened is instructive.

With the onset of the stagflation crisis—which in Denmark was accompanied by mounting government fiscal deficits and national debt—traditional corporatist institutions, as well as the conventional ideological positions of the political parties, and business and labor organizations proved to be insufficient for making sense of and resolving the nation's economic problems. Tripartite corporatist arrangements were transformed in various ways. Moreover, a search for alternative sensemaking approaches ensued. Three things were especially important in this search.

Firstly, several people told us during interviews that during the 1980s almost everyone began to temper their ideological differences and political partisanship. And many policy research organizations—especially in the private sector—soon learned that nobody would take them seriously if they came to policy negotiations and debates wearing their ideology on their sleeves. Ideological arguments were no longer credible.

Secondly, this led to an important change in sensemaking approaches. Policy research organizations began to turn more toward the scientific analysis of data in order to better understand the nation's economic problems and devise policy solutions for them. Their credibility came to depend increasingly on their ability to make convincing arguments based on solid data analysis. As a result, everybody began to elevate their analytic game by developing better data sets, more sophisticated statistical and modeling capacities, and the like. Even some of the scholarly research organizations reported that they came under greater pressure to improve their in-house analytic expertise in order to compete more effectively with each other and with the Ministry of Finance in influencing policy. The Ministry played a key role here, insofar as it sponsored the development of a variety of macroeconomic and microeconomic models to better understand the national economy and where it was likely headed; models that were often made available as a public good to any organization that wanted to use them. The tendency, then, was for most policy research organizations to use the same basic analytical toolkit.

Thirdly, policy research organizations began to cooperate with each other in producing data, forecasts, and other analytic practices. All of the major forecasting groups inside or very close to the state—such as the Ministry of Finance and DØR, respectively—and farther from the state—including AE, LO, DA, and the large banks—began to use similar data sets and analytic models, although they often modified them for their own purposes. Today there is much sharing of data and information about analytic technics. For example, the DA and LO research shops routinely do this with each other and DA shares much of the data it collects from its members with other organizations, including Danmarks Statistik, Denmark's national statistics office. Cooperation is apparent in other ways too. Notably, LO and DA sometimes collaborate in order to define problems for which they believe research is necessary. Sometimes they work together on these research projects and craft joint policy recommendations. And together they sometimes even lobby the government to act on their recommendations.

What occurred, then, in Denmark was the development of a new knowledge regime that set aside traditional ideological arguments in favor of a more analytic approach. This, of course, represented a shift from a replication to an abstraction-based form of sensemaking to understand the nation's economic problems. This was led in large measure by the state, particularly the Ministry of Finance, which began to establish various public and semi-public policy research organizations whose operations were dominated less by the social partners and more by experts in policy analysis, modeling, and forecasting. This also involved more cooperation among state, scholarly, and advocacy policy research organizations. In much of this the Ministry also began to play a more forceful and active role as gatekeeper to policy analysis and policy deliberations, whereas until the early 1980s organizations participated in public policy-making through formalized channels granting peak organizations a near monopoly of representation in public commissions and administrative councils. So, the Danish knowledge regime is less competitive than the American one. It is also less partisan and more cooperative. And it is more consistent in terms of turning away from replication toward abstraction-based learning as the chief approach to sensemaking. Much of this is reflected in the DØR's reports from the period.

2.4.2 Consistent Recommendations from the DØR

The DØR is a semi-public policy research organization funded by the government. It has a council with representatives from government, labor, business, and the financial institutions as well as a chairmanship of four independent economists—the so-called "Wise Men"—appointed from universities by the government. By law the council is mandated "to contribute to the coordination of different economic interests" and tries to facilitate consensus among the representatives on the council from the social partners, government, and others, although it does not always achieve it.[16] The council meets twice a year to give comments to biannual reports prepared by the Wise Men. Several aspects of the Danish knowledge regime's transformations are reflected in the reports prepared by the Wise Men for the DØR.

Firstly, because the Wise Men's mandate is in part to help facilitate consensus among the social partners on the council—who have long been involved in a variety of corporatist negotiations aiming for consensus in labor market and other economic matters—these reports exhibit none of the flip-flopping characteristic of the American CEA reports. They are much more even-keeled. Extreme positions are avoided. And in this regard they do not adopt a rigid philosophical tone assuming either the inevitability of market failure or market efficiency. In fact, the Wise Men have long recognized both possibilities and argued for a middle ground position.[17] This is an artifact of the cooperative and consensus-oriented nature of sensemaking in Denmark.

Secondly, this sort of consensus-oriented moderation led to consistency across reports. In other words, sensemaking is a less erratic process than it is at the American CEA. For instance, acceptance of supply-side reasoning appeared quite late.[18] The 2007 report was the only one we reviewed to accept supply-side measures, and only because of specific concerns in this period about an insufficient supply of labor.[19] In contrast, the 1987 report only discussed supply-side policies in negative terms, deeming them useful only under very particular circumstances, such as these. Furthermore, in 1987 the supply-side approach was said to be less effective than demand-side policies in managing the national economy.[20] Even when a supply-side approach was accepted in the 2007 report, it was supposed to be mixed with a demand-side approach, which was clearly preferred by the Wise Men. Notably, when the Wise Men recommended in 2007 that growth in government spending be reduced, they also acknowledged the positive economic consequences that the growth in public expenditures had had up until then.[21]

Thirdly, the Wise Men maintained a clear aversion to neoliberalism even as they warmed to some supply-side possibilities. This we presume stemmed from the inclusive nature of Danish sensemaking. Indeed, organized labor was always represented in the council and even representatives from the business community subscribed to certain basic social democratic principles.[22]

---

[16] Law no. 574 of June 6, 2007.
[17] *Dansk Økonomi*, May 1987, chapter IV, pp. 68–9. Chapter IV also discusses different types of market failure.
[18] *Dansk Økonomi*, spring 2007.
[19] *Dansk Økonomi*, spring 2007, pp. 3, 27, and 93.
[20] *Dansk Økonomi*, December 1987, p. 22.
[21] *Dansk Økonomi*, spring 2007, pp. 4 and 96.
[22] In an off-the-record comment to Campbell during an interview a representative from a major business association remarked that at heart everyone in Denmark holds dear some social democratic principles.

In particular, from 1987 through 2007 they endorsed the use of public expend-itures as demand-side automatic stabilizers.[23] The extensive use of automatic stabilizers, of course, represented the institutionalization of decades-old compromises among the social partners and government. It was also a throw-back to Keynesianism. And we found no example of the neoliberal idea of rolling back the state. Instead, the emphasis was more on controlling public expenditures and on reforming the public sector so as to make it more efficient. The one exception was that the Wise Men raised concerns about fiscal sustainability in their 2007 report. They worried that a social contract existed between the government and the people, which included promises of pensions and health care, and that it was unclear whether the state would be able to meet its obligations under that contract as the population got older and there would not be enough workers in future generations to financially sustain these programs. The idea of fiscal sustainability was couched in rational expectations models and microeconomic analysis in order to lay the ground-work for mid- and long-term structural reforms in these programs and to address the issue of an insufficient supply of labor.

The aversion to neoliberalism is especially clear if we compare specific policy recommendations from the Wise Men and the American CEA. Generally speaking, in 1987 the Wise Men held fiscal policies to be more effective than monetary policies for stimulating the economy, and lower taxes to be less effective than lower wages for improving trade and the balance of payments.[24] More specifically, by then the CEA was already calling for supply-side tax cuts as the most important means for creating incentives and improving American economic competitiveness.[25] But in Denmark tax reform was viewed primarily as a means of income redistribution and only secondarily as a vehicle for creating economic incentives.[26] Furthermore, in Denmark the Wise Men took wage competitiveness to be the most important factor affecting the inter-national competitiveness of the economy, not taxes. This argument was usually followed by an emphasis on the role of the social partners in negotiating wage moderation, and on the need for the government and social partners to coordinate their decision making.[27] Calls for institutionalized negotiations like this were a far cry from the more neoliberal approach of the CEA. In short, demand-side fiscal policy still ruled the roost in Denmark insofar as stimulating the economy was concerned.[28] And in this regard it was not tax cuts, but rather public expenditures and public investment that the Wise Men

---

[23] *Dansk Økonomi,* December 1987, chapter, pp. 16 and 22; *Dansk Økonomi,* spring 2007, p. 110.

[24] *Dansk Økonomi,* spring 2007, pp. 75ff.

[25] *Annual Report to the President,* January 1987, pp. 83–96.

[26] For the use of taxation to establish incentives, see *Dansk Økonomi,* May 1987, pp. 11–12. See for consistency *Dansk Økonomi,* spring 2007, pp. 95–6.

[27] *Dansk Økonomi,* December 1987, pp. 76ff.

[28] *Dansk Økonomi,* December 1987, p. 148.

viewed as the more effective way to accomplish the job.[29] This is certainly why the Wise Men provided many pages in their 2007 report discussing how demand-side policies could be used to stabilize the economy.[30]

Fourthly, we found evidence in the Wise Men's reports of the move toward ever more scientific analysis—that is, abstraction-based learning. For example, in the spring 1987 report there were only a few references to academic papers, international databases, or the work of international research organizations. However, in the spring 2007 report the number of references to academic journals increased dramatically, as did references to international databases and research organizations.[31] And as in America the style of argumentation increasingly resembled that found traditionally in academic journals and papers.

In sum, the Wise Men's reports illustrated a very different approach to sensemaking than the CEA's reports in the US. It was a much more cooperative and consensus-oriented approach than in the US—a clear reflection of how things were conducted in the knowledge regime in general. This meant as well a much more stable process in the sense that the Wise Men did not flip-flop around ideological or politically partisan poles. Only gradually and recently did supply-side understandings emerge and then in ways that eschewed neoliberalism and remained mostly subordinate to traditional demand-side Keynesianism to which most members of the council remained committed. This reflected the broader knowledge regime too, insofar as it was associated with inclusive cooperative sensemaking practices. And it was generally and consistently a more science-based approach than in the CEA reports. In this regard, the Wise Men were more inclined toward abstraction-based learning than replication learning. As a result, sensemaking in Denmark was less competitive and therefore less schizophrenic than in the US.

2.5 CONCLUSIONS

The most important insight here is the fact that, insofar as economic policy analysis and advising is concerned, sensemaking varies according to how it is organized in national knowledge regimes. The two knowledge regimes made sense of economic uncertainty in rather different ways with the American knowledge regime becoming more competitive and the Danish knowledge regime becoming more cooperative. In both cases people questioned the conventional ways of making sense of the national economic situation and

---

[29] *Dansk Økonomi*, December 1987, p. 130.
[30] *Dansk Økonomi*, December 1987, chapter II.
[31] See the comprehensive reference list in *Dansk Økonomi*, spring 2007, pp. 305–14.

made some changes. The abstraction-based learning approach gained ground in both countries. But in the US the number of advocacy organizations increased significantly with the result being that the knowledge regime became more competitive and partisan, and replication learning became more prominent—even to the point of jeopardizing the credibility of some policy research organizations that had opted for the abstraction-based approach. In contrast, ideology and the replication learning approach to sensemaking were largely set aside in Denmark. People started to question the conventional political-ideological sensemaking approach and so developed a less politicized way of sensemaking. And in Denmark in many respects the state orchestrated this, but in ways that enhanced the collaborative and cooperative nature of sensemaking.

These broad changes in each knowledge regime were evident as well in each one's national council of economic advisors. In effect, the organization and sensemaking dynamics of each one reflected in microcosm those of their respective knowledge regimes. The American CEA exhibited much partisan flip-flopping and was more inclined to extreme points of view—that is, neoliberalism—than its Danish counterpart. In contrast, the DØR's reports were steadier and more moderate in perspective, with little of the ideological gesticulation of the American CEA reports.

It is important to reiterate that replication and abstraction-based learning involve both retrospective and prospective sensemaking. The American CEA made sense of the past in both ideological/replication and causal/abstraction terms. The analysis of past performance was based on both ideological inter-pretations and econometric modeling. Similarly, the lessons gleaned from the past were projected into the future through ideological predictions of whether free markets would perform well or not, as well as econometric forecasts. So it is difficult to disentangle retrospective from prospective sensemaking in this case. Retrospective and prospective sensemaking also bled together in Den-mark. The DØR based its forecasts on econometric analysis of past perform-ance. Indeed, most policy research organizations are in the business of examining and understanding the past in order to make predictions and policy recommendations for the future. This is what econometric modeling and forecasting is all about. Hence, differences in the two knowledge regimes are best suited for understanding how policy research organizations engage in either replication or abstraction-based sensemaking rather than retrospective or prospective sensemaking.

We have, of course, treated both the US and Danish knowledge regimes in isolation from each other. As we have explained, national knowledge regimes are sometimes linked to each other through various formal and informal arrangements (Campbell & Pedersen, 2014). Professional econo-mists, for instance, travel in international circles and read the international literature. The OECD, the EU, and other international organizations certainly facilitate linkages among knowledge regimes too. But we found little evidence during our interviews that the effects were so significant as to overwhelm the structures and practices of national knowledge regimes. And even when ideas did diffuse across borders, notably the movement of neoliberal and supply-side ideas from one country—often the US—to another, this process was mediated by institutional arrangements in national knowledge regimes. Indeed, despite the fact that the Wise Men were well aware of neoliberal supply-side economics in the United States, they were not so enamored with it to abandon demand-side traditions or call for the state to cease being a key player in the economy. They were, after all, supposed to facilitate consensus and compromise among the DØR members, some of whom, notably organized labor, were adamantly opposed to neoliberal austerity policies.

One caveat is important. The American CEA reports frequently discussed monetary policy. The Danish Wise Men's reports did not. This, of course, is because the Danish kroner was pegged to the German deutschmark in 1982 and then the euro in 1999, thus putting monetary policy largely out of reach for Danish policy-makers. This is why a turn toward monetarism was far more evident in the CEA reports than the DØR reports.

Whether changes in knowledge regimes and the sensemaking practices of their principal actors—policy research organizations—mattered for economic performance and institutional competitiveness is an open question. On the one hand, the international competitiveness of both economies recovered in the 1990s and early 2000s. Even today after the 2008 financial crisis sent shock waves through both countries, they are still ranked among the ten most competitive economies in the world (World Economic Forum, 2012). Hence, one might infer that the manner in which people in both countries made sense of their situations eventually contributed to economic policies that were successful. This would be consistent with those who have argued that there is no one best route to success for advanced capitalist countries (Hall & Soskice, 2001). On the other hand, there are no guarantees that policy-makers necessarily listen to whatever ideas they might receive from their knowledge regimes. Policy-making is complicated and involves much more than just sensemaking per se. Further research is required to determine the degree to which the policy decisions that actually affected national economic competitiveness were influenced by what happened in these knowledge regimes or something else. But if knowledge regimes were influential, then how they are organized and operate is certainly implicated in the institutional as well as the international economic competitiveness of nations.

3

Productive Enterprise in Search of a Regime

Moving Sensemaking from Past Phantom Communities to "Ends in Sight"

Peer Hull Kristensen

3.1 INTRODUCTION

Though the Fordist production regime dominated in the post-World War Two recovery—both mentally and organizationally—many countries did not simply import the model (Zeitlin & Herrigel, 2000). Rather divergent institutional legacies and adaptations helped to foster many different ways of combining institutions with business enterprises. Thus, instead, capitalist countries could be seen to gradually develop a diversity of *competition models*—for example, Fordism, craft production, flexible specialization, diversified quality production, the "opportunistic" model, the "flexible mass production of differentiated goods and services" model, and the "discontinuous innovation" model (Whitley, 2010). Whitley argues that each of these competition models depends on particular sorts of labor power, particular sets of knowledge, and particular types of capital, which are produced by a variety of different institutions, which differs in their composition among capitalist countries. Put differently, with more emphasis on the formative processes behind such competition models, we should imagine that, dependent on the professional identities of different social groups at a given time and space, they will tend to form the nature of firms and institutions so that they enlarge the social space that allows their respective aspirations to thrive. Obviously, such a process neither unfolds without conflicts among the groups involved, nor in a neat and rational way. An emerging competition model is only attractive for a grouping if it allows for fulfilling given aspirations or offers prospects for even more promising life worlds (Kristensen, 1999). A *competition model* could be said to be subjectively attractive, if this is achieved, whereas it has to be "objectively" sustainable in the competitive selection process.

Whitley's competition models could be seen as those that were "objectively" sustainable during a period where Fordism dominated. With the crisis of Fordism after 1975 some of the other models showed comparative advantages, but today it seems as if globalization has broken with this previous form of complementarity. The variety of national competition models are now rather contested on their ability to search for a new role in an emerging production regime, tentatively characterized by global value chains, networks of innovation, etc. where the competitive advantage of firms—in particular multinationals—is dependent on the ability to combine comparative advantages across countries in disintegrated production and innovation networks (Kristensen & Morgan, 2012).

Such transformations, however, only come easy to external academic observers. Both the formation of the old competition models and the search for the new ones involve actors that try to make sense of the world and of the situation, probably in the first instance trying to protect the competiveness of their past model, which also sets the scene for forming their current identities and future expectations, to use James March's (2010) wording for replication forms of dealing with ambiguity. The question is, however, whether such a replication approach may trigger an abstraction-based attitude so that it leads to improved search and understanding of causes and needs of novel perspectives.

3.2 MAKING SENSE BY COMPARING SENSEMAKING

Debates of how social communities make sense of situations and structure actions accordingly have become intense with a myriad of academic approaches making it difficult to assess when making sense of sensemaking has been done in a satisfying way. Previously, the task seemed manageable as sensemaking was about adding a certain dose of *Verstehen* to a basic scheme of functional or causal explanation, *Erklärung*, as in the Weberian tradition. Now it is expected that causalities operate primarily by triggering sensemaking processes, and that it is when these are intellectually narrated as causalities that causes do actually emerge. This has made the job of making scientific explanations very difficult, especially within an organization studies framework that tends to focus on micro-level interactions and is generally reluctant to broaden the analysis to understanding larger patterns.

It is likely that most scholars would expect the job to increase in magnitude and complexity if asked to perform such analyses comparatively. Against such expectations it is my contention that, without a comparative view, it is almost impossible to capture idiosyncratic sensemaking processes and use them to help understand how processes of change take on divergent routes in different time periods (Foucault, 1970) and societies (Herrigel, 2010). Comparative studies might accidentally bring the researcher to a situation where previous observations in one field can suddenly be compared with ongoing observations in another field. Contrasting the two may reveal many of the core concerns of how participants sensemake their situation, narrate the process of change that they go through, and use these understandings to interact and assess actions and decisions. Furthermore, such accidental discoveries make it possible to use comparative material to capture entire configurations of social life and thereby overcome the dualisms of micro and macro (Ragin, 1987).

3.3 ACCIDENTAL DISCOVERY OF DIFFERENCES IN SENSEMAKING

Such an accidental discovery of different sensemaking processes happened in 2000, when we were researching different subsidiaries of a multinational in different countries (Kristensen & Zeitlin, 2005). We were interviewing the team leader (TK) of one of the new production cells that had been created in an American subsidiary in Lake Mills a couple of years earlier, as part of the ongoing process of changing production in tune with a trajectory scheme towards lean production (Strauss, 2008). As we were finishing the interview, TK said:

> "If you meet Flemming in Horsens [where a Danish subsidiary of the same multinational was located], please send him my best wishes and tell him that we have neither changed the architecture of the cell nor the programs of the individual CNC machines since he set up the cell two years ago. It is very impressive."

Thinking that Fleming was the managing director of the Horsens plant and knowing that he was very busy after he had become business area manager of twenty-two subsidiaries around the world, I said:

> "I will, but how could Fleming get time to do this with all his other duties and not being very skilled in CNC programming?"

> "Oh, no," TK said, "I didn't mean Fleming, the manager, but Fleming, the machine worker, a guy with an extreme mass of technical courses, you know. Though a worker, like me, he came here for half a year and helped restructure the whole plant, but it was really impressive that he could go into such detail that he was able to devote the individual machine for specific tasks and make the actual programming of it."

"Aha, that Fleming. I have already heard about him and will pass on your regards, when I am interviewing him next month to learn about his working career and his current role in the Horsens plant."

TK's remarks were highly significant. Not in isolation. But because of their contrast to what I had learned just a few months previous during a visit to the Horsens plant. Here the situation was almost the opposite. CNC machines were frequently reprogramed, or programs were being modified as new and better work sequences were discovered. Furthermore, machines were constantly being newly programed for producing new blanks with the continuous incremental change in products. The machinists were in general frustrated by having to use flexible machines for repetitive tasks and wanted to liberate the flexibility of these machines by investing in automats or by outsourcing the most repetitive tasks. Where Lake Mills were opting for devoting machines and manpower for repetitive tasks, Horsens' workers were trying to get rid of such tasks. At the same time, the business area manager, the other Flemming, and the Horsens convener had agreed that "We cannot bill customers for resetting time, so we have to be better at doing it quickly." Consequently, the whole plant was engaged in a comprehensive game of bringing down resetting time—factory workers, technical and sales staff, logistic planners—and for every 20 percent decrease, there would follow a general increase in salaries for all groups of employees. Thus, they were searching for novel ways of collaborating and interacting through such a new incentive scheme to increase the benefits and reduce the costs of being flexible. Being competitive in the US was associated with doing repetitive tasks, while in Denmark it was related to being speedy in flexibility and getting rid of such repetition; two very different ways of chasing competitiveness.

A closer look at the workplaces that constituted the work organization of the two plants would reveal even more significant differences. In the American plant, a cell consisted of fairly repetitive workplaces, the meaning of which was given by the overarching architecture of the plant. In the Danish case, teams were organized according to a series of machines, which workers could make use of for highly different tasks during a day, and the Danish workers would frequently work at their desks and construct new programs to run new manufacturing tasks, be collaborating across teams and departments to make a new blank, etc. The Danish plant could be seen as a whole set of independent suppliers working under one roof, whereas Lake Mills had a fixed division of labor.

After the transition towards lean production, American plant workers were stimulated to learn to run more than one machine via a "learn to earn" scheme that helped stimulate rotation; whereas in the Danish plant, to learn to run a set of machines properly, to be able to reprogram them frequently, etc. generally took many months, and rotation was inhibited by workers who would constantly sophisticate their workplaces with new equipment, add-ons, and testing procedures. The latter were exploring the opportunities of materials, tools, and different forms of computer steering, and machine workers said it took more than a decade to learn to exploit the full potential of a new CNC machine. The balance between exploration and exploitation differed considerably between the two plants.

Contrary to the American plant, workers in the Horsens plant, at the end of a long series of on-the-job training sequences and numerous sophisticated further training courses, received no extra pay. Continuous training and learning was seen as a part of their renumeration. The Danish convener said: "Should we, after having invested heavily in further training of workers also pay them extra for our investments? This would create very wrong inducements for stimulating learning." The "learn to earn" of the Lake Mills plant thus would have been considered totally alien in a Danish context.

Do not miss my point. The organization of work at the time of observation in both Lake Mills and Horsens was inspired by ongoing transitions to Japanese forms of work organization and manufacturing management. On the one hand, in many ways Lake Mills came closer to this ideal template by keeping the cells focused on a well-defined set of tasks and rotating men among machines within the cell by up-skilling them. On the other hand, skills and abilities to make changes and improvements in Horsens lived up to the highest imaginable standards for up-skilling, but this was used to continuously change and sophisticate the individual workplace for flexibility.

3.4 MAKING SENSE OF HOW ACTORS MAKE SENSE IN DIFFERENT FIELDS

It is a common argument among organization analysts that differences in how work is organized is the outcome of local translations of an otherwise basically isomorphic transformation of industry (Meyer & Rowan, 1991; Delmestri, 1998). That may be, but then it is very difficult to see exactly where the differences in translation happen. In this case, a Horsens worker had restructured the American plant under the auspices of a business area manager in Horsens, also acting as manager of Lake Mills. The translation seems to happen by institutionalizing similar practices in highly divergent ways. But why and how?

There is no question that changing towards Japanese templates of organization has been seen as a source of serious disruption of normal routines and habitual acts for the social groups involved—both in the US and Denmark. In the words of Mead's social psychology, when situations are normal, people align their actions by "taking on the role of others and forming a *me*" (Mead, 1934). But if situations, for some reason, become abnormal and do not perform normal roles this triggers some role holders to "raise an *I* against *me*" (Mead, 1934), that is, to become reflective of the *me* that performs habituated actions. Mead's framework, however, raises a major problem concerning how individualized reflectiveness transforms into collective reflectiveness. How do an *us* and a *we* become constituted?

At a given time, "mes" have been constituted as an endless history of "taking an I against me," by which the individual become institutionalized in their community and the community in them. In the introductory chapter this was referred to as "identity construction", with a reference to Weick and March (2010). A similar thought is found in Selznick (1957), who speaks about *character* or *organizational character* when institutionalization of an organization has taken place. Character formation happens through a sequence of incremental and irreversible commitments between community and individual, and between organization and community/society. If this happens gradually and incrementally, and without rationalization and justification, both the individual and the organization may be quite unaware of its character or identity.

But when changes confront past character formation, individuals, groupings, and organizations may become conscious of their character and, for each new step in the new direction, they become more and more aware of the dimensions that constituted the old character and the community in which it was embedded. Maybe it is a break with past expectations to the future that make organization members discover their identity and the community in which these expectations could be fulfilled? In this way, the notions that March connects with replication forms of dealing with ambiguity may be activated.

But this step may have great consequences. Weick (2001) has shown how spontaneous interaction may gradually become self-conscious, first by a mutual justification of the rationality of interaction by the interacting parties and later by inventing a description of the world in which this interaction becomes of importance. This process of interpretation justification is at the forefront and the outcome of discovering an *us* by a justifying *we*.

In this way, organization members come to discover that they share a general idea of the idealized community they prefer and see it as giving space for their diversity of aspirations; an abstract *generalized other* (Mead, 1934) is being socially constructed. Athens (2007) has called such a generalized other a *phantom community*, as it is only depiction of the "objective" community from the needs of justifications that are evoked by a concrete situation. But it may well be one in which it is possible to see the place and prospects of oneself and others as a set of idealized role holders and roles. Thus, a phantom community may be used to measure whether practices and roles are moving in the right direction for/by different groupings. Thus phantom communities may provide models to guide, search, and construct causalities, and are hereby preparing for what the editors of this volume call an "abstraction-based approach." When reacting to a novel situation actors may tacitly or by reflective deliberation try to implement the new changes by institutionalizing practices that create as much of the imagined phantom community as possible that they share, while ignoring other parts of the changes. In terms of competitiveness, they are trying to make the past phantom community competitive by making use of changes to protect as much as possible the ideals of a community. Mostly, when referring to "phantom communities," we mean those evoked as idealized versions of a past form of living, community, or society. Sometimes, as pressures for change persist and groupings align themselves in role matrices that reflect this future, take on new aspirations, and formulate new group interests, they may imagine futuristic phantom communities, but here we will refer to these as "ends in sight," following Dewey's notion (Ansell, 2011). When the latter occurs, abstraction-based search and causality construction may enter an even higher level of sophistication.

3.5 THE DETECTION OF PHANTOM COMMUNITIES

Though phantom communities are very difficult to detect empirically, as they normally rest in the minds of individuals and groups, it becomes much easier to iterate towards approximation when two or more fields of actions are compared, as the comparison reveals sets of signifiers. Though this is the case, described collective phantom communities will always be the result of an observer's engagement with and analytical work on an empirical field, and can only be an approximation to the ones held by its participants. With these reservations our comparative analyses came to understand the phantom communities of the two plants broadly in the following way.

In Lake Mills workers and local managers agree that the age of grandeur was in the 1960s, when the firm became large, vertically integrated, and a primary player in the American oligopolistic market, so that the co-evolution of jobs in manufacturing, engineering, sales, and management constituted a hierarchy of heterogeneous specialties, in which the growth of some led to the growth of all. Seniority rules under the surveillance of strong unions determined how safe employment was, and the longer a worker operated the same job, the higher their qualifications rated and the easier their access to higher levels of the hierarchy or to a repositioning in jobs with plenty of overtime pay when positions became vacant. As the corporation was dominating the small community of Lake Mills as the single largest employer, the growth of the community, town, and the corporation were deeply interdependent. In many ways the plant and the corporation offered the basic framework also for the social stratification of citizens, and its rules of and roads toward promotion were consequently among the strongest conditioners for social mobility of its citizens. Of course, as in every vertically integrated plant that grew incrementally, there was both a tendency to co-evolve the capacity of machines and workplaces proportionally to the needs of the general turnover, but also a tendency for inconsistencies to emerge. The latter created an abundance of possibilities for running machines and jobs on an overtime basis, giving some job holders opportunities for overtime pay. This explains why devoted machines and jobs played an important part in the company: The more devoted machines and workplaces were, the more probable it would be to get the fringe benefit of overtime as a factory designed in this way will have shifting bottlenecks dependent on conjunctures for different products. At the same time, the more routine and rule-bound jobs were, the easier it would be to see how to make use of them in a sequence to create a career appreciated by peers of the local community. Managers owed their position in the plant and community to such careers, but were devoted to this phantom community. The plant had given space to several strong unions, which constituted their power by organizing the holders of job positions. In many ways, the importance of unions stemmed from handling (with managers) the grievances that emerged by working together within this structure of stable positions in markets of shifting conjunctures. Speaking of complementarities, this construction of a phantom community contains them in abundance.

Employees in Horsens shared a very different phantom community. In a distant past the plant had been an engineering craft plant producing a heterogeneous set of machines for food processing and, being a very small firm (especially compared with Lake Mills), workers had been used to do highly shifting types of work. The core workers were craft metal workers, but they were assisted by skilled specialized workers (would-be craft workers) (Sabel, 1982). The craft metal workers' union dominated the plant, but engaged the specialized workers in a coordinated effort to secure the continuous training and up-skilling of all factory workers to enlarge the roles of the factory against, in the eyes of workers, intruding technical office staff. After a series of mergers and acquisitions the plant had been forced to specialize on some few core products (pumps and valves), but had turned this narrow set of products into an abundance of types and variants that could be customized in very flexible ways through investment in CNC machines and developing computing skills for workers. The favored craft form of work organization thus had defined a market segment in which workers were continuously challenged by new customer needs. The plant had been reorganized for continuous flow, can-ban production, and was operating on just-in-time principles. However, though the plant architecture thus reflected devoted machines organized into cells, the very fact that machines were often used as capacity suppliers for other cells and for shifting variants made the individual workplace much more demanding in terms of skills and reduced the need for overtime payments. With the workers increasing they became not only involved in customizing existing pumps and valves, skills and competences but were often engaged in ad hoc project groups that were preparing for new product generations, making the whole plant both a factory and an experimental laboratory, searching for new ways of serving customers in complicated ways. Workers' interests did not lie in mastering archaic and repetitive tasks, and these were often outsourced. The skilled workers in particular had a dominant influence on conceiving the phantom community and saw the plant as an ideal community provided it allowed them to progress in skill levels at a greater pace than other regional plants, allowing them to increase their potential career mobility and search for even more challenging jobs in other firms. In this way, people originating from the plant could be found in high positions in other firms, in local union offices, in local politics, and among instructors in further training institutions. The plant was thus a cell for organizing itself and the community as a craft community.[1]

3.6 SELF-NARRATION OF PROCESSES OF CHANGE IN FIELDS WITH DIFFERENT PHANTOM COMMUNITIES

The phantom community of the Horsens plant in many ways resembles how Whitley (2007; 2010) characterized the *industrial district*, while the Lake Mills plant resembles the *compartmentalized integrated conglomerate* of Fordism, and therefore have different operative logics, patterns of strategic interactions among stakeholders, and habits of reflecting on strategic actions toward local contexts. But these differences only become visible for the academic comparative business analysts and not for the participants of the two plants. To them it is natural to expect "the other" to behave in similar ways as they do themselves. To each the other plant belongs to the same engineering industry, using similar technology and skills. So while comparative characterization helps the analyst to see the reasons why they have constructed different phantom communities, for the participants of the two plants the "other" behaves and speaks in ways that makes less and less sense (Hotho & Pedersen, 2012). One could say that the more an idiosyncratic phantom community is formed and

---

[1] The two contrasting cases suggest that it is not the nature of the firm that determines the way it is composed of social groups, but that the causalities also work in the opposite direction, as suggested elsewhere (Kristensen, 1999) and studied in greater detail for Denmark (Kristensen, 1989).

becomes inclusive of more and more organizational traces, social groupings, and the neighboring community, the more it becomes blind to its idiosyncrasy and becomes a self-referential frame for local rationality, increasingly difficult to understand for outsiders from different idiosyncratic phantom communities. The better they understand their own, the less well they may understand the phantom community of the other.

The *trajectory scheme* (Strauss, 2008) of change in manufacturing, under the heading of Lean, that took hold among top managers toward the end of the twentieth century, combines a new set of management practices favoring continuous improvement and innovation, outsourcing, reductions in manpower, up-skilling of employees, focus on core competencies, etc. In our case study, the headquarters (HQ) of the multinational in London used this trajectory scheme to assess and reflect on what needed to be done in its subsidiaries. Obviously, the interactions among fields of actors that use such different frameworks for reflecting on practices constitute highly complex polities that do not necessarily lead to a common and inclusive shared phantom community. Instead, it leads to highly diverse ways of narrating change, measuring progress and failure, and assessing acts of others. For the HQ, these sources of misunderstanding led executive officers to believe that they were facing opportunistic strategies from subsidiaries and that these should be counterbalanced by more and finer grained control measures, performance indicators, and audits. For the subsidiaries, HQ interventions and their consequences led to the narration of change in which the elements in the new trajectory schemes of management took on an entirely new meaning, mostly classified as "stupid" from the standpoint of their respective phantom communities.

3.6.1 Narrating Change on Behalf of the Phantom Community of Lake Mills

This was particularly the case in Lake Mills. For obvious reasons, outsourcing is the most alienating element of the new idiom for a vertically integrated corporation seeing its progress as the gradual growth of a whole set of interdependent functions. Having ignored for years soft HQ requests to start outsourcing, Lake Mills were forced to do so by being ordered to sack 200 employees. This constituted for the plant a "real event" (Bourdieu, 1990: 73), which was self-narrated in approximately the following terms: to choose who had to be laid off in Lake Mills, the HQ appointed a group of foreign managers to select who had to go from the employee lists. When the "chosen" got their dismissal notices, however, they would use the seniority rules—as agreed between unions and local managers, and which foreigners had ignored—to pass on their notices to people with lower seniority. By the end of this process, dismissal notices winded up among a large group of newly recruited young CNC machinists, the training of whom had been a major investment in what Lake Mills had expected to become a future core competence. Instead, this competence would now have to be provided by external suppliers, whom the plant ironically had supplied with skilled labor at great costs. Where the HQ in London saw its intervention as a tough but necessary way of redirecting its "subject," the phantom community by which Lake Mills assessed this event could come to no other conclusion than that HQ was ignorant, making badly informed decisions and that it had to find ways to insure itself against such crazy HQ decisions in the future.

To repair the damage Lake Mills engaged in two activities that were simultaneously seen as leading in the right direction by both HQ and Lake Mills. From the perspective of Lake Mills the actions were seen to have been taken to insure itself against London and to move closer to a return of the preferred phantom community of a vertically integrated plant. Firstly, by setting up a scheme for training workers in several plant-specific jobs instead of a single task, Lake Mills wanted to make sure that they kept jobs and skills inside the plant even if they were forced to lay off more employees. HQ endorsed this scheme as an attempt to up-skill workers for flexibility. Alongside the training scheme came the introduction of a "learn to earn" scheme, which was not a matter without complication. The unions were inscribed in existing job classifications and workers benefitted from rigidities in the form of overpay. The solution was to let unions and HR managers work in tandem so that the social space of all parties was retained within the new order. Workers could earn more by learning extra skills instead of working more hours; unions and managers could solve conflicts from moving workers around shifting work stations, etc.

Secondly, Lake Mills engaged in developing an entirely new and highly sophisticated ice cream machine, by mobilizing internal resources and manpower across normal organizational divides. Where HQ saw this as a move toward welcome innovation—a view that found support when Lake Mills won prizes for the quality, pace, and methodology of its innovation—Lake Mills saw it as a way of recapturing lost terrain, so that internal balances between various organizational functions could be re-established and form the basis for the quantitative growth of the vertically integrated plant, which both its employees and the local community saw as tantamount for future prosperity. Had the narrative stopped here, it would be a story about how two diverse phantom communities learned to live together; but neither events nor self-narration stopped here. Following its trajectory scheme, HQ sold off the newly created ice cream machine on the conviction that it was not part of the core competence of the multinational. To Lake Mills this confirmed that London was crazy, and after demonstrating this in its attitude toward London, made HQ launch a general attack on Lake Mills. This attack came in the form of taking Lake Mills apart in such a way that different functions and sections of the plant came under different business area managers in different countries, with the effect that the very narration of a collective phantom community became impossible. Interestingly, however, the increase in new ways of managing, measuring, and reporting never became part of the critical narration of *us* against *them*, and seems to have progressed almost with ease and to the satisfaction of those who held power in the functional units that the vertically integrated plant had already established. Lean management practices were to Lake Mills nothing but Taylorist management practices writ large.

Lake Mills' path in many ways follow the general pattern of American plants to have absorbed Lean as a set of new managerial practices without really changing more fundamentally how plant workers operate (Kristensen & Lotz, 2011). Simultaneously, Lake Mills' self-narration recalls the vicious circle of gradual managerial destruction of the general American corporation that played an important role in organizing the life of communities, such as the one in Lake Mills. A general trajectory that Davis (2009) has made painfully clear.

3.6.2 Narrating Change on Behalf of the Phantom Community of Horsens

The self-narration in the Horsens plant constitutes a very different story. Here the biggest challenge was to counteract headcount reductions and a specialization pattern that would reduce the variety of production tasks, which made it a challenging plant for skilled workers. Attempts from business areas managers to evoke such specialization led Horsens to follow a dual strategy by which the plant subversively took a counteracting direction in sales, promising customers—especially within the multinational itself—extraordinary services by customizing products and reducing delivery time. This way of using subversive strategies against orders from some quarters of the multinational and become known and highly reputed as a very collaborative supplier resembles in many ways the approach Horsens took in narrating its past customer relations. If the coherence of a "we" through the production of a narrative is a sign of the strength of an agency (Carr, 1986), the "we" in Horsens was very strong indeed. But, interestingly enough, it didn't view other actors as potential enemies; rather, a strongly embedded partnership between a union convener, shop stewards, and the plant manager made it possible to mobilize multiple resources from the institutional context (Karnøe et al, 1999). In the current situation this strategy helped the plant increase turnover to such an extent that there was no problem in demonstrating that there were fewer employees compared to sales; rather, the reverse became the result, and increasing sales could only be met by extensive outsourcing to the local industrial district. On the one hand, this helped the plant get rid of the most simple and repetitive tasks, making it possible to up-skill unskilled workers to constantly move to increasingly complicated or novel tasks, and shifting between continuous and ad hoc innovative teams. On the other hand, it was easy to reduce transaction costs and make agreements with industrial district suppliers, many of which had recruited employees from the ranks of the highly reputed labor force of the Horsens plant. In effect, Horsens emerged in the eyes of HQ as a template of best practices of its ideal trajectory scheme of lean production. Consequently, the Horsens manager was promoted to business area manager, responsible for a considerable part of the subsidiaries around the world, and the Horsens employees, including blue-collar workers, found new challenges by acting as consultants in reshaping plants around the world.

This up-skilling was made possible by making use of vocational training and welfare schemes in a very creative way, by collaborating with local union offices. Though measured performances came out right in the eyes of London, they had not emerged as a result of the change towards lean managerial practices. Rather, by decentralizing responsibilities to internal work teams and external suppliers to an extreme degree, and letting people operate and interact in highly informal ways, the system produced extraordinary good outcome metrics. Few would see that this system totally lacked the attributes of lean management and ways to make systematic and continuous improvements. Rather, Horsens' work organization, by being highly responsive to new and frequently shifting customer needs, was effective in making small incremental innovations. These continuous incrementalist refinements translated into frequent introductions of novel product generations, making it impossible to compare across years how the plant performed. In many ways Horsens saw the completion of reporting schemes as a ritualistic task that had to be undertaken for the sake of London, but, as long as the bottom line of the plant was good, London would probably not care very much. And they were right. Firstly, London was so overburdened with reports from subsidiaries that nobody really had time to use them diagnostically and names of the executive officers changed so frequently that no narration of progress on behalf of the different subsidiaries took place over years. Lean came without monitoring.

Framed by the twin reflective phantom communities of London and its own, Horsens developed to become an increasingly skilled highly sophisticated producer, collaborating tightly with customers through an increasing number of services, which made it possible to identify to an increasing extent what customers would like from the next generation of pumps and valves. In many ways this narrative predates the larger pattern of business firm evolution that took place in Denmark (Kristensen, Lotz, & Rocha, 2011; Kristensen, 2006) by making use of welfare, the labor market, and vocational training institutions to reposition itself in global production and innovation networks.

3.7 FROM SENSEMAKING PROCESSES IN
DIFFERENT ORGANIZATIONAL FIELDS
TO COMPARATIVE OUTCOMES

Our analysis reveals how different the local narratives are that make sense of what seems, from an external observer, to be similar "trajectory schemes" (Strauss, 2008: 55) for change, in casu the scheme held by the London HQ. But are outcomes really as different as the self-narration and the phantom communities of the different fields suggest? Several analysts see the outcomes to be similar, but affected by different institutional environments (Delmestri, 1998) and processes of restructuring.

My view is that the search for new production and innovation regimes is an ongoing experimental process in which past phantom communities will be gradually transformed to ends in sight. Many elements of the managerial templates seem to become similar, but as they combine with highly different forms of underlying work organization, both the challenges and the ends in sight will constantly differ between fields.

The best data to illustrate this view was given to us in a paper by Lorenz and Valeyre (2003) where they inverted data results from the third working conditions survey made by the European Foundation for the Improvement of Living and Working Conditions. By using the answers from respondents from different countries they could determine whether people were working either in traditional, Taylorist, Lean, or learning forms of work organization and then construct a comparative picture of how different countries are clustered dependent on whether they have over-representations of certain forms of work organization.

What we learn from this is that Denmark is among the countries where the majority of people are working in a learning form of work organization (60 percent of respondents). The learning form of work organization is characterized by highly autonomous workers, actively learning new things by solving novel problems, being less engaged in repetitive tasks, but working neither under some of the defining managerial templates of lean production (such as job rotation and norms), nor under hierarchical or horizontal constraints on work rates that are associated with both Taylorist and lean forms of management. Ireland and the United Kingdom—the two countries of the sample that most clearly can be classified as liberal market economies (Hall & Soskice, 2001) or be seen to be represent compartmentalized business systems (Whitley, 2007)—have evolved most clearly towards the formal traits of lean management, as was the case of Lake Mills. Southern European countries don't seem to have moved far from Taylorist practices and constitute a very clear contrast to Scandinavia and other small countries with developed welfare states, whereas the typical examples of coordinated market economies—such as Germany, France, Belgium, and perhaps Finland—have a much more even representation of the four forms of work organization.

Whereas the Taylorist, the Lean, and even the traditionalist forms of work organization have rather well-understood forms of managerial authority, the learning form of work organization constitutes an enigma in this respect. This enigma was underlined by findings that emerged from the Fourth Working Conditions Survey, which found that not only did Denmark (and the other Nordic countries) have the highest level of worker autonomy, but also some of the highest productivity, only paralleled by countries with much less worker autonomy (European Foundation for the Improvement of Living and Working Conditions, 2007: 60). The European Foundation called the Danish/Nordic an "Active Working Organization" and tried to search for causes as to why workers were working with this high intensity. Neither the influence of bosses nor a higher pace of machinery, which are weaker and lower than in any other cluster of countries, could explain the enigma. Rather "demands from customers" turns out to have a significant impact on work intensity in the Nordic countries and part of the autonomy is that employees of all categories interact directly with customers much more than in any other country.

According to the European Foundation, for instance, France, the United Kingdom, and Ireland are placed in a mixture of "low strain" and "passive work organization," while Germany falls into the category of "high-strain work organization." According to Maurice et al. (1986) there are large differences between the managerial authority relations in France and Germany, so perhaps it is not enigmatic that transition processes over the last couple of decades have resulted in divergent performance outcomes between Germany and France.

To our knowledge researchers have not accounted for how organizations in the two aforementioned countries have made sense of ongoing changes, neither in terms of phantom communities, nor the self-narration of change. Clearly, similar trajectory schemes of change as in the London HQ have been in play among German and French managers (Boltanski & Chiapello, 2007; Woywode, 2002). Woywode's (2002) comparative study of the introduction of work teams in the French and German auto industry, however, bear witness to the contours of phantom communities and self-narrating processes that have been in operation in the two countries. In France the initiatives for transforming work organization came solely from managers, who formed teams without alteration of the previous managerial hierarchy, with only initial and formal approval from unions, and therefore it is quite clear that no employee phantom community has been evoked to reflect on and influence the creation of the new work organization. Woywode (2002: 517) gives an extreme example of this:

... in one of the French plants, the workers we spoke to had not actually realized that they were working "in groups". For them, working in the old system (without working groups) and working in the new system (with working groups) appeared to be more or less the same. It was the management that had introduced the term "team work" to refer to the work organization of the final assembly without giving significant substance to it.

Woywode's account of France in many ways recalls Crozier's (1964) study of French bureaucracies, in which managers introduce organizational change to retain power by evoking uncertainty on lower levels of the organization, but without disturbing the highly fragmented authority structure on which managerial power and legitimacy depends, and assured of the absence of a worker collectives that could otherwise raise a voice in local negotiations. But can and will workers take on the new roles of new forms of work organization if they are not taking part in the sensemaking processes?

In Germany, contrastingly, union and employee representatives are actively engaged in co-constructing the novel work organization by negotiations in work councils and activists in local union offices (Herrigel & Wittke, 2005). In Germany, too, work teams are installed in the previous hierarchy, which is, however, more level than in France; but this installment happens by changing position roles and adding new ones. For instance the *Meister*, from being directly involved in the practicalities of work, becomes a coordinator and consultant for a set of work groups. In systematic contrast to France, in Germany a new position as work group spokesman or team leader is created (in all plants) with the job of interacting actively and proactively with the entire organization and of organizing job rotation within the team (Woywode, 2002). Thus in Germany, the change is clearly demarcated and enters into the everyday life of employees, in contrast to France.

Ironically, so it seems, the French way of introducing the formal schemes of management practices resembles, to a high degree, what was observed in Lake Mills. And the German transition seems at the surface to resemble the Horsens case. But there are, in the last comparison, huge differences. High skills in Germany have been used to ease job rotation, whereas in Denmark they were used to sophisticate and make the individual workplace play flexible roles within the larger organization. In both countries, however, direct employee involvement in changing work organization has led to high work intensity, whereas this seems much lower in both France and the liberal market economies.

One of the key features in comparing France and Germany is that the transitions in Germany have led to changes in roles and positions. Such processes depend highly on "identity work" and the formation of organizational character, which again triggers complicated and serious personal reflectivity. Using Mead's notions again: "I" will be forced in chain reactions to take the position of "me" in past practices and will need to reconsider future identities with past aspirations. Such processes will radically raise the propensity to become engaged in fields of micro-politics, forcing people into deliberations, justifications, and sensemaking. It could be that, in countries with an active or high-strain work organization, we should expect reflections and experiments with a novel regime of growth and development, and novel comparative advantages to be the most intensive, while life has continued more habitually and routinely in low-strain and passive work organizations. The ability to go from replication to abstraction-based forms of learning may be very unequal among countries and may make it more or less possible to reform institutional competitiveness.

3.8 IN SEARCH OF *THE* NEW PRODUCTION REGIME: ARE THERE ENDS IN SIGHT?

The differences in terms of performative advantages are most clear when comparing countries with lean and learning forms of organizations. The hierarchical control of the lean management system makes systematic and continuous improvement possible in the US, United Kingdom, and Ireland. But the scope is limited as the focus is on work teams with clearly defined and limited responsibilities, and autonomy for experimenting. In learning organizations the scope and distribution of room for maneuver is much higher for making innovations (in every meaning: product modifications, changes in production methods, and processes, such as ways of collaborating, and modes of interaction between teams both internally and externally), often referred to as "employee or user-driven innovation." But this innovative performance is often unsystematic, frequently ignored by all others but the individual innovators, who are therefore often reinventing the wheel simultaneously in several places even within the same organization. This may be the reason why in Denmark low productivity coexists with high work intensity, and conversely high productivity and low strain coexist in the United Kingdom and Ireland. Clearly, learning organizations offers a better preparation for participating broadly in open innovation, but the lack of systematic monitoring and documentation of achievements would limit the benefits harvested from such increasing engagement with external actors.

Thus, for countries that build their comparative institutional competitiveness on learning forms of organizations, the question is how to make learning more disciplined, systematic, and targeted. In case this shall happen under high degrees of professional autonomy, the challenge is to find a monitoring system that constantly makes it possible for different professions to diagnose problems, codify, and diffuse solutions to create a moving target of standard-ized best practices on which continuous improvements can be based. By comparing school systems in the US, Denmark, and Finland we actually identified the basic elements for such a system in Finland, but it was very far from the phantom community that the Finns had constructed for themselves (Sabel et al., 2011). What seems to be the case—after lengthy and careful investigations—is that an education system has been created in Finland where the least able 20 percent of the students are systematically diagnosed, then best current practices are customized to help the individual student cope with their special learning problems. These interventions are made by a corps of highly educated specialized teachers. The system is highly developed in registering progress, and when sudden and impressive results are achieved, these are investigated, codified, and distributed through courses to the corpus of specialized teachers. Thus, in the Finnish school system a decentralized experimental search for novel ways to solve problems happens in interplay with a body of knowledge of best practices, that can be further improved by new successful experiments.

In all likelihood, similar procedures of monitoring, diagnosing, reporting, and diffusion of results are needed to be installed to overcome the potential weaknesses of the learning organizations of the Nordic countries if they shall harvest intense work efforts productively. Unfortunately, moves towards such novel systems of governance are hampered by a situation in which the phantom communities of professionals stand in stark contrast to the trajec-tory templates of both public and private top managers that strive for lean and new public management. What are called for are narratives of processes by which the two phantom communities become integrated and turn out a third visionary trajectory projection with new ends in sight (Follett, 1951).

3.9 CONCLUSIONS

In this chapter we have tried to make an inquiry into how sensemaking enters into processes of change in organizations. We have seen that different loca-tions of actors and groupings make sense of novel tendencies from past visions of idealized phantom communities or trajectory schemes, so that progress and failure is accounted for in these schemes rather than a depiction of what is going on in the very process of change. Causalities explaining the past and models that are used to construct the future are created, yet it is unclear whether these abstraction-based endeavors are so high intellect after all. This can both explain cases that lead to both miserable and desirable results, but the point is that the polity in which more comprehensive understandings may be deliberated is rarely constructed, so that new ends in sight can be constructed by the multitude of participants. This illustrates the need for a new analytical practitioner—a comparative historical analyst that is able to see the directions taken in sensemaking and transformative practices in different communities/ societies and is able by comparative assessment to see what has been achieved and what is still missing in each of the societies, so that ends in sight may be identified. It is such an analytical practice that the chapter has sketched and demonstrated, to diagnose what the next step in improving competitiveness could be for the Nordic countries.

4

Reforms of National Innovation Policies in Europe

Coordinating Sensemaking across Countries

Susana Borrás

4.1 INTRODUCTION

National innovation policies were subjected to considerable reforms in 2000–10, a decade in which the political currency of the discourse on the "knowledge-based economy" put innovation policies at the center of public action for enhancing competitiveness and growth. In Europe this thrust towards reform has basically been on a national level, with widespread discussions and debates about the pillars of competitiveness. However, this debate has also related to political initiatives at the EU level in the context of the Lisbon Strategy—an EU-level strategy applied from 2000 to 2010—the aim being to foster and to stimulate a series of reforms at the national level. The mechanism used to stimulate those reforms has been the "open method of coordination," (OMC) bringing together national civil servants in a series of topic-specific meetings. This OMC aims at synchronizing national reforms by creating a common language and learning from mutual experiences among national civil servants. The focus of the OMC on the sharing and learning from national experiences, and its emphasis on analysis and forward-looking approaches to national reforms render this method a good example of an organizational mechanism willing to promote a prospective sensemaking process. In other words, it provides an excellent case for studying the cross-national dimension of sensemaking in the context of national institutional reforms, and how *prospective* and *abstraction*-based processes of sensemaking operate.

This chapter studies the features of coordinating sensemaking at the EU-level, and the conditions under which this had an influence on national debates and national reforms. In particular, it examines the civil servants' sensemaking of national reforms in four countries with very diverse traditions in innovation policymaking and types of socioeconomic innovation systems. With this in mind, this chapter compares the reforms undertaken in four European countries—namely, Denmark, Sweden, Germany, and France—and studies the sensemaking process of their respective civil servants during the reform period and in the context of EU-level coordination. The civil servants of these four countries actively participated in EU-level OMC, which aimed at synchronizing national reforms by creating a common language and by providing a platform for learning from their mutual experiences. Hence, the main research questions that this chapter addresses are what features characterize the coordination of the sensemaking process of national civil servants in a cross-national setting? And to what extent has this had an influence on the national debates about national reforms?

The findings show that the process gave an overview to participants and created international networks of influence, and to a lesser degree upgraded national knowledge competences, and developed common concepts and approaches. The findings also point to the fact that the OMC had some influence on the national debates, depending on the organization of national public administration, the timing of political attention, and the technical nature of the topic. The concluding section reflects upon these findings and discusses the process of sensemaking in complex settings such as innovation policy reforms.

4.2 SENSEMAKING, NATIONAL REFORMS, AND EU-LEVEL COORDINATION

Theories of institutional change have repeatedly underlined the predominance of gradual change over radical change, and the tendency for change to be largely dependent on past events. There is now extensive recognition that these traits are particularly evident in the changes of national institutions of the capitalist economies, as a high level of institutional complexity is believed to reinforce these gradual, path-dependent, and structurally shaped changes. Recent theoretical advances in institutional and organizational theories have started to consider a somehow disregarded element of change processes, namely the role of ambiguity. Interestingly, however, they have done so in a different way. From the perspective of institutionalism studies, the different degrees of ambiguity of institutions tend to generate a sort of "open space" within which agents-of-change operate by triggering/stimulating specific types of institutional change (Mahoney & Thelen, 2010). Here ambiguity can be seen as an opportunity structure that is utilized intentionally by agents who seek power and change. From the perspective of organizational studies, ambiguity is somehow different in that it refers to the inherent inconclusiveness of the individual organization's experience (March, 2010). Experience never provides unidirectional or clear-cut lessons for change, and therefore the lessons of experience are difficult to grasp and require an intellectual effort.

This chapter takes as the point of departure these agent-based and ambiguity-based approaches that offer important and complementing venues to examine different outcomes of institutional change. However, these previous studies have somehow disregarded the fundamental issue of how agents engage in building up meaning when defining courses of action. "Building up meaning" refers to the cognitive and interpretative process by which agents induce institutional change. This is what the introductory chapter identified as sensemaking—a key process in the construction of decisions that inform institutional change. From this perspective, the process of institutional change is one where agents of change make sense of the existing institutions and of their general experience. Therefore, sensemaking is a process where goals and means are constantly exposed to multiple forms of interpretation and reinterpretation through different agent interaction mechanisms. The introductory chapter provided an analytical framework that differentiates the types of sensemaking processes based on whether they are *retrospective* or *prospective* (looking backwards, justifying past actions or looking ahead, defining future actions), and whether the intellectual process is based around replication or abstraction (when actors involved in the sensemaking collect specific forms of knowledge sources in their process of making sense).

The sensemaking approach to institutional change is a particularly interesting theoretical framework from which to analyze cross-national differences in institutional reforms of innovation policies in European countries in the first decade of the 2000s. These salient national reforms (Borrás, 2009a) have been strongly linked politically to some emblematic efforts for institutional reforms in Europe, namely the Lisbon Strategy, 2000–10 (continued under the name Europe 2020). The Lisbon Strategy is a governance architecture defined by a set of ideational components (discourses) and a set of organizational components (OMC) (Borrás & Radaelli, 2011). Its overall goal is to provide a strategic and coordinated venue for policy reform at the national level. However, ambiguity has tended to dominate much of this governance architecture. The ambiguity refers to the hybrid and somehow undetermined nature of a reform agenda that encompasses an ample repertoire of open-ended discourses, such as "competitiveness," "knowledge-based economy," and to the constantly tinkering and informal nature of its organizational aspects, such as the coordination procedures and the role of the European Commission (Borrás, 2009b).

Since 2003 the Lisbon Strategy has attempted to coordinate national reforms in the field of research and innovation policy through a series of OMC cycles. During each cycle CREST (the advisory committee made up of national top civil servants in this policy field) agree on a limited set of policy issues and install specific working groups of national representatives to discuss these issues. At the end of each cycle working groups report back to CREST, which draws some general conclusions and, where appropriate, formulates some policy recommendations. From 2003 to 2010 there were four completed cycles of the OMC. However, in spite of these efforts, there are still diverse views on the effects of the OMC. Some authors argue that the coordination of national research and innovation policies through the OMC has been a failure as it has not reached its goals (Shaw & Laffan, 2007; Kaiser & Prange, 2005), whereas other authors are more positive about the overall convergence trends and national attitudes towards reforming national research policies more generally (Gornitzka, 2005; Morano-Foadi, 2008; Mcguinness & O'Carroll, 2010).

There are several reasons for such a diverse response to the Lisbon Strategy call for national institutional reforms. Authors in the literature have argued that the voluntary nature of this open coordination does not generate the incentives for national change (Schäfer, 2006). The lack of obligations and legally binding rules means that there are no possibilities of sanctions from the EU level and, hence, no real "shadow of hierarchy" (Scharpf, 1999) to force non-compliers. This might be an interesting argument when it comes to regulatory policy areas (typically associated to the single market), but it is far less so for expenditure-related policies such as research policy. Other authors in the field of Europeanization point to the hypothesis of the pre-existing "goodness of fit" to explain variation, identifying those countries whose national institutional frameworks are closer to the institutional solutions proposed at the EU level, where change is most likely and the costs of enforced change are relatively low (Radaelli, 2000).

These previous accounts of the factors that determine institutional change and reform in the context of cross-national coordination in the Lisbon Strategy are valuable and rich in empirical evidence. However, taken together, they suffer from two explanatory limits. The first limit is the analytical failure to acknowledge that the ideational and organizational nature of the Lisbon Strategy is intrinsically ambiguous. Most of the studies have focused on the "strength" or "softness" of the organizational dimensions in the implementation of the Lisbon agenda, namely its voluntary nature and lack of binding regulatory requirements. However, the ideational nature of the same agenda is equally important (Schmidt, 2010), as the ambiguous nature of the Lisbon Strategy has left open considerable leeway for different national responses, questioning whether coordination attempts are actually working. The second explanatory limit has to do with the underestimated role assigned to agency and actors as forces for change. Gwiazda's study is one of the few that puts the role of agency at the forefront and helps to balance the eminently structural accounts from previous studies (Gwiazda, 2011). However, she focuses only on one type of agent: the political color of the government in power. While this is naturally a very important aspect, the role of national stakeholders and civil servants as agents of change is an understudied factor.

Taken together, these two blind spots indicate that the previous literature on the Lisbon Strategy coordination of national reforms has tended to have a rather simple top-down approach to institutional change at the national level, disregarding not only the intrinsic ambiguity of the Lisbon Strategy both in organizational and ideational terms, but also the relevance of agents of change at the national level beyond the color of the government in power. Willing to bring the role of agency back into the equation, as well as having an eminently bottom-up approach to institutional change in the national context, this chapter studies the processes of sensemaking among national civil servants participating in the cross-national coordination exercises, and the influence of these processes on their respective national reforms of innovation policy.

4.3 THE CASES, THE DATA, AND THE ANALYSIS

This study concentrates on four European countries: Denmark, Germany, France, and Sweden.[1] They represent different traditions in innovation policy, as well as different varieties of capitalism. Following Ergas's distinction in his seminal work (Ergas, 1987), France and Sweden have traditionally followed a mission-oriented approach, as their governments have had a strong hand in innovation processes. They actively select specific technologies, support large industrial efforts, and organize research through large public institutions. In contrast to this, Germany and Denmark have been more diffusion-oriented, as in both cases the state has not been actively involved in specific technological areas, but has paid more attention to indirectly promoting intermediary organizations bridging science and industry, and upgrading knowledge competences in a more distributed manner in the economy. These four countries also conform to established types in the varieties of capitalism literature, as Germany and France are considered to be coordinated market economies (CME) (Hall & Soskice, 2001), whereas Denmark and Sweden are "hybrid"

---

[1] The data of this chapter is based on thirty-eight personal interviews with civil servants in four EU member countries (Denmark, Sweden, France, and Germany) and on four reports conducted by national experts who conducted the interviews. These were conducted by the European Commission in 2008 in the context of an evaluation of the open method of coordination in innovation and research policy areas under the Lisbon Strategy. The interviews were based on a series of semi-structured qualitative questions formulated in a specific and homogeneous interview questionnaire. The questionnaire consisted of seventeen questions and took approximately one hour for each respondent to complete. The questionnaire was also pilot tested in different national systems to make sure the questions were understandable and suitable in different national and administrative contexts.

Table 4.1 Features of the four countries under study

	Coordinated market economy	Nordic/hybrid market economy
Mainly diffusion-oriented	Germany	Denmark
Mainly mission-oriented	France	Sweden

models, in between coordinated and liberal market economies (Campbell & Pedersen, 2007). The four countries are world leaders when it comes to levels of innovation performance in the economy, and are actively involved in EU-level policymaking and policy discussions on such issues. Table 4.1 provides a quick summary of their key characteristics.

The focus of this chapter is on national civil servants' views on the OMC as a process put forward by the EU's Lisbon Strategy to coordinate sensemaking across boundaries. With this purpose in mind, the chapter has two overall goals: to study how *prospective* and *abstraction*-based processes of sensemaking operate, and to study the cross-national dimension of sensemaking in the context of national institutional reforms. Hence, the first step in this research design is to define how to approach the study of sensemaking. This chapter uses thirty-eight interviews conducted in 2008 with national civil servants who were involved in the OMC (ten in Sweden, ten in France, eight in Germany, and ten in Denmark). The interviews were conducted by national experts who produced summary reports including some analytical remarks on the interviews. These four summary reports have also been used in the analysis, as they contain interesting material from the expert. The analysis is not based on the exact formulation of words and sentences, but on the overall messages and ideas of the respondents. In other words, this chapter does not conduct a narrow text analysis of concrete language samples, but an analysis of the overall concepts provided by respondents.

The research design of the analysis is based on three steps. The first step is a succinct description of the major national reforms in the corresponding national innovation policy. This serves as the background to grasp the nature and extent of national reforms, and the issues at stake when national civil servants attend meetings in Brussels on these matters. The data on this, which is essentially of a secondary nature, is based on accounts of national reforms by the existing literature. The second step of the analysis examines the views of the national civil servants on two crucial aspects that deal with the two research questions: the features of the OMC as a process of coordinating sensemaking, and the conditions under which this has had an influence on the national debates on national reforms.[2] The technique used to obtain this

[2] The data collected is qualitative and based on the personal opinions of the respondents concerning different aspects of the CREST-OMC. For obvious reasons, this data is treated anonymously and does not represent official views of the countries. The sample of respondents

data is to assign a code to the responses, which form patterns according to their similarities. The responses regarding the OMC as a sensemaking process are clustered into four distinct coding items: (1) the upgrading of national knowledge competences of national civil servants, (2) providing an overview of other countries' initiatives and activities, (3) the development of common principles and approaches across countries, and (4) the creation of inter-national networks of influence. The responses concerning "conditions for influence of OMC process in national debates" are coded into three items: (1) the timing of political attention at the national level, (2) the technical nature of the topic under debate, and (3) the administrative organization at the national level.

Following on from these national-focused analyses in steps (1) and (2), step (3) examines these elements in a comparative manner.[3] The description of national reforms give some general clues about the respective nature of the reforms, indicating the extent to which it is worth noting changes of direction in the type of innovation policy (mission-oriented or diffusion-oriented). The final analysis gathers these together and compares national civil servants' overall views on the features of OMC as a cross-national sensemaking process and on the conditions under which OMC influences national debates on reforms.

4.4 DENMARK

Although the institutional reforms of innovation policy in Denmark during 2000–10 were quite extensive, they mostly comprised addendums and adjustments rather than path-breaking changes (Lindgaard Christensen, Gregersen et al., 2008; Aagaard & Mejlgaard, 2012). The reforms largely

---

was selected carefully and had one main profile, namely national civil servants who have been participating in the OMC process. Regarding the reliability of the data, it is important to note that it is based on the personal opinions of the respondents and there are no reasons to believe that respondents, knowing the anonymity of the interview, have not answered in an honest way. Regarding the representativeness of the data, it is very important to underline here that the data gathered in the interviews is representative only in the sense that it comes from approximately ten different respondents in each country. That is to say that there is no statistical representa-tiveness in our data, but a set of fixed criteria that allow a degree of certainty that *we have been able to collect the widest possible spectrum of qualitative data regarding opinions* related to the phenomenon under study, given that only a selected number of national civil servants regularly attend OMC meetings and activities in the field of research and innovation policy.

[3] Steps (2) and (3) of the analysis are based on data from the forty-two interviews mentioned above, which has been coded and analyzed using the software NVivo 10. It is important to keep in mind that the data of this chapter is qualitative in nature, and that issues of statistical significance are not to be applied here.

concerned three main elements. The first was the addition of new strategic and technology-focused research instruments, mainly the creation of three new research funds or councils.[4] Parallel to this, the traditional research council was slightly reorganized as the Council for Independent Research (formed from six scientific-discipline-oriented councils), which, together with the National Research Foundation (Grundforskningsfond), form the backbone of independent and curiosity-driven research funding mechanisms in Denmark. These reforms essentially involved the process of appending new strategic instruments to the existing framework rather than truly reforming them (Aagaard & Ravn, 2012). Experts have noticed this form of institutional change and a certain exuberance in Denmark's research policy instrument portfolio (Lundvall, 2008; ERAC Expert Group, 2012).[5]

The second big transformation in Danish innovation policy was the reform of universities and public-sector research organizations, which was perhaps the most in-depth reform in the Danish innovation policy landscape during the first decade of the 2000s. In 2003 the university law[6] introduced extensive transformations in their governance structures. Furthermore, in 2007 virtually all sector-oriented state-owned public research organizations were absorbed by universities, and at the same time several universities were merged.[7] The third reform was the transformation of the structures relating to knowledge transfer. Danish policymakers have been concerned with Denmark's relatively low levels of patenting ratios. The Danish diffusion-oriented policy has very successful bridging institutions like the GTS centers,[8] supporting knowledge transfer to small and medium-sized enterprises (SMEs). The new law of technology transfer has abolished the traditional university "professor's privilege" principle,[9] granting patent ownership to the university rather than to the individual professor. Yet, since then, universities have struggled to make that work due to their lack of experience in technology transfer activities (Lissoni, Lotz et al., 2009).

This chapter examines this EU-level coordination of the sensemaking process among civil servants across national borders in the area of innovation policy, asking how this process was characterized, and the extent to which it had an influence on debates relating to ongoing national reforms. When asked

---

[4] The Council for Technology and Innovation (2001), the Council for Strategic Research (2002), and the Advanced Technology Foundation (2004).

[5] Weekly *Mandag Morgen*, 2012.

[6] *Lov om universiteter (universitetsloven)*, Law no. 403, law adopted May 28, 2003.

[7] *Bekendtgørelse om ændring i styrelsesregler for en række universiteter som følge af sammen-lægning med andre forskningsinstitutioner*, Statutory order no. 280, adopted March 21, 2006.

[8] *Godkendte Teknologiske Serviceinstitutter.*

[9] The Professor's privilege principle allows him/her to claim ownership of the patents based on their research results and their work at the university. This was abolished in 1999 in Denmark by the Act on innovation at public research institutions: *Lov om opfindelser ved offentlige forskningsinstitutioner*, no. 347, adopted June 2, 1999.

about the features characterizing the OMC, the ten Danish respondents emphasized issues of knowledge upgrading at the national level, the importance of expertise of the OMC groups chairmen in terms of being able to create a common language through concepts that could be shared in the group, and the fact that the OMC induced the creation of a cross-national network of civil servants that has been active since those meetings. A Danish senior civil servant remarked that "at the beginning it was difficult to find out what to talk about, because the concepts are different in Europe; the groups need to create a common language and basic understanding." Another senior Danish civil servant stated, "OMC is not only a process inducing learning from others, it is also a process that is an advanced continuous training for junior and senior experts."

Regarding the conditions for influencing the national debate, Danish respondents seem to have emphasized the timing of political attention. One of the respondents indicated that,

> The timing of the topic explains why some OMC topics are more diffused than others, and there is more awareness than with other topics. For example: we were very interested in the "internationalisation" working group because Denmark was about to develop its own strategy towards China. We used the work and ideas in the working group actively.

As for the administrative organization at the national level, the Danish respondents showed that this seemed to be relevant in terms of limiting the influence of OMC results in national debates:

> The difficulty is that there is no clear procedure about what will happen at national level once the report is finished. In Denmark we try to use it to inspire the internal leaders of the ministry. But in general it is important that there is a political leadership that channels the process for making the most of the reports and work of the OMC-CREST within the member states.

Likewise: "There is a very rapid circulation of personnel inside the Danish ministry and across ministries, so they do not have the time to go deeply into the issues." Or as another respondent put it: "There is a sharp division of labour in Denmark between departments that are in charge of EU matters and those that are not." The technical nature of the topic in the debates seems to be important as well, with one respondent giving a clear example of the fact that this positively affected the debate at the national level because it was in the hands of a few experts: "Intellectual Property Rights: there is relatively few people in the ministry that follows this topic, and they were involved in the working groups." The important reforms of this particular area in Denmark (as mentioned above) indicate that this expertise was influential in the political debates at the national level.

4.5 SWEDEN

The Swedish innovation system also experienced some changes during 2000–10. However, those changes involved the addition of some new elements and the consolidation of pre-existing trends rather than transformation of the system as such. Most of the institutional reform effort has been justified in terms of addressing the paradox that Sweden has a high level of expenditure in research and development (R&D) activities but a relatively low ratio of innovation outcomes (Bitard, Edquist et al., 2008). This paradox is relative, though, as Sweden continues to be one of the most innovation-strong countries in the world. The traditional structure of the Swedish innovation system is based on strong universities, large firms conducting R&D, and a small number of user-oriented sectorial research organizations. These features of the innovation system have been in the spotlight ever since Sweden needed to consider innovation not only in technology and R&D, university-based knowledge production, but in non-technological innovation as well (Thorslund Granat, Elg et al., 2005; OECD, 2012).

The introduction of the innovation system approach in Swedish policy-making resulted in several reforms during the period examined, the most relevant of which are, firstly, the creation in 2001 of VINNOVA, which is a continuation and expansion of the remit of the previous agency NUTEK. An important part of VINNOVA's goal is to fund and foster collaborative activities between universities, firms, and research organizations, but its budget is smaller than similar agencies in other countries. Secondly, the creation in 2001 of Vetenskapsradet as a major research-funding agency composed of different sub-councils. The council is the result of a merger of existing organizations, and is the most prominent funding agency for basic and academic research in the country today. And thirdly, the creation in 2004 of the first national innovation strategy,[10] an all-encompassing document with specific goals for a coordinated policy directed towards the improvement of economic competitiveness. It is worth noting that this strategy is strongly linked to the multi-annual financial commitment of the Research and Innovation Bill approved by the Swedish Parliament. Despite these reforms, Swedish policy has some features that do not seem to have changed as profoundly during the period 2000–10, for example, the structure of universities (Lundvall, 2008). Furthermore, in contrast to most European countries, Sweden has not abolished the "professor's privilege" at universities, the so-called "lärarundantaget," presumably due to the traditional strength of the senior members within the academic community (Magnusson, McKelvey et al., 2009).

---

[10] Government of Sweden (2004) *Innovative Sweden—A strategy for growth through renewal.* Ds 2004: 36. Available at <www.sweden.gov.se/sb/d/2026/a/32551>.

It is important to keep in mind that Sweden is a leading country in levels of innovation performance, and it has played an important role in EU-level discussions regarding the Lisbon Strategy and innovation policy measures in particular.[11] Sweden's presence in Brussels' research and innovation policy debates is remarkable, particularly given its small size. Moreover, Swedish civil servants were actively involved in the Lisbon Strategy and particularly in the OMC cycles in the field of research and innovation policy. For that reason, it is worth looking at the way in which Swedish civil servants view this OMC process, and the extent to which they believe this has exercised some influence on the national reform debate in Sweden.

The interview data with Swedish civil servants is unfortunately not very strong, and the richness of the qualitative data is limited. Taking this into account, we can see that the number of responses is relatively lower than the other countries. Regarding the issues about the features of the OMC as a sensemaking process, Swedish civil servants seem to have emphasized the OMC as a process providing an overview and creating international networks of influence. As one respondent mentioned: "There has been a lot of learning from these groups. This is coming through participation, not from documents." And that "These groups are in the core of the Union. Working together, creating networks, sharing experiences. Really updating your skills and competencies and creating new possibilities."

Turning to the conditions for influencing the national debate, the content and technical nature of the topic were the most relevant item mentioned. Here are a couple of the respondents' views: "Not all the working groups, but some have spread [their results] and been discussed in Vinnova because the content is interesting." "Some of the topics given [from the action plan] were very focused like the Tax refunds and IPR. Others were very broad. We managed to further identify some good topics for our group."

4.6 FRANCE

The 1999 Innovation and Research Act (*loi Allègre*)[12] was the starting point of sweeping reform and political attempts to bring about a profound transformation of the French innovation policy in 2000–10. Behind this law was the concern that the French system was too rigid and underperforming in terms of

---

[11] One example of this is the Swedish Presidency in Spring 2009 successfully putting forward the notion of "grand societal challenges" to guide EU and national research and innovation policies, complementing the traditional principles of advancing human knowledge and economic growth that have traditionally guided public support for basic and applied research.

[12] *Loi n 99-587 du 12 juillet 1999 sur l'innovation et la recherche*, initiated by Claude Allègre, the then Minister of Research.

getting public research outcomes to benefit innovative activities of firms. A further concern was that there was the need to create incentive conditions for public researchers' initiatives in these innovation-oriented activities (Llerena, Matt et al., 2003). Ten years later, however, the high ambitions of the law have not been entirely fulfilled, as there continue to be obstacles, particularly cultural obstacles with public researchers giving priority to academic activities rather than collaboration with industry, even if the number and operations of incubators seem to be quite successful (Academie des sciences, 2010). Nonetheless, the innovation law was a fundamental step in three crucial aspects: (1) bridging the traditional gap in France between the extensive public research sector and industry, (2) focusing on start-ups and SMEs in contrast with the traditional focus on large firms, and (3) creating a horizontal mechanism other than the traditional industrial sectoral focus of much of the French system since WWII (Muller, Zenker et al., 2009).

Each of these three aspects was also extended in a series of subsequent reforms and strategic initiatives that followed shortly after, in what can be considered the building blocks for a major turnaround of the French system. The 2006 Research Programme Act[13] and the 2007 Universities Freedom and Responsibility Act[14] introduced an increased degree of autonomy to universities and governance structures, the explicit "third mission" task for universities, a regulatory framework for university ownership of patents, and the possibility of creating foundations for professionalized partnerships with firms. Another important goal of this reform was to cut public spending in the sector. This university reform also introduced the *pôles de recherché et d'enseignement supérieur* (PRES),[15] aimed at creating further interactions between universities, grandes écoles, and public research organizations (CNRS, etc.) in order to create critical mass in some specific areas of public research (Laperche & Uzunidis, 2011).

Three further significant novelties in the French research and innovation system were: (1) the creation in 2005 of the ANR, the French research council (followed by a substantial increase in the amount of research funding that is based on competition), (2) the new scheme for research-industry collaborative activities funded under the "Instituts Carnot" scheme, and (3) the creation of Oséo in 2005, providing support to innovation activities in SMEs, by bringing together ANVAR (French innovation agency for the regions— Agence nationale de valorisation de la recherche) and BDPME (SME development bank— Banque du développement des petites et moyennes entreprises).

Another three crucial factors in the public research-industry relations in the French system were: (1) the expansion of the "industrial PhD" scheme

---

[13] *Loi n 2006-450 du 18 avril 2006 de programme pour la recherche.*
[14] *Loi n 2007–1199 du 10 août 2007 relative aux libertés et responsabilités des universités.*
[15] PRES was introduced in the 2006 Research Programme Act.

(Conventions industrielles de formation par la recherche—CIFRE) created in 1981, (2) the creation of the *pôles de competitivité* at regional level in 2005, and (3) the expansion of the regional *Centres d'innovation et de transfert de technologie* (CRITT). This denotes an important change in the state of mind of the actors in the system in terms of public research-industry relations.

All in all, the French system is experiencing profound changes, and the intention is to introduce a more horizontal approach to research and innovation policy, in contrast to the vertical and academic approach from the 1950s. Reforms in France seem to be aimed at making the system more similar to other European countries (Thèves, Lepori et al., 2007). The reforms have resulted in expanding the number of actors and in increasing funding and flexibility, but they have also increased the complexity of the system. Critical voices regarding problems of coordination and planning were directed at the creation of the national research and innovation strategy in 2009 (Stratégie nationale de recherche et d'innovation—SNRI).[16] It is also important to underline that, in spite of introducing multiple diffusion-oriented instruments bridging the gap between academic science and industry (Robin & Schubert, 2012), the French innovation policy continues to be eminently mission-oriented, as it still has a preference for supporting specific scientific and technological areas, and is implemented by means of a hands-on approach from central state authorities (Robin & Schubert, 2012).

French civil servants were actively involved in the Lisbon Strategy in general and in particular in the OMC process in research and innovation policy during the period under study. This active involvement was evident during the interviews with the French respondents and the fact that many senior high-level civil servants were participating in these OMC meetings. This was not the case in other countries, which tended to send more junior civil servants to those meetings. Regarding the OMC as a sensemaking process in a cross-national context, the French respondents emphasized that the process provided them with learning and networking opportunities: "The peer review process is very useful to open minds and learn from other national contexts." "The participants had a shared expectation: to exchange experiences and avoid repeating errors. The fact that the participants had different types and history of experiences was a very fruitful element of the exchanges." "The dialogue was frank and free, and the learning was good." Another remark in this vein was:

> In the first phase, the work was analytical and it was expert work. The profiles of participants were quite different; this was useful to produce a rich report. The report involved a comparative analysis of policy instruments, an identification of "good" and "bad" policy tools and how a government could choose the "good" tools, i.e. the right tool for the right objective. In the second phase, the work was

---

[16] "Stratégie nationale de recherche et d'innovation".

more of a political nature. The profile of the participants was more of an institutional type rather than experts.

Another remark: "This group was a 'group of influence' to advance some proposals and inspire future Community proposals."

As observed above, the French innovation policy underwent very important reforms during the period in which the OMC was unfolding. French respondents seemed to be particularly positive as to the influence that this OMC process exercised on the reform debates in France. Hence, regarding the condition for the influence on national debate, these respondents tended to emphasize the timing of the political attention, as well as the administrative organization at the national level (but not always in a positive way). A respondent said: "A difficult point is that a [OMC] report, to get an audience, should come at the right time with respect to the policy agenda." With regard to national administration: "There is little absorption capacity and little diffusion of European documents. One reason lies in the fact that they are generally not very concrete, not oriented towards operational questions. They are often not in line with the national subjects of interest." And again: "There is a lack of strategic watch units on EU matters, composed of people who understand both the national context and EU developments. The absorption and diffusion rests on very few people who take the decision to pay interest and diffuse this work or not." Nonetheless, in spite of these individual remarks, the OMC process had a clear influence on the French reform debate, both in terms of timing and the active participation of senior-level civil servants in the Brussels meetings.

4.7 GERMANY

The German research and innovation policy has also experienced important changes, which amount to more than the usual adaptation, but do not constitute a substantial transformation. Some observers point out that some of the novelties introduced by policy reforms in the 2000–10 period were characterized by a strong emphasis on mission-oriented innovation policy instruments (Frietsch & Schubert, 2012). This is noteworthy as the German system has traditionally focused on fostering collaboration between industry and academia. One of the most significant novelties in innovation policy was the creation in 2006 of the High-tech Strategy, which has been recently relaunched as High-tech Strategy 2020. The main objective of this strategy is to focus on industry-science collaboration as well as on the commercialization of research results. It has enhanced the cross-ministerial coordination, brought together several policy instruments, and created new target-oriented ones (such as the "cluster competition" initiative focusing on some thematic clusters). Another important initiative is the "Excellence Initiative" of 2006, which has granted universities the possibility of applying for additional funds to create excellence graduate schools, excellence-based collaborations, all of which have basic science and excellence at universities as the main focus. Germany has also reformed the funding of the research conducted at universities, which is today mainly funded by competition-based external sources rather than basic government endowment to the universities. This is somewhat similar to other countries' trends (Lepori, van den Besselaar et al., 2007). Likewise, the new law in 2002 on university patents abolished the "professor's privilege" and granted universities the right to obtain intellectual property rights (IPRs), although this has so far had limited effects on the system (von Ledebur, Buenstorf et al., 2012).

Germany is one of the largest research and innovation countries in Europe, and it holds particular weight in political discussions in Brussels. This is clearly reflected not only in the traditional side of EU R&D and innovation policy at the supranational level, but also in the OMC process of cross-national coordination under the open-ended Lisbon Strategy. German civil servants are generally experienced, and the size of the country means they have a critical mass of highly specialized as well as generalist civil servants. The large size of the country may also make some German civil servants more sceptical about the need to coordinate and share experiences on a cross-national level than those in smaller and less science/technology-intensive countries, which are more dependent on knowledge sources from abroad. The German civil servant respondents were more aware of these differences among participants in the OMC sensemaking process, but they were generally positive when describing the features of the process in terms of providing overview and creating international networks of influence. As one respondent put it: "What all countries shared in the group was to get an overview of what kinds of methods and instruments exist, how they function, why they are employed in specific contexts, and how success is measured in different countries." Along similar lines: "The discussion was very active, and did not come to a standstill; all were very involved and active. The aim was to deliver common ideas." And also, "I would even go further and characterise the group as having a kind of scouting function."

Something similar can be found among the German respondents' views on the conditions for influence at national level. Here the emphasis was on diversity and the importance of the technical nature of the topic under discussion in the cross-national context. "We have taken note of some of the [OMC] reports because we try to match our own policy recommendations and research activities with these policy recommendations." And in regard to the differences across national civil servants:

The expectations were very diverse due to many different backgrounds and starting positions. Example: Romania, Bulgaria and other new countries are not advanced enough to be able to talk about excellence in science. Their expectation is to learn the basic elements of evaluation methods, get best-practice examples and collect experiences from other countries.

4.8 COORDINATING NATIONAL REFORMS AND SENSEMAKING

Processes of institutional reform are complex and tend to involve many different actors. This is the case of the extensive reforms in innovation policies during the first decade of the 2000s in the four countries examined. Virtually all of them perceived the need to introduce some novelties and structural changes in their innovation systems as a way to improve the competitiveness and productivity of their national economies. This chapter does not examine the extent to which this has or has not been achieved, as it corresponds to other types of analyses evaluating impact and results. Instead, this chapter examines the way in which some of the most prominent actors involved in the reform processes have viewed those processes in the context of the cross-national EU-level interactions among civil servants. The OMC under the overall EU-level Lisbon Strategy provided a platform for the interaction of civil servants involved in these important institutional reforms at the national level. To a large extent, these EU-level civil servant interactions and informal open coordinations were taking place simultaneously with the national-level processes of institutional change. The forward-looking and analysis-based interactions of these national civil servants' meetings in Brussels indicate that the OMC was designed as a process for mutual learning. This provides a unique opportunity to study the way in which prospective and abstraction-based processes of sensemaking operate in a cross-national context where institutional reforms are taking place concurrently.

A total of forty-two qualitative interviews with national civil servants in France, Denmark, Sweden, and Germany were coded and clustered around two main issues: the views of the respondents on how the OMC process was characterized as a process of sensemaking, and the views of the respondents on whether the OMC at EU level influenced the national debates during the institutional reforms. Tables 4.2 and 4.3 summarize the frequency with which national respondents pointed to some specific associated items. These figures do not reflect a systematic quantitative outcome of qualitative data. Instead, they reflect the frequency of respondents' associations to some specific items, when asked generally on their views of the process of which they were a part.

Table 4.2 Number of references indicating codes referring to the OMC process as sensemaking, by nationality of respondent

	Wrong premises	Upgrading knowledge competences at national level	Providing overview	Developing common principles and approaches	Creating international networks of influence
Danish respondents		2	2	1	2
Swedish respondents		1	2		1
German respondents	2	2	5	1	2
French respondents		2	12	2	4

Table 4.3 Number of references indicating codes referring to respondents' views on the influence of the OMC process on national debates

	Timing political attention	Technical nature of topic	Administrative organization at national level
Danish respondents	7	5	5
Swedish respondents		5	
German respondents		3	
French respondents	4	2	8

The results in Table 4.2 show that the OMC (designed as a platform for cross-national sensemaking processes among national civil servants) gave participants an overview and created international networks of influence. To a lesser degree it seems that this also contributed to upgrading national knowledge competences among national civil servants, and to developing common concepts and approaches across different countries. Regarding the issue of influence on the national debates, the findings in Table 4.3 show that the EU-level coordination of national civil servants had some influence, but that this was related to national-level features such as the organization of national public administrations and the timing of political attention. The technical nature of the specific topic discussed was also relevant in this regard, because the more technical the nature, the less influential EU-level sensemaking processes on the national debates.

Apart from these tables, sections 4.4–4.7 have shown the differences in the reforms introduced by the national innovation policies, as well as the different views and perceptions from national civil servants who took part in the EU-level OMC. The cross-national differences are remarkable, not only in the nature of the reforms, but also in the views and understanding of how this EU-level induced process of sensemaking across national boundaries was characterized and influenced national debates.

With these results in hand, it is worth turning back to the definition of sensemaking provided in the introduction. This book sees sensemaking as a key process in the construction of decisions that inform institutional change, reflecting and transforming related socioeconomic discourses, and therefore as a necessary element in the construction of social knowledge. The OMC under the Lisbon Strategy provided a platform for this process to take place among national civil servants in the period 2000–10. More concretely, it provided a platform for the prospective and abstraction-based processes of sensemaking that were forward-looking and analysis-based. From the findings in our study on civil servants' views on this process, it is possible to conclude that these types of *forward-looking* and abstraction-based sensemaking processes are related to some important "external" patterns in which the process of sense-making is ultimately embedded. These external patterns refer to the know-ledge bases of the participants and the environment from which they come, the differentiated national-level political timing of the discussions, and the administrative organization at national level where such cross-national sense-making processes are to have an influence. Likewise, the way in which prospective and abstraction-based sensemaking processes are conducted is somehow related to the features of the topic at hand, meaning that the technical or less technical nature of the topic does have a different context for the sensemaking processes, and for their effect outside the circle of participants.

One of the most significant findings of this study is that the participants interviewed indicated that the development of common principles and approaches (a common language) within the group was not an easy or automatic task. Even in contexts of abstraction and prospective sensemaking processes among experts, this was not as easy as one might expect at first sight. National differences in terms of conceptual frameworks and levels of expertise among participants were visible and represented a challenge for this sense-making process in a cross-national setting. Taken together, these remarks indicate the complexity of cross-national processes of sensemaking, even when they take place in contexts of specialized policy areas related to specific socioeconomic institutions, or abstraction-based and prospective-oriented sensemaking processes.

5

Sensemaking in Public Management Reform in Denmark

Carsten Greve

5.1 INTRODUCTION

Public management reform has been a part of public sector restructuring globally. For many, public management reform is a product of the increasing globalization that leads nations to compete amongst each other for positions in the global economy (Andrews, 2010; McNutt & Pal, 2011; Pedersen, 2011; Roberts, 2010). For others, public management reform has become wired into the everyday practice of a changing public sector in every corner of the globe in pursuit of improved performance (Kettl, 2005). After more than thirty years of reform, we have a better understanding of what works (OECD, 2010; Pollitt & Bouckaert, 2011), but there is still no conclusive evidence on performance (Pollitt & Dan, 2013). There are recent calls for "new analytics" for the next steps in public management reform analysis (Grindle, 2011). So, *why and how have public management reforms developed?*

The chapter looks empirically at the Danish experience. Denmark is a particularly relevant country for the study of public management reform. Two reforms are examined in particular: The structural reform and the quality reform. Denmark has been steeped in rhetoric in the New Public Management (NPM) era, while in practice it has been oriented toward collaboration and digitalization. Denmark's standing in various worldwide indexes affirms its top position in public sector performance. New indexes have shown the Danish public sector to be effective. These indexes include the World Bank's Worldwide Governance Indicators, the Organisation for Economic Co-operation and Development (OECD) Better Life Index, the OECD Government at a Glance project, the World Economic Forum, the Transparency Index, and the United Nations on internet use and government's preparedness for the digital era. Denmark is doing remarkably well in all these indexes, strongly indicating that Denmark's institutional competiveness for the public sector is impressively high and robust. The Danish public management reforms are on a par with many reform initiatives in the NPM era that other OECD countries are pursuing.

The chapter is divided into four parts. Firstly, the theoretical framework of sensemaking in public management reform is presented. The second part examines the cutting edge of public management reform theory. Thirdly, a comparison between two recent public management reforms in Denmark is made and we look at how key actors have made sense of public management reform developments in Denmark. The fourth part offers a short conclusion.

5.2 THEORETICAL FRAMEWORK: SENSEMAKING IN AN INSTITUTIONAL CONTEXT

Where do the ideas for reforms come from? Who pushes for reforms? How do reforms become institutionalized? These are some of the questions that historical institutional theory and the sensemaking approach can help public management reform scholars answer. Historical institutional theory focuses broadly on social processes in time, and especially on their political aspects (Steinmo, Thelen, & Longstreth, 1992; Pierson, 2004, Streeck & Thelen, 2005; Thelen, 2004, 2009). Historical institutionalists do not see a mere socioeconomic pressure dictating events, but are interested in the way a crisis is socially constructed (through "ideas"), how actors push for reforms and try to respond to pressures ("interests"), and how change processes are possible when there are already institutionalized elements in place ("institutionalization"). Furthermore, historical institutionalists examine the change processes through longer time periods and view short-term explanatory arguments as unsatisfactory. Ideas are studied by scholars such as Campbell (2004); interests and actions are studied by Streeck & Thelen (2005) and others; while the longer time perspective is forcefully presented by Pierson (2004) and others. The focus is on institutional change processes. It is expected that looking at these processes will reveal discussions of ideas and interest. The discussion on the historical institutional view on institutional change can be divided into two subsections on path dependency and gradual change.

Path dependency means that once a course is set, development will take place within a designated path for a considerable period of time. Change of direction takes place during critical junctures that set off another path. Historical institutionalism starts with the assumption that change takes place in critical junctures that create different paths for further development (Thelen, 1999).

Researchers within historical institutional theory have long been displeased with the strict interpretation of the path dependency concept, and research now focuses more on institutional change mechanisms (Campbell, 2004; Streeck & Thelen, 2005). Campbell (2004) used the term "bricolage" (see also Roberts, 2010) to describe a process where institutional change happens more gradually and through a set of different social change mechanisms. Thelen (1999; 2009) argues for a more dynamic view of change where institutional change is ongoing rather than only occurring in ruptures or in the critical junctures followed by long paths of "frozen action." Thelen argues that focus should be on the mechanisms of reproduction in institutions, and how the factors affecting change and stability can be the same and should not be separated in the analysis.

Streeck and Thelen (2005) have elaborated on this argument and they point to five different strategies for institutional change that signal more dynamic approaches, each seeing a gradual transformation of the original institutional settlement: displacement, layering, drift, conversion, and exhaustion. Later, these approaches were reduced to four modes of change, leaving out exhaustion. Displacement characterizes "slowly rising salience of subordinate relative to dominant institutions" (Streeck & Thelen, 2005: 30). This could be done in various ways, one of them being an "invasion" of foreign practices. Layering describes situations where "new elements attached to existing institutions gradually change their status and structure" (Streeck & Thelen, 2005: 30). Drift is when existing institutions are "neglected." This neglect can be deliberate, but it can also be because of changing environmental circumstances, making the old institution less important in new surroundings. Conversion is a situation of "redeployment of old institutions to new purposes" or "new purposes attached to old structures" (Streeck & Thelen, 2005: 30).

The advantage of the more incremental approach to institutional change is that it allows for more sensemaking by organizational actors and individuals. Sensemaking in this volume, following Borrás and Seabrooke, is understood as the cognitive and interpretive process through which organizations and actors (agents of change) give meaning and define their interactions with each other and the institutional set-up. From this view, sensemaking directs our attention to the constitution and co-creation of changes to institutional environments, as well as organizational goals and practices. There is also the advantage that it allows for a more detailed process view on how change processes actually occur. Organizations may move from layering processes to conversion approaches to institutional change. Determining the conditions under which they use which change mechanism is of pivotal importance to trace. Streeck and Thelen (2005) have pointed out how institutional systems are inherently unstable and how organizational actors involved in them need to reassert their position constantly and strategically. As Borrás and Seabrooke noted in Chapter 1, organized interests can use ideas to further their strategies. A crucial point is that "uncertainty creates an open space for re-interpretation over the nature of problems and of possible solutions, searching new angles and considerations about how the economy should work" (see Editors' Introduction). The disadvantage of the change mechanisms' approach is that it can get too complicated to follow the different strategies through a process (see also Campbell's point about the empirical research conditions related to the approach). The Streeck/Thelen/Mahoney approach is based on the view that organizational actors tend to concentrate on gradual change and not path dependency, and that the focus is on how different forms of gradual change are informed by the various roles performed by change agents (Mahoney & Thelen, 2010).

Sensemaking is an approach that builds up from the ideational and discursive approaches of institutionalist theories, as well as American pragmatism and organizational sociology. The sensemaking approach provides two important novelties: it first brings forward an agency focus in the ideational and discursive institutionalist approach of previous studies, while looking at the different experiences and backgrounds of agency; and secondly, it puts emphasis on the process of making sense rather than on the outcomes of this process. The chapter is inspired by James March's latest book on the ambiguity of agents' experience, and the low and high intellect ways of dealing with this ambiguity, understood by the editors of this volume as abstraction and replication.

How does sensemaking of institutional competitiveness take place? It is not an objective feature of national institutions, but the way in which agents make sense of how institutions work in their economies and the way in which they aim to change those institutions in order to improve their competitiveness. Sensemaking is a process by which agents gather (ambiguous) experience about how their economic institutions work and need to work in order to improve the national economy's competitiveness.

5.3 PUBLIC MANAGEMENT REFORM ANALYSIS

Public management reform has been the topic for both researchers and individual countries (Bresser-Periera, 2004; Goldfinch & Wallis, 2009; Kettl, 2005, 2009; Pollitt & Bouckaert, 2011). Increasingly, international organizations such as the World Bank, OECD, and the European Union also discuss their views, announce their approaches, and engage in debates. The current debate over ideas in public management is centered on whether there is a shift from the NPM (Hood, 1991; Christensen & Lægreid, 2011) to a post-NPM situation or, if there are new concepts such as New Public Governance (NPG), Digital Era Governance (DEG) (Dunleavy et al., 2006; OECD, 2011a), and Public Value Management (PVM) (Hartley, 2011). Public management reform is a process by which both the makers of reforms (the central actors) and the takers of reforms (the recipients in lower-level public organizations) strive to formulate strategies and create meaning about what reforms consist of.

Public management reform has been defined as follows: "Public management reform consists of deliberate changes to the structures and processes of public sector organizations with the objective of getting them (in some sense) to perform better" (Pollitt & Bouckaert, 2011: 2). "*Comprehensive* public management change is the occurrence of some change in institutional rules and organizational routines within a national government in *each* of the areas of public policy management policy just listed as a result" (Barzelay & Gallego, 2006: 545, emphasis in original). We will explore those further below. Rephrased to institutional theory, a working definition could be: reforms are intentional attempts by reform actors—through use of reform ideas—to systematically change institutions and processes in order to make them work better/make them more performance-oriented/create advantageous institutional positions/create salience on political issues.

A prominent theme has been the relationship between reform and performance. Much like the argument about a competition state that engages in institutional competiveness (Pedersen, 2011), the public sector is an important part of each country's institutional competitiveness profile. There is growing literature collecting evidence on different countries' experiences with reform (OECD, 2005; Pollitt & Bouckaert, 2011; Pollitt, 2011). Van der Walle (2009) raises a key point in his award-winning article on reform and performance. Van der Walle distinguishes between economists' approaches to performance and political scientists' measures of performance. The latter is more focused on institutional advantages, and securing institutional strongholds. Hartley (2011) covers some of the same issues when she asserts that the judgment of whether public organizations create public value is a dynamic issue that cannot be settled, and that a democratic interpretation will always play a part in assessing performance. There are a number of indexes that measure public sector performance, as noted above in section 5.1.

Pedersen (2011) has shown how countries are adapting to the globalization of the economy, and how they are promoting their own countries' position in the global race. Following Cerny, Pedersen names this development "the competition state." Pedersen notes how Denmark is in a state of permanent reform because of the need to make the public sector efficient in playing its role of serving the private sector in competing in the global economy. Roberts (2010) has advanced the argument that the financial discipline associated with markets is putting pressure on all of the public sector, which he termed "the logic of discipline." Governmental systems are themselves "matters of contention" and not stationary (Barzelay & Gallego, 2010: 299–300). It is important to note the politics of public management reform (Barzelay, 2001; Barzelay & Gallego, 2006; Radin 2006).

In summary, it can be said that there are a number of theoretical approaches to public management reform even within a broad theoretical church of historical institutionalism. A historical institutional theory has focused on the broader path dependency development. The focus on dynamics and more subtle institutional change mechanisms is evident in the transformative and political approaches. The sensemaking perspective helps us see how reform actors are engaged in arguing and promoting public management reforms.

5.4 PUBLIC MANAGEMENT REFORM IN DENMARK: MAKING SENSE OF TWO REFORMS

Danish public management reform can be compared to the main international trends. Danish reforms are usually placed in relation to NPM countries or other traditions. Denmark is traditionally viewed as being a skeptical NPM-implementing nation, but developments in the 2000s would place Denmark alongside high NPM countries with focus on managerialism and markets. The reforms have been in focus, but Denmark has lacked the overall reform narrative and sweeping reform statement that other countries have experienced, such as the Australian Government's "Blueprint" for reform, the US Government under President Obama's focus on the themes of "transparency, collaboration and participation" (Coglianese, 2009; Obama, 2009), and the UK Government's idea of "the Big Society."

Public management reform in Denmark was shaped by a critical juncture in the early 1980s with the advent of a serious economic crisis. The economic crisis led to a new "modernization program" being launched in 1983. The sensemaking approach to modernization was initiated by the then Conservative-led government. The modernization program consisted of five elements: (1) budget reform and focus on performance management, (2) executive management and human resource management, (3) competition and choice, (4) deregulation and cutting red tape, and (5) e-government. These focus points were the topic of subsequent management initiatives by other governments (Bentzon, 1988; Pedersen & Lægreid, 1994; Ejersbo & Greve, 2005). In 1993 the Social Democratic government continued the modernization effort under the heading "A New Perspective on the Public Sector," which largely contained the same elements, but with a slightly different priority. In 2002 the Liberal-Conservative government headed by Prime Minister Anders Fogh Rasmussen announced a program of "Citizens at the Steering Wheel," and a companion program on "Public Services and Choice," which emphasized the choice agenda to public management. For three decades the themes of budget reform and performance management, management/leadership and human resource management, competition, deregulation, and e-government have been developed further. This has followed the path largely associated with the NPM reform agenda in the OECD world. A couple of new themes were added; most visible of these was innovation, which appeared on both the international and national agenda. The path was continued by Prime Minister Lars Løkke Rasmussen who took over from Anders Fogh Rasmussen from 2008 to 2011.

During the 2000s two underlying themes were prominent in the Danish approach to public management reform. Firstly, the Fogh Rasmussen government gave priority to competition and choice. The government wanted to extend choice to citizens, to create competition for public service delivery wherever possible, and to open up markets for private companies and associations. Secondly, the government was focused on securing Denmark's competitive advantage as a country in the global economy and viewed an efficient public sector as a helping hand for a thriving private sector.

In the 2000s the government started to introduce more formal and informal reforms in a number of policy areas. Some of these reforms involved the five themes, but regrouped under new headings. The reforms were all top-down initiated changes aimed at systematically changing public management structures and/or processes. Public management reforms included the choice reform, the public sector top executive reform, the budget and accounting reform, the digitalization reform, the structural reform, the welfare reform, the globalization reform, the police reform, the courts' reform, the university reform, and the quality reform. Many of these reforms were official reforms, while others merely possessed the characteristics of reform (these reforms have been discussed in detail in other texts, for example, Greve, 2012; see also Table 5.1).

5.4.1 The Structural Reform

The structural reform in Denmark involved 271 local governments merging into ninety-eight local governments, and thirteen counties were merged into five new regions. Local governments are delivering public services close to citizens in Denmark and can raise their own tax revenue. Regions are mainly responsible for health services and run all of the main public hospitals in Denmark. Contrary to the counties before them, the new regions cannot raise their own taxes, but are dependent on a grant from the central government. The economy of both local governments and regions are planned each year in negotiations between the Danish Ministry of Finance and the peak associations Local Government Denmark and Danish Regions. Local government

Table 5.1 Examples of key public management reforms in Denmark in the 2000s: three dimensions of sensemaking

Reform	Timeline (start and end date of official reform activities)	Contents
Choice reform	2002	Compulsory "free choice" legislation for all local governments
Budget and accounting reform	2001–	Introduction of accrual accounting principles
Digitalisation reform	2001–	Digital-era governance solutions
Code of public governance reform for top executives	2001–05	Code with nine recommendations for actions for top executives in the public sector
Welfare reform	2005	New financing of welfare services for the future
Globalization reform	2005–06	Preparing for Denmark in the global economy
Structural reform	2002–07	New structure in local government: from two hundred and seventy-one to ninety-eight local governments, and from thirteen counties to five regions
Police reform	1997–2007	Huge reform of all aspects of the police, including change from fifty-four to twelve police jurisdictions
Court reform	1998–2007	From eighty-two to twenty-two primary courts
University reform	2006–07	From twelve to eight universities
Quality reform	2006–08	Process initiatives to improving quality of public services

reform has a long tradition in Denmark. In 1970 the last major reform was made which merged the then 1,300 small local governments into a new structure. More tasks, especially those concerning the welfare state tasks, were decentralized to the local governments in the 1970s and 1990s. An attempt at a new reform was made in 1998 when a "task commission" (the *Opgavekommissionen*) reported on where tasks in the public sector should be located organizationally. The report from the *Opgavekommissionen* reached the conclusion that the tasks were spread effectively between local government, counties, central government, and the European Union. One of the main ideas of the *Opgavekommission* was to see if the structure and power of the Copenhagen local government could be challenged. Copenhagen local government has 500,000 inhabitants, making it the largest local government by far. The 1998 reform attempt did not succeed in breaking up Copenhagen local government. In 2002 an attempt to reform the local governments was again put on the table. The Minister of the Interior took the initiative—after some pressure—to establish a Structural Commission to examine the size and organization of local governments in Denmark. The Structural Commission was more successful than its predecessor. The commission worked for over one year on its proposal. One of the proposals was to reduce the number of local governments. Research has since shown that Danish Industry, the key national employers' association, was very active in lobbying for fewer local governments (Christiansen & Baggesen Klitgaard, 2008). Danish Industry's preferred number of local governments was 100, compared to 271 municipalities in existence prior to the reforms. When the commission's report was presented, there was a big event held in Vejle in Jutland. All mayors and politicians with a stake in the outcome were present. The commission's chairman presented the report and the Minister of the Interior spoke as well. The meeting changed the attitude toward reform. After the event, mayors and politicians were convinced that a reform was going to happen. The reform was presented in 2005 after a short public hearing and consultation period. The government took in the report's main findings, and then proceeded to make its own recommendations of ninety-eight local governments and five regions to "future proof" the organizational structure of the Danish welfare state. The new local government structure came into law on January 1, 2007.

Politicians and civil servants made sense of the structural reform in mainly efficiency and effectiveness terms. Denmark would have a "future-proofed," efficient, decentralized public sector according to the government. The way to present efficiency and effectiveness as key terms had started already back in the 1980s. A previous attempt at changing the local government borders in 1998 with the *Opgavekommission* had failed to deliver a result. But in 2002–07 with the structural reform, a new and successful attempt was made. There was a reform impetus and dynamic that had been present throughout the last few decades. The government was actively trying to lay the ground in communication terms toward a new structure. Opponents were dealt with and sidetracked (including the political parties in opposition to the government who left the negotiations before the final bill in Parliament was agreed). There has been active sensemaking by key government actors during a sustained period of time. The commission was part of the active sensemaking process.

5.4.2 The Quality Reform

The quality reform was initiated by the Danish Government in the summer of 2006. The final reform was presented to the public in late summer 2007. The majority of the reform proposals were agreed in Parliament by March 2008. The main elements of the reforms were: (1) users at the centre, (2) attractive workplaces, (3) management reform, (4) quality development in public services, (6) strong local government, (7) cutting red tape, (8) more public employees, and (9) investments in future welfare service and infrastructure (mainly the building of new hospitals in Denmark).

The reform was going to be placed in the institutional context of previous reforms, but with more emphasis on the quality and consumer choice aspects. The government made it clear that the reform was not designed to abolish or attack the public services, but to boost and improve the quality of the public services. The timing was at the height of the economic prosperity of the 2000s, just before the global financial crisis set in.

On June 17, 2007 the agreement with the trade unions was confirmed and a "tripartite agreement" was secured. The government made the agreement with Local Government Denmark (employers' association), Danish Regions (employers' association), LO (the Danish confederation of trade unions), and AC (academics' association). The initiatives included support of public management education, including a flexible master in public management and governance for DKK 80 million and "evaluation of public managers that includes employees" for DKK 200 million. On July 1, 2007 the last of the trade unions, FTF (Danish confederation of professionals), entered an agreement. The agreement was between the government, Local Government Denmark, Danish Regions, and FTF. The government became committed to prioritize competency development for FTF's members, including a special pot of money worth DKK 250 million and further education of teachers of DKK 75 million.

The tripartite agreements on June 17 and July 1, 2007 showed that the government was now committed to allocating substantial resources to the improvement of public services. The trade unions had managed to secure substantial funds and benefits for their members, but were now also in support of the government's reform agenda for public services. As July is a month of summer holidays in Denmark, the government chose to wait until August 21, 2007 to publish the final report on the quality reform. A media conference was called for that date. There were initiatives amounting to DKK 50 billion, with DKK 25 billion allocated to the health sector.

How can the quality reform be interpreted? Here we turn to the analytical framework in the beginning, that of the relationship between ideas, interests, and institutions. Regarding the ideas, it has become apparent that the quality idea itself was not new. The government did not promote the reform as something new or ground-breaking. The government was very vague as to how quality should be conceptualized, and only made a sketchy definition when pressed to it. Here the government opened for different sensemaking activities related to the concept of quality. The origin of the words "quality reform" has been traced back to a Liberal Party proposal around ten years ago. Interests were organized to promote the quality reform. The obvious reformers were the prime minister and the Prime Minister's Office, but there were many other organizations and actors involved in the process. The institutions that were to be reformed by the quality idea were open to such attempts. The quality idea was not designed or interpreted to be an attack on the existing institutional foundation of public service delivery, but can be interpreted as boosting or underpinning the institutions associated with public service delivery. The reform was very much a plus-sum game where every organization involved gained something. The government therefore didn't meet any strong resistance to any of the proposals or initiatives. The issue of time should be kept in mind. This was a "reform episode" in Barzelay's terms, where there are previous events, contemporary events, and later events, but where the focus is on the main events connected to the reform. Others would be more interested in the place of quality reform in the larger reform agenda, and the longer term reform program and initiatives. The quality reform in its content is rooted in the previous decade's efforts to "modernize the public sector" in Denmark.

The quality itself was remarkable for at least three reasons: (1) The quality reform built on previous and existing public management reform ideas, but gave it a twist of quality. (2) The prime minister was in the driver's seat and made an effort to include many organizations in the reform process, which also meant a clear media communication strategy. (3) It was aimed at all levels of the public sector as public service quality improvement involves ministries, regions, and local governments, and even private sector organizations. In that way it was not only a governance reform but also a more comprehensive reform. The reform can be analyzed from many perspectives, but in this chapter we highlight two important features: the politics of the quality reform and, related to that, the organization of the reform process and the interest groups involved.

The reform was a political act, not an administrative, technical adjustment of the way public services were delivered in Denmark. The reform was political and aimed at sensemaking in the following ways: (1) addressing the issue of the government's standing in opinion polls, (2) the decision to take and show leadership (prime minister versus Ministry of Finance), (3) the decision to include many organizations, including trade unions, in the process, (4) the decision to keep the opposition out of the process, (5) the communication strategy aimed at dominating the political agenda for a continued period of time, and (6) the objective of the general election campaign.

The reform was perceived mainly as a response to opposition parties' rise in the opinion polls in spring 2006. The government was about to conclude the globalization reform with a report on Denmark in the global economy and was launching a university reform in late June. The structural reform was due to commence on January 1, 2007, so the local governments had enough on their hands. There was no technical or rational reason for a big reform effort at this particular point in time. However, the government saw that the reform efforts made so far had not paid off in the opinion polls and was trying to claw back the initiative. Mr Fogh Rasmussen hit on the idea of a quality reform that he could use to stall the opposition parties. The prime minister gained by keeping momentum that sustained his own leadership position. Under ordinary circumstances, the reform of the public services is traditionally a policy area for the Ministry of Finance. The prime minister had led the globalization reform process with great authority and was widely praised for his committed leadership. He brought that leadership role to a different but related area: public management reform. Normally, you would not see a prime minister devoting a great deal of his time to such a subject matter as public management reform. The prime minister sensed that this was important with voters and could see it in the opinion polls also. The Ministry of Finance and the Finance Minister were temporarily sidelined while the chief executive took charge. In other countries this is the norm also in public management reform, but the Ministry of Finance had a strong track record of management reform in Denmark. The prime minister built explicitly on his experience with the globalization reform process, and began to invite a number of organizations and interest groups to participate in the quality reform process. Organizations were invited to the meetings, but were also encouraged to send written submissions on each particular topic. Organizations and experts were added to the list of invitations gradually. In the end, almost no one was left out, except for the political parties in Parliament who had to wait until the official negotiations for the state budget legislation a year after the reform was started.

The prime minister succeeded in splitting the opposition, and gained the trade unions' support for the government's reform process and not the opposition's reform proposals. The strategy had the effect that the government came to dominate the news agenda related to the public sector for a whole calendar year. From August 2006 until the first proper reform paper was released in November 2006, the media was full of stories wondering what form the government's next big project would take. Anticipation of the "next big thing" filled media stories, and the prime minister contributed to this by mentioning the reform ideas in key speeches throughout the fall, without giving away details of the reform proposals. When the thematic meetings began in November 2006, the government dominated the media for the week the meeting was scheduled. Stories were leaked to the press Sunday evening. On the Monday morning the papers carried stories of the quality reform theme of the week. Ministers gave interviews to various media leading up to the meeting. The meeting was held on a Thursday, so Friday's papers were then occupied with reports on the findings of the previous day's meetings. The weekend papers could then be devoted to more in-depth stories and reviews of the week gone by. This went on for the first three meetings until there was a crisis in the reform process in March 2007 and the game changed. The ultimate objective was the election campaign of 2008; the government made no secret of it and used the quality reform as its main policy document showing government policy toward public service improvement. Once the election was over, and the government had won, the prime minister and his office quickly lost interest in the quality reform. The prime minister used it to advance his own political interests, which in the short term centered on re-election in 2008. In hindsight the reform process paid off politically, but it was not without risks along the way. The government was close to losing support and legitimacy in March 2007 when public knowledge or backing proved to be almost non-existent. The government also took a risk with the economy when it devoted many resources to public services. The Conservative Party sensed this during the summer and demanded tax cuts to satisfy their segment of the voting public.

The organization of the reform process consisted of (1) inviting organizations and securing an alliance, (2) taking leadership and setting up a task force, (3) planning of meeting schedule and briefing the media, and (4) adjusting the meeting schedule and appointments. The government continued the seemingly successful process of the globalization reform and invited all bigger interest organizations and trade unions to participate in the talks. The process of inclusion continued (except again for the opposition parties in Parliament). A number of organizations and experts received invitations along the way. In spring 2007 the government formed new groups and committees using the pool of organizations already involved. The new organizational forums included the two special envoys who acted on behalf of the prime minister, and "the Quality Group" and the "9 Principles Group" that formulated principles for good public service management. The result was a reform coalition consisting of the government (Prime Minister's Office and the Ministry of Finance), Local Government Denmark, and Danish Regions (employer organizations and key stakeholders also), the key industrial and trade organizations, and the trade unions. This reform coalition had previously been engaged in making the globalization reform, and before that some of them had helped design the structural reform of the local governments. Now they were together again, this time focusing on making a quality reform. The key players all knew each other and they knew that they were all going to be called to another reform meeting sometime in the future. This instance of what economists call "iterated (repeated) games" means that the incentive to cheat or to extract bountiful promises is not an immediate option if you want to stay in the coalition.

The Prime Minister's Office established a small task force and also drafted key people from selected ministries, including the Ministry of Finance. They organized the thematic meetings, kept track of the tasks ahead, and ordered policy papers and briefings from other ministries. The person in charge of the operation was later promoted to permanent secretary in another ministry (the person in charge of the globalization reform was later promoted to chief executive officer of the Danish Competition Agency). The task force kept the website going and briefed the media on the development of the quality reform process. In short, the process was flexible enough to accommodate the new events that occurred from March 2007 onwards.

5.5 DISCUSSION

Focusing on the changes in the 2000s, and using the lenses of institutional change mechanisms and sensemaking, we can analyze the developments. The early part of the reform period was characterized by layering activities. The government was putting more layers on modernization with the choice reform from 2002, and the budget and accounting reform (from 2001) that introduced accrual accounting principles, and especially digitalization or digital-era governance reforms (from 2001). The middle part of the period was characterized as drift, with some institutions gradually losing importance to newer institutions arriving on the scene. The top executive reform that installed principles for good public governance for top managers in the public sector left strong veto possibilities for politicians and for top executives themselves, but these were avoided. There remained a high level of discretion as to how the code for good public governance would be interpreted and implemented. The same goes for the two economic reforms in the middle period: the globalization and the welfare reforms both signaled change, but not overnight. The globalization reform and the report "Denmark in the Global Economy" signaled the change toward a "competition state" (Pedersen, 2011), but not a state that would immediately alter the welfare state. The change was going to be gradual. The change from one type of financing welfare services to the proposals in the welfare reform of 2004 were not designed to be implemented right away. The later middle period from 2005–07 is characterized by displacement. It introduced a number of far-reaching structural reforms for the public sector: The structural reform for local governments (from 2007), the police reform (from 2007), the courts' reform (2007), and the university reform (2008) were all quite radical reforms that changed the structural landscape of the public sector in Denmark. In the later part of the period (2007 onwards), Denmark entered a conversion period. The quality reform was not meant to change either structure or processes, but the government tried to renew the thinking of what quality meant in the public services.

How can we explain the sensemaking processes related to Danish public management reforms by comparing the structural reform with the quality reform? Reform actors in the reform coalition are constantly interpreting and reinterpreting what reform means for the Danish public sector.

The key actors engaged in sensemaking are considered here. A coalition between the Ministry of Finance, Local Government Denmark, and Danish Regions exists in shifting combinations. Key politicians (the individuals), including the different prime ministers and the executive directors of the local government organizations, shaped the transformation of the Danish public sector in pursuit of a sensemaking process that should add better performance in the political and administrative vocabulary. The dynamics of the reforms are especially fascinating. Maybe the reforms should not be viewed as pearls on a string, but should center around one really important reform (the structural reform) that other reforms relate to or are entangled with. Reforms are seldom "finished," but continue to unravel and have ripple consequences. The structural reform has had many "aftershocks," related to work environment and to ongoing discussions about making more structural changes. The quality reform was meant to supplement or address the need for more content in public management reform that was not addressed by the structural reform. Thereby, both reforms supplement each other in a sensemaking perspective.

The two reform processes show how public management reforms rely on actors to actively introduce new reform ideas and to campaign for them. At the same time, the structural reform and the quality reform were clearly parts of a longer reform effort, and part of a sensemaking process that had been ongoing for several decades in the Danish public administration.

5.6 CONCLUSIONS

This chapter has examined the relationship between sensemaking and public management reform in Denmark. The theoretical framework of institutional change mechanisms and sensemaking activities within an institutional context has been laid out. There is a broad path dependency toward public management reform, which started in the early 1980s. Recent reforms have also been following the reform path. Denmark has been compared to the more anglo-phile NPM model. Focusing on recent Danish reforms, more subtle institutional change mechanisms are at play. Two recent reforms have been investigated and discussed: the structural reform, which changed the local government structure; and the quality reform, which emphasized improved quality of public services. They covered both the structural and the process perspectives. These institutional change mechanisms allow a greater role for political action of key interests. Danish reformers actively pursue a sense-making approach by emphasizing efficiency and effectiveness of the reforms. Key reform actors, including the prime minister, other central ministries, and peak local government organizations, are interpreting and reinterpreting what public management reform might mean by constantly developing new reforms. The broad reform path has not been strayed from, and has become more refined over time as key actors have actively made sense of the reforms in terms of efficiency and effectiveness.

The key reform coalition has been able to disengage alternatives to the dominant reform agenda. The reform coalition has also promoted a logic of reform that creates sensemaking by first legislating on a structural reform that altered the borders of local governments and then making a quality reform that changed the contents and processes in public service delivery. The reform coalition have used a variety of means, including a commission, a government council, an elaborated meeting agenda that involved key stakeholders, and the publishing of reports and statistics, to support the reform agenda. All this was achieved in a way that creates sense for the public management reform effort. The Danish Government was an active sensemaking actor in the 2000s and it made sure that public management reform had a place on the political agenda.

6

Making Sense of Change and No Change in Employment Policies

Søren Kaj Andersen

6.1 INTRODUCTION

The financial crisis that hit the world economy in 2007–08 can be characterized as the biggest shock to the world economy since the depression in the 1930s with severe effects on GDP and, subsequently, employment levels. Within the European Union (EU) five million fewer people were in employment in early 2010 compared to the onset of the crisis in mid-2008. Still, focusing on labor market institutions and policy responses in EU member states to declining employment levels, the crisis has prompted very limited changes in existing labor market institutions. In this chapter, we argue that rather uniform responses have been made, while, at the same time, these reactions have tended to follow well-known trajectories of existing employment relations regimes.

Looking back on the last decade, the European Commission, as well as various European research centers, has produced policy papers and reports on the need for labor market reforms emphasizing the need to enhance the mobility on the labor markets. Often they have been targeting too strict rules regarding dismissals that hinder the mobility of the workforce. In other words, the basic idea was to improve the *external* mobility of workers, typically emphasizing the need to introduce flexibility to the regulation of dismissals, severance pay, etc. and thereby easing the transition of workers from one workplace to another. The policy idea of "flexicurity" became prominent in the debate on potential reforms, claiming to embrace both (job-to-job) flexibility and (income) security. Further, principles of flexicurity were adopted in the European Employment Strategy (Mailand, 2010).

Contrary to the flexicurity debate and other reform ideas emphasizing the external mobility of workers, short-time work is all about *internal* mobility of workers within the company. Short-time work schemes can be defined as a temporary reduction of working time aiming to maintain the existing employer–employee relationship. The schemes may involve anything from a limited reduction of the working week to a full suspension of the working contract (zero hours week), however, in all cases, maintaining the employment contract. Typically the wage compensation varies between 50 percent and 80 percent of normal pay. In most European countries the schemes for short-time work and temporary lay-off are based on tripartite dialogue or consultations between employers' associations, trade unions, and the state. Accordingly, rules and regulation on wage subsidies and social security contributions are typically laid down in legislation. Still, employers and trade unions often conclude agreements that set out terms and conditions of the short-time work or temporary lay-off arrangement. These agreements are normally concluded at sector or company level. Finally, measures have to be approved by a governmental authority like the public employment service. Often employers, trade unions, and government agree that training should be provided and in some cases it is mandatory (European Foundation, 2010; European Commission, 2010).

It can be argued that the basic idea behind the claim for labor market reform inherent in the European flexicurity debate was to strengthen the institutional competitiveness of individual states—c.f. the Lisbon Strategy and the aim to become the most competitive and dynamic, knowledge-based economy in the world. The successes of the Dutch and Danish flexicurity systems were repeatedly highlighted as examples of how different national institutions, via specific institutional complementarities, were able to create high levels of employment in relatively successful economies (Wilthagen & Tros, 2004; Madsen, 2004). More specifically, this includes, in the Dutch case, the wide-spread use of atypical work within a secure regulatory framework for these workers, and, in the Danish case, easy access to dismissals cushioned by relatively generous unemployment benefits and an active labor market policy. Contrary to this, the idea of introducing or expanding the use of short-time work clearly goes against policies stressing the external mobility of workers.

This raises the question of what motivated the expansion of, or in some cases the introduction of, short-time work schemes and, further, how could these schemes be perceived to enhance the institutional competitiveness of individual states? There are at least two dimensions to the answer of these questions. Firstly, the financial crisis and the specific consequences for employment created a radical change of agenda and, therefore, also raised new questions regarding how to enhance competitiveness and subsequently employment levels. This in turn leads to a focus on new types of policy initiatives. Much has to do with how to make sense of the crisis in the initial phases: should this be understood as a temporary shock where the rapid drop in demand would eventually also lead to a quick recovery? If so, it would make sense to secure employment within the company and thereby being able to bring workers back to full-time work as soon as demand re-emerged. Secondly, we should expect some states to be more inclined to introduce short-time work schemes than others. This happens as short-time work is inherently associated with the tightness of employment protection and especially the level of severance pay. High firing costs potentially have the effect of deterring companies from laying people off. However, a massive drop in demand can force the company to do so anyway, with severe consequences for both employers and employees. Accordingly, we typically find that in states with tight employment regulation, characterized by a high Employment Protection Legislation (EPL) index,[1] there tends to be generous short-time work schemes. Conversely, we expect to see that states with low levels of EPL unemployment benefits tend to be generous. In other words, there exists a certain complementarity between the level of EPL and the disposition of states to have either generous short-time work schemes or generous systems of unemployment benefits (European Commission, 2010). In short, from the perspective of key agents—representatives of governments in office, employers' associations, and trade unions—two questions appear to have been urgent with regard to policy responses to the increasing levels of unemployment in the early phases of the crisis. Firstly, how to understand, or make sense of, the specific nature of the crisis: is it purely a financial crisis or does it have structural consequences for the real economy? Will it be a short or a long-standing crisis? Secondly, what would be considered adequate responses to increasing levels of unemployment within the specific national institutional framework, considering, for instance, the national levels of employment legislation protection?

Due to the complementarity between levels of employment protection legislation and the generosity of short-time work schemes, we can have specific expectations regarding how states with different varieties of capitalism have treated short-time work. For example, Germany is characterized by a high level of EPL and we should therefore expect a strong focus on short-time work arrangements. The UK is characterized by a low level of EPL, which should indicate that short-time work would play a minor role in response to the crisis. Denmark scores a rather low EPL level, also in this case indicating that short-time work would not become a prominent tool in responding to increased levels of unemployment.

Before turning to the analysis of the national responses, first we look at an outline of our analytical framework. This is followed by a presentation of short-time work policy initiatives or absence of such initiatives with a focus on the Danish case. This leads to the analytical part, still centered on the

---

[1]   OECD *Employment Outlook*, 2004.

Danish case. Before reaching conclusion, the role of cross-border and Euro-pean dissemination of knowledge on short-time work is reflected on as part of the sensemaking processes.

6.2 ANALYTICAL FRAMEWORK

In institutional theory it has long been a dominant idea that, as described in Carsten Greve's chapter in this volume, economic systems and subsystems such as employment relations systems are characterized by strong path dependence, and that change typically occurs during periods of crisis. This happens as crises destabilize existing institutions, create uncertainties where the institutional equilibrium has been temporarily punctuated, and where interest groups seek to defend their interest via the reshuffling of existing or creation of new institutions. As emphasized in the introductory chapter, this account raises problems. One of them concerns the poor conceptualization of critical moments (economic crisis, natural disaster, etc.); how much uncer-tainty do we need in order to have openings for institutional change? The aim in this context is not to produce an answer to the question. However, it does form a point of departure for the analysis in the sense that, looking at the European labor markets, it appears somewhat surprising that a deep economic crisis has not led, at least so far, to any fundamental de-legitimization of existing labor market institutions or any sudden significant institutional change.

On the other hand, it is rather well documented that employment relations regimes in European states have changed quite significantly over the last two decades. This includes more decentralized collective bargaining institutions; this has happened both in the form of organized (coordinated) decentraliza-tion and disorganized (liberal) decentralization (Traxler, 1995), the latter dismantling multi-employer bargaining and often leading to fragmentation of labor market regulation. Labor market policies have also changed, generally characterized by a stronger focus on active labor market policies—emphasizing education, training, and workfare policies (Peck, 2001). Also in this case, the distinct characteristics of national regulation regimes impact on actual institutional development. In general, these processes of change are far more evolutionary than revolutionary or, put differently, incremental change of labor market institutions seems to have had quite significant consequences for European labor market institutions (c.f. Mahoney & Thelen, 2010; Marginson & Sisson, 2004).

Based on the understanding that labor market institutions do change, but they tend to do so in a rather incremental manner, the assumption in the following is that, in spite of the crisis, labor market institutions in European states continue to change in an incremental fashion. By introducing sense-making we will put a strong focus on *agency*—in this case the key-actors in labor market regulation: representatives of employers' associations, trade unions, and the government in office (in particular, the Minister for Employment). From this understanding of sensemaking, it is viewed as a cognitive and interpretative process through which organizations and individual actors (the agents of change) give meaning to and define their interactions with each other and with the institutional set-up (see the editors' introduction to this volume). Drawing on James March (2010), we argue that organizations are confronted with the fact that their experiences are rarely unambiguous, but rather points toward several potential solutions. In other words, when organizations try to make sense of their experience, that experience turns out to be ambiguous. For March, this leads to two distinct modes of learning and consequently sensemaking. Firstly, learning through replicating success—a mode called "replication" learning—where actions associated with success are replicated. Organizations seek to enhance their performance and therefore turn to actions associated with success and try to reproduce them, and likewise seek to avoid actions associated with failure. This mode of sensemaking/learning is furthermore linked to three different mechanisms of learning: trial-and-error learning, imitation, and selection. The second mode identified by March is learning through "stories and models"—called "high-intellect" learning or "abstraction" in this volume—which is a process of making sense/learning that "operates by devising explicit understandings that fit the events of experience into a causal explanation through a natural language narrative, an analytical model, or a theory" (March, 2010: 42).

Further, sensemaking puts the focus on *process*, meaning in this case how ideas, positions, and potential policy initiatives (or lack of initiatives) are developed and formulated by the key-actors over time. Emphasizing the temporal dimension, we make a distinction between the prospective and retrospective processes of sensemaking. We see prospective replication-based sensemaking as focusing on *expectations* and retrospective replication-based sensemaking as focusing on *identity*. With regard to abstraction-based sensemaking, we see the *prospective* form leading to *search systems* and the *retrospective* form leading to *causal analysis* (see the editors' introduction to this volume). In this chapter we are going to analyze how to understand the processes of sensemaking among the key-actors regarding the regulation of short-time work at the time the financial crisis hit the real economy and impacted on employment. The focus is on the Danish case and the period from early 2009 to late 2010.

Finally, it needs to be emphasized that the processes of how key-actors make sense of the need to use (or not use) short-time work regulation as a prominent tool to shelter workers and companies form the effects of the crisis that are seen as being intimately linked to how the same key-actors believe they can preserve or, even better, optimize the national *competitiveness*.

The case in focus here will be Denmark. However, before turning to the Danish experience, we will briefly describe responses regarding short-time work in the broader European context, especially in Germany and the United Kingdom. The overall aim is to present both how a coordinated and liberal economy reacted regarding short-time work during the crisis. More specifically, the aim is to acknowledge that Danish key-actors in the labor market closely follow trends on the German labor market and in the German economy as such, as the much smaller Danish economy in many aspects is dependent on its southern neighbour. This was also the case regarding the use of short-time work in the early phases of the financial crisis.

6.3 VARIETIES OF SHORT-TIME WORK

Looking across Europe, the various forms of short-time work regulation, at least to some extent, mirrors the different regimes of labor market regulation, or industrial relations regimes, in Europe. In many west European states short-time schemes have long been part of the regulation. Still, in many of these countries, schemes were extended as the downturn hit—the prominent case being Germany.

Triggered by the crisis, short-time work schemes were for the first time introduced in eight east European EU member states: Poland, Bulgaria, Czech Republic, Hungary, Latvia, Lithuania, Slovakia, and Slovenia. Compared to the west European states, these schemes are typically less generous in terms of duration and benefits, and impose stricter conditions for the initiation of the scheme. Further, this regulation often only runs for a certain period of time—supposedly covering the period of recession (European Commission, 2010).

As the crisis accelerated, the German Government chose to expand the coverage of their short-time work scheme (*Kurzarbeit*) twice. Coverage was expanded from six to eighteen months in 2008 and in spring 2009 with additional six months, so that the scheme offered state-financed wage compensation for up to twenty-four months. Consequently, the number of workers sheltered by the scheme more or less exploded over winter and spring 2008–09 to more than 1.4 million workers in June 2009. Wage compensations covered up to 67 percent of normal pay, often topped up by company agreements on further wage compensation.

During 2010 it became obvious that Germany was able to reduce the number of persons involved in short-time work significantly, while at the same time reduce the overall unemployment rate. From the peak in mid-2009 of 1,443,000 in *Kurzarbeit*, the number was 220,000 in September 2010.[2] Many observers pointed to the risk that German unemployment could explode as large groups of workers reached the twenty-four–month limit of the short-time work schemes. Among others, in 2009 the OECD predicted that the number of unemployed could move towards 5 million in 2010 (OECD, 2009). By October 2010 Germany had 2,945,000 unemployed. Even German economists describe the development as "unexpectedly positive." Two explanations were highlighted for the robust development on the German labor market. Firstly, the extensive use of short-time work made it possible for companies to initiate a prompt increase in activity, as the global economy loosened up, and the export-oriented German economy could benefit from increased demands, particularly in Asia and Latin America. Secondly, employers and trade unions managed throughout the crisis to maintain moderate wage increases, making it the focal point in securing workplaces (Sachverständigenrat, 2010). Furthermore, Germany could note the largest fall in unemployment observed in the EU between October 2009 and October 2010—from 7.5 percent to 6.7 percent (Eurostat 2010a; Eurostat 2010b).

In the United Kingdom no state-financed programs on wage-compensation linked to agreements on short-time work were found. Regulation does exist on statutory guarantee pay in case of workless days. Still, within the European comparison, this is a very limited scheme, covering a maximum of five workless days in any three-month period, paid by the employer and left to the employer to decide whether or not to introduce it. Further, the effects of the financial crisis have led to no British policy initiatives in this area (European Commission, 2010). It could be argued that a traditional liberal approach has been followed by British policymakers.

Still, company-based short-time work arrangements did occur in the United Kingdom. At the large construction equipment manufacturer, JCB, an agreement on cutting working hours was concluded in November 2008. This agreement attracted considerable media attention as negotiated—and not imposed—short-time working arrangements are uncommon in the United Kingdom. A 2010 policy discussion paper from the Advisory Conciliation and Arbitration Service (ACAS) confirms that similar agreements were concluded in an unprecedented number of companies: "A shorter working week and pay cuts were evident in previous recessions but not to the extent that we are seeing now, nor were there the variety of options currently being explored by unions and employers" (ACAS, 2010: 3). Basically, such agreement must be seen as resulting from concessionary bargaining, hollowing out workers' terms and conditions as they are not backed by any public scheme providing worker compensation.

---

[2] Monatsbericht, November 2010, Bundesargentur für Arbeit.

6.4 SHORT-TIME WORK: THE DANISH EXPERIENCE

In Denmark clauses in the collective agreements give access to short-time work for a period of thirteen weeks; however, it can be prolonged to twenty-six weeks, that is, six months. It is stipulated in the agreements how employers' and employee representatives (shop stewards) can negotiate short-time work arrangements. Social security contributions in the form of supplementary unemployment benefit are linked to short-time work (*arbejdsfordeling*) arrangement concluded by the social partners in the collective agreements. The wage compensation for a skilled worker will normally make up around 50–60 percent of the normal wage and, contrary to the German case, there will be no company top-up, meaning that all in all the Danish scheme is clearly less generous than the German.

As the crisis hit the real economy in the early months of 2009, an increasing number of workers, especially in manufacturing, were reported to be on short-time work schemes. From a couple of thousand workers in January 2009, the number increased to around 18,000 on reduced working-time in April 2009. Subsequently, the number declined.[3]

As the use of work-sharing increased, the debate on the scheme intensified. In a policy note from January 2009, the Danish Trade Union Confederation, Landsorganisationen Danmark (LO), criticized the scheme for being too rigid.[4] It was argued that there was a need to soften the rules so that companies could initiate short-time work in a quicker and more flexible way. Among other things it was criticized that a person on short-time work had to stay off work, following the sequence of one week at work, one week off work. Parallel to the discussion of the scheme being too rigid, some trade union representatives began to voice the need for a prolonged scheme. The Minister for Employment of the center-right government in office rejected the idea, arguing that it made no sense just to "distribute unemployment among workers."

Already in February 2009 it became clear that the Employers' Confederation, DA, supported the idea of more flexible rules, leaving more room for employers and their employee representatives to conclude local agreements on short-time work. In March the Minister for Employment presented new legislation relaxing the rules on how time off is organized within the framework of the existing short-time work scheme. In its own way this legislative initiative is typical for the partly corporatist character of Danish labor market regulation, in that, if the dominant employers' and trade union confederations agree about specific reform proposals, the government in office tend to embrace the proposal and implement the necessary legal steps (Due et al., 1994). Still, the duration of the scheme remained unchanged.

---

[3] Denmark. "Work-sharing saves jobs," European industrial relations observatory online, 2010.
[4] LO, *Stort behov for opkvalificeringspakke* (January 2009).

In spite of some trade union representatives having expressed the idea of expanding the duration of the scheme, a key representative on the trade union side, chairman of industrial employees in the trade union 3F, was pleased with the fact that the minister had not prolonged the duration of the scheme. He argued that the scheme's duration was an issue to be dealt with in the collective agreements, that is, in the bargaining process with the employers. He also added that the minister could change the rules on supplementary unemployment benefits, but had refrained from doing so. He hereby addressed the issue of the period where a partly unemployed person can receive the supplementary unemployment benefit. In early 2008 this period had been reduced from fifty-two to thirty weeks. The dominant employers' organizations had long been exerting pressure on the government to initiate this reduction. They claimed that the supplementary unemployment benefit was misused, especially in the public sector, as they forced public employers to accept that employees stayed on in part-time work, receiving supplementary unemployment benefits, even though full-time jobs were available in the private sector. The pressure from the employer side was motived by labor shortage in a number of private sectors during the boom years leading to the financial crisis.

As economic compensation during short-time work is dependent on the supplementary unemployment benefit, if workers ended up in unemployment after twenty-six weeks of short-time work, they were now risking having only four weeks of supplementary benefit left. Leading trade union representatives stated that in practical terms this meant that unemployed workers in this situation were forced to find full-time jobs, as part-time jobs would lead to a substantial loss of income. Still, the question of reversing the cut-back in weeks on benefit was utterly rejected by the Minister for Employment and the dominant employers' confederation. Even though labor shortage problems diminished drastically as the crisis hit, the employers' confederation did not change position.

Somewhat surprisingly, the harshest criticism of the unchanged duration of the short-time work scheme came from large and traditionally very influential industrial employers, especially Danfoss, one of Denmark's largest companies (a joint-stock company operating globally and producing valves, pumps, and motors for refrigeration and heating). Management representatives went to the media on several occasions and argued that they were forced to lay off core-workers, as unlike their German counterparts, they could not take advantage of the internal flexibility created by the extended short-time work schemes. They claimed that this gave the German companies a competitive advantage. Other major companies such as the industrial employer, Grundfos, and the toy producer, Lego, supported the idea. Still, the dominant employer's association maintained their support of a no-change policy on the duration of short-time work. A newspaper headline reported that government policy on short-time work "splits the business community".[5]

Danfoss continued their pressure for a prolonged scheme and addressed the minister directly, who once more rejected the idea of a German-style model. Once again the dominant trade unions emphasized that they could only support a prolonged scheme if the rules on supplementary unemployment benefits were expanded as well. Further, the unions argued that short-time work should be combined with education and training. A survey conducted in this period shows that 70 percent of the workers in the private sector believed that short-time work was a useful instrument if it prevented dismissals.[6]

During August and September 2009 articles began to appear in daily newspapers on the German success to keep workers in work. A lead paragraph in the daily paper, *Børsen,* stated that "at least 23.000 Danes could have kept their job if we had been half as efficient as the Germans in using short-time work".[7] In other words, a prolonged short-time work scheme could have saved jobs. In the same article the argument is supported by a former Wise Man, a professor in economics. An LO representative also stated that the full potential of short-time work had not been accomplished in the Danish context. A survey from the trade union 3F showed that only one in six workers who had been on short-time work eventually ended up unemployed. The Minister for Employment, employers, trade union representatives, and a researcher all agreed that the short-time work scheme had been an important tool in sheltering jobs.[8]

Looking back at employment figures for industrial workers, the financial crisis had a dramatic impact. From the fourth quarter of 2008 to the second quarter of 2010, 66,000 workers lost their job; this corresponds to 17.6 percent of the total employment in the sector.[9] Further, it was argued that, once these workplaces were lost, they would never come back to the Danish sites. Once global demand returned, new jobs would be placed in subsidiaries in low-cost countries.

6.5 MAKING SENSE OF SHORT-TIME WORK: THE DANISH EXPERIENCE

In the introduction, sensemaking was defined as a process by which agents gather ambiguous experiences about how their economic institutions work

[5] *Information*, March 20, 2009.
[6] *Ugebrevet* A4, March 25, 2009.
[7] *Børsen*, August 20, 2009.
[8] *Berlingske Tidende*, September 21, 2009.
[9] Arbejderbavægelsens Erhvevsråd (Economic Council of the Labor Movement), "Beskæfti- gelsen før og efter krisen. Mange store erhverv hænger forsat fast i krisen." October 21, 2011.

and need to work in order to improve the national economy's competitiveness. In the following, we seek to identify the specific processes of sensemaking, characterizing first and foremost how key-actors on the Danish labor market chose to use, or rather not use, the potential of short-time work regulation. We then turn to some comments on the German and the UK trajectory regarding short-time work, and, finally, look at European institutions' roles in formulating short-time schemes.

As Denmark experienced a historically sharp increase in unemployment—particularly in the manufacturing sector—in the early months of 2009, key actors like some trade union representatives and representatives from some major industrial employers began to argue for an expansion of the Danish short-time work scheme. This could be interpreted as a *prospective* move from these actors characterized by an abstraction-based search for, if not a new system, then an expanded system of short-time work safeguarding workers from the effects of the crisis. On the other hand, this could also be seen as a, by and large, egoistic move from employers who would like to see state finance supportive measures in times of great economic uncertainty. Likewise, it could be seen as logical if trade unions would view expanded protective measures like short-time work as a policy gain. Yet again, as the success of the German short-time work regulation became evident in the second half of 2009, almost all relevant key-actors recognized that short-time work had proven to be a very efficient tool in sheltering employment. Economists did suggest that more than 20,000 jobs could have been saved if Danish regulation had followed the German path.[10] Still, this led to no change in the regulation of the Danish short-time work scheme.

Two arguments appear to have been decisive for the Danish no-change policy regarding a more active German-style use of short-time work. Firstly, as mentioned, the dominant employers' associations had for a long time been pressing for a reduction of the period in which partly unemployed workers were entitled to supplementary unemployment benefit. The government reduced the period to thirty weeks in early 2008. Accordingly, a prolonged short-time work scheme adding to the existing twenty-six weeks would quickly move beyond the thirty weeks during which workers could obtain public support. A scheme with no public support would never be accepted by the trade unions, and a roll-back of the reduced period of supplementary unemployment benefit was not a policy option on the employer side, nor for the government in office. This created in a sense an institutional deadlock. The dominant employers' organisations were under pressure as some large and very influential member companies were publicly arguing for a prolonged short-time work scheme. Still, the employers' organisations maintained a

---

[10] *Børsen*, August 20, 2009.

policy of no change regarding the rules on supplementary benefits. Besides changing the rules on supplementary unemployment benefit, the trade unions also argued still more persistently that workers on short-time work should be offered access to education and training before they could support the idea of a prolonged scheme.

The second argument concerns the so-called flexicurity character of Danish labor market regulation. As flexicurity became a prominent part of the European employment strategy in 2007, Danish labor market regulation was also promoted as a European role model of flexible rules regarding the hiring and firing of workers, as well as the security of unemployment benefits and active measures directed toward the unemployed. The flexible rules on hiring and firing underpinned the basic idea governing Danish regulation that schemes supporting jobs in companies lacking demand (and therefore possible lacking a competitive edge) endangers the economy and accordingly does not offer stable employment for the future. In a sense this policy embraces the idea of *creative destruction*; non-competitive companies must close down and, via entrepreneurship and a high level of mobility on the labor market, create room for new companies and new jobs. In view of that, the Danish labor market regulation is a mixed regime of liberalism and corporatism—coined by Pedersen (2006a) as "negotiated" liberalism.

Both employers' organisations and trade unions embrace and support the flexicurity character of the labor market regulation along with a majority of political parties. In line with this, key representatives emphasize that introducing a German-like model of expanded use of short-time work would mean a break-away from traditional Danish regulation, giving priority to external numerical flexibility. Employers' representatives have long argued that easy dismissal procedures—the external numerical flexibility—is crucial for the large majority of small and medium-sized companies in Denmark. Therefore, in their view, expanding the short-time work scheme would be a "move in the wrong direction." Likewise, some trade union representatives argued for the overall importance of the flexicurity dynamic and voiced skepticism toward an expanded short-time work scheme. Other trade union representatives held more mixed positions, arguing that they could support a prolonged scheme if the period of supplementary unemployment benefits were prolonged as well. Still, obviously, this was not going to happen.

Putting it all in the perspective of sensemaking, the Danish *agents of change*—that is, employers' organisations, trade unions, and the government in office—for somewhat varying reasons end up in a no-change policy regarding the short-time work scheme. In the first phase of the crisis this happens in what can be termed a *replication* process of sensemaking via a *prospective* response, where the dominant actors seem to expect that the existing flexicurity character of Danish regulation, giving primacy to the external numerical flexibility, will serve the economy best in securing competitiveness and eventually job creation. In a later phase of the crisis—during the second half of 2009—when it became clear that Germany had successfully sheltered jobs through short-time work, the Danish representatives recognized the potential of the short-time work arrangement. But this led to no policy changes. Even when the Swedes in early 2012 introduced new legislation on short-time work, which includes a maximum of twelve months on reduced working time, no new debates on the issue surfaced in Denmark. Swedish employers' representatives expressed somewhat limited enthusiasm toward introducing such a scheme. However, they wanted "a level playing field," meaning that such schemes were seen as an important regulatory element in neighbouring economies, and therefore it was perceived as necessary to introduce similar regulation in Sweden. The idea was to have the same policy tools available, when the next (financial) crisis hits the economy or, put differently, to make sure that a potential competitive disadvantage was eliminated. In the sensemaking perspective, the introduction of this new legislation in Sweden can be seen as a *prospective replication*-based process of learning, as the successful schemes form neighbouring countries was, by and large, replicated.

A brief remark should be made from the sensemaking perspective on the German and British trajectory regarding short-time work and responses to the crisis. On the one hand, it can be argued that the decisions among the German key-actors to initiate an expansive use of short-time work were *replication* and *prospective* decisions based on the expectation that the crisis would be short and workers on reduced working time would be able to return to full-time working. This basically became the outcome; however, there was a great deal of skepticism and ambiguity surrounding the decisions in the first phase of the crisis. On the other hand, it might be that these decisions were first and foremost based on *identity*, meaning that they mirrored how the Germans traditionally have handled the effects of economic bursts. As a German labor market researcher has commented, in Germany "the idea to dismiss hours and not workers seems to be well accepted" (European Foundation, 2009). The United Kingdom did not initiate any form of national policy initiative regarding the short-time schemes or anything similar. Debates on possible policy initiatives in this field have been limited. Consequently, the United Kingdom is one of very few EU states taking no initiative in this policy field; as unemployment levels increased a well-known policy path was maintained or replicated. Despite the no-change policy regarding national schemes, some companies introduced local arrangements on short-time work. In a sense this reflected a search for new (local) systems in order to handle the employment effects of the crisis.

Summing up we will return to the observation—as stated earlier—that we should expect some states to be more inclined to introduce short-time work schemes than others. This happens as short-time work is inherently associated with the tightness of employment protection and especially the level of severance pay. Therefore, we typically find that states with tight employment regulation, characterized by a high EPL index, tend to have generous short-time work schemes. On the other hand, we expect to see that in states with low levels of EPL, unemployment benefits tend to be generous. Basically, the observation is that there exists a certain complementarity between the level of EPL and the disposition of states to have either generous short-time work schemes or generous systems of unemployment benefits (European Commission, 2010). Due to this complementarity we had specific expectations regarding changes in the regulation and the use of short-time work in specific states. Germany is characterized by a high level of EPL and we should therefore expect a strong focus on short-time work arrangements—and so we did. The United Kingdom is characterized by a low level of EPL, which should indicate that short-time work would play a minor role in response to the crisis—and actually it played virtually no role at all. The case we have been focusing on, Denmark, also holds a rather low EPL score, indicating that short-time work would not become a prominent tool in responding to increased levels of unemployment—again this was basically what we witnessed. In spite of pressure from leading national companies, some trade union representatives, and the successes of the German policy, we did see some policy initiatives breaking away from the expected regulatory path. We can say that the crisis with regard to this specific, but nevertheless very important regulatory tool—short-time work—only led to policy changes that, by and large, strictly remained within the framework of existing national regulatory institutions.

6.6 SHORT-TIME WORK AND CROSS-BORDER LEARNING

In the broader European view, short-time work schemes were expanded in many western European states and for the first time introduced in many eastern European states in early phases of the financial crisis, in 2008–09. European reports and policy documents on short-time work first and fore-most appeared during 2010, indicating that this has not been a policy process where European policy formulation had been diffused to nation-state level. Rather, the parallel policy responses suggest that the cross-border dialogue and learning process has been rather intense in the early stages of the crisis. Accordingly, European reports and documents on the issue primarily appear to evaluate these policy responses, discussing the effects and consequences for future regulation.

All in all, nine EU member states introduced short-time work schemes for the first time during the early phases of the crisis; most of them being eastern and central European states. Most of these schemes are less generous than schemes found in western European states, and we can also identify elements of adaptation to existing national regulatory systems in order to create institutional fit. Nevertheless, the similarities between the schemes in different EU states are far-reaching. So, processes of sensemaking leading to the introduction of such schemes must be characterized as *replication* (c.f. March, 2010). It can be questioned whether or not it is correct to link these processes of sensemaking to the *replication* mode. Still, it does not appear meaningful to link these processes to the rather abstract *abstraction* mode of learning through stories and models. March also emphasizes that "behaviour that is commonly described in high-intellect terms actually may reflect rules learned through low-intellect replications of actions associated with success" (March, 2010: 35–6). Further, it can also be questioned whether short-time work schemes were associated with "success." Back in time the German experience on reduction of working hours has been mixed and policy recommendations at the European level has, over the last decade, emphasized the need for increasing the external numerical flexibility (e.g. relaxing rules of dismissals), thereby also reducing the importance of internal flexibility (e.g. short-time work).

Both the European Commission and the European Foundation for the Improvement of Living and Working Conditions published comprehensive reports on short-time work schemes in 2010. They confirmed that these schemes had become a prominent policy tool during the crisis. In addition, it was emphasized that these schemes have widely been seen as "successful in mitigating the worst effects of this very serious recession", and it was concluded that even if an upturn in the business cycle should reveal negative aspects of these schemes (e.g. lower job transition rates) "they do appear to have been a successful business-cycle instrument" (European Foundation, 2010: 1).

Further, the success of the schemes has influenced European-level policy recommendations. Flexicurity emphasizes a move from job security to employment security, promoting the employability of the workforce rather than protecting a specific job (c.f. the Danish case). Still, the European Foundation (2010) argues that flexicurity is an intangible concept, lacking conceptual rigour (Schmidt, 2010). Therefore, the foundation promotes the distinction between *external* and *internal* flexicurity. In empirical terms the *external* flexicurity is basically referring to Danish regulation while the *internal* flexicurity is referring first and foremost to the German experience on short-time work. Nevertheless, these considerations potentially have a larger impact as they suggest that regulatory systems like the German—often criticized for being rigid—have potentials to cushion effects of an economic crisis effectively. And, of course, this argument is backed by empirical evidence.

Nation states are competing and labor market regulation is primarily embedded within the realms of national policymaking. But policy responses—and in this case the responses to the impact of the financial crisis—have been largely formulated on a cross-national basis. In other words, the generation of ideas on adequate responses—in this case short-time work—is formulated in cross-national processes. It should be noted that the basic concept of short-time work does not originate from any European policy institution. The concept is well known and has long been part of employment policies in many western European states. What has highlighted the concept to the European institutions has been the apparent success of this policy tool in using and, not least in the German case, expanding the scheme significantly during the crisis. Successful policy instruments catch the attention of European policy institutions, which leads to the inclusion of such policy instruments in various forms of papers and policy recommendations.

6.7 CONCLUSIONS

We have explored the diverse processes of sensemaking behind policy choices on short-time work regulation in order to shelter workers and companies from the effects of the financial crisis. The focus is on the Danish case, and on positions and attitudes of agents of change. German, British, and, more generally, European experiences on short-time work regulation have been studied. We have found that diverse policy choices on short-time work followed existing national policy trajectories to a large degree. In other words, the external shock created by the crisis did not prompt institutional change. Rather, short-time work initiatives—or lack of such initiatives—can be interpreted as an adaptation within the framework of existing national institutions.

Further, in spite of the varying responses in Denmark, Germany, and the United Kingdom toward the use of short-time work, it could be argued that they have all responded in ways that the key-actors believed to be in accordance with their national competitiveness profile. The British have, as one of very few European states, refrained from introducing any form of national short-time scheme and thereby confirmed the liberal character of British regulation, with a comparatively low level of risk-reducing regulation aimed at employees. In this sense it can be interpreted as an example of institutional fit *not* to take any initiative in this field. Turning towards the German case, it could also be said that expansive use of short-time work is an expression of institutional fit too. As we have seen, there seem to exist a complementarity between public short-time work arrangements and EPL, meaning that high levels of employment protection can be compensated by short time-work schemes. Put differently, companies can avoid costly firing procedures by utilizing short-time work (European Commission, 2010). This again underlines the ambiguities of Danish policymaking during the crisis. Dismissal rules are liberal, but a relatively high level of risk-reducing regulation for employees is also in place. Together these characteristics deploy the mixed or hybrid character of the Danish political economy (Campbell & Pedersen, 2007). This can be seen as an explanation as to why the lack of a policy initiative to expand the short-time work schemes became debated, and especially caused controversies within the dominant employers' association. Yet, there was no break-away from the flexicurity path, highlighting the positive effects of external numerical flexibility, that is, the ease with which workers can be dismissed. In short, the two decades of success with policies of high external numerical flexibility was replicated.

7

Making Sense of Generational Change and Institutional Competitiveness

Leonard Seabrooke

7.1 INTRODUCTION

Discussions of national institutional competitiveness seek to explain why some societies have a greater capacity to replicate institutions that create social and economic success. Variations in how institutions within national economic systems complement each other go a long way to explaining why some societies are able to sustain social and economic success, while others face severe difficulties when placed under stress. This chapter suggests that institutional competitiveness is really all about socioeconomic *regeneration*, and that thinking through sensemaking via prospective replication calls us to reflect on norms and attitudes concerning how the economy should be renewed and sustained. I suggest that a source of national institutional competitiveness is how societies regenerate themselves over generations, and that intergenerational conflicts over expectations of access to socially valued assets, such as housing, suggest potential weaknesses. This chapter puts forward the view that expectations about how the economy will work differently for different generations is a consequence of a sensemaking process that is about socioeconomic regeneration. Included here is what is referred to in this volume as "replication-based sensemaking," which stresses identity and normative aspects concerning appropriate behavior from others (parents and children, the young and the old), as well as strategic behavior on how to anticipate changes in markets that will have adverse effects on future generations. Sensemaking narratives about plausible futures may highlight generational conflict in some societies, the importance of intergenerational equity in others, or reinforce other types of relationships, such as financial ties between parent and child in more familial-based systems (Schwartz & Seabrooke, 2008). This chapter puts forward an exploratory framework for understanding generational change within what we now understand as a range of liberal and coordinated economies that intersect with a range of welfare state types (Hall & Soskice, 2001; Esping-Andersen, 1990; Campbell & Pedersen, 2007).

The basic logic here is that sensemaking, when related to institutional competitiveness, is not only about the local situation, but involves reflection and prediction about social change to the nation or polity. From this perspective actors engage in sensemaking processes among their social groups to give meaning to their actions and inform themselves of how the economy does and should work. Changes to how people engage markets, such as housing, reflect not simply responses to rational incentives, but sensemaking about what is normatively and strategically plausible as to the reasons why change has occurred and how it can be justified for one's own and other generations (Boudon, 2001). For example, the rapid increase of parent-bought properties for children in Denmark (known as *forældrekøb*) is not simply a rational response to market incentives, but a form of intergenerational transfer among those who can afford it. By contrast, the Australian housing market has become increasingly concentrated around landlords who receive tax breaks on real estate investments permitted by early access to pension funds. Both the Australian and Danish examples provide forms of intergenerational pressure (see also Mortensen and Seabrooke, 2008). I comment on these examples in this chapter, and also note important trends and concerns for intergenerational change, conflict, and equity in Organisation for Economic Co-operation and Development (OECD) countries. I suggest that structural pressures create conditions for sensemaking not as a rational economic actor, but in a process of prospective replication-based sensemaking where cultural and normative attitudes must be considered alongside strategic aims. As elsewhere, I consider individual actions as "saturated" by economic social norms and that they also contain expressions reflective of new ideas and practices that will inform future actions that have an effect on intergenerational and intragenerational relationships (Seabrooke, 2006; 2007a).

Meaningful actions from sensemaking can be affirmation of identity and also normative and/or strategic. When isolated, identifying sensemaking within small groups allows us to understand organizational variety, as the literature on sensemaking in organizational studies has demonstrated very clearly (Weick, 1995, see also the editors' introduction to this volume). When aggregated to the national level, sensemaking activities provide a plausible account of why things are the way they are, and such narratives have a serious impact on institutional complementaries and national institutional competitiveness. Sensemaking processes, when aggregated, inform discourses about which institutions are appropriate for a population (Weber & Glynn, 2006). In this way sensemaking can be seen as a micro-foundation of discourses that can be identified through narratives and variations in behavior (see the conclusion to this volume). We can understand this broader phenomena through a range of lenses, including through national identity, or conflict between different socio-economic classes (Seabrooke, 2006), as a reflection of mobility and welfare provision within a population (Kenworthy, 2004), to name but a few. Studying intergenerational issues provides a potent way of understanding broader sensemaking processes. This chapter deals with some of the conceptual issues involved in putting forward intergenerational relations as a source of national institutional competitiveness.

The chapter is structured as follows: first I discuss the issue of social regeneration and intergenerational relationships within the common frame-works applied in Comparative Political Economy. I then discuss the notion of generations as studied by experience or by cohort, and the implications of the focus of analysis for understanding sensemaking processes and institutional competitiveness. This leads to a discussion of how to locate sensemaking and generational change as a *prospective replication* phenomenon. After discussing some general trends with intergenerational change in the OECD, I provide vignettes of housing-related pressures on prospective replication-based sensemaking in one liberal market economy (LME), Australia, and one coordinated market economy (CME), Denmark. I conclude the chapter by reflecting on the importance of understanding broader social processes, such as concerns with intergenerational equity, for comparative explanations of the sources of national institutional competitiveness.

7.2 SOCIOECONOMIC REGENERATION AND COMPARATIVE CAPITALISMS

The worlds of Comparative Political Economy and Welfare Studies provide us with a number of leads or opportunities to make connections between sense-making, intergenerational change, and national variation among systems. After all, the literature on comparative capitalisms is essentially about how institutions provide opportunities for the maintenance or transformation of social order. Intergenerational issues are implicit in the *Varieties of Capitalism* (Hall & Soskice, 2001) and *The Three Worlds of Welfare Capitalism* (Esping-Andersen, 1990) frameworks, and common forms of sensemaking would seem to follow from the established institutional configurations: from CMEs and conservative welfare regimes that maintain the status quo, to CMEs that have universal welfare regimes to provide mobility with steady government and business support, to LMEs and liberal welfare regimes that are designed to permit mobility for the entrepreneurial. These systems have different ways of distributing benefits to not only different socioeconomic groups within the population, but also different generational cohorts.

Theories of institutional change that emphasize how change takes different forms, depending on the underlying drivers, also have an implicit under-standing of the intergenerational dynamics involved in socioeconomic regen-eration. Recent explanations of institutional change focus on forms of change characterized as "displacement," "layering," "drift," and "conversion" (Mahoney & Thelen 2010: 15–16; Streeck & Thelen, 2005a) that follow rules and their removal, neglect, change, and introduction. The ultimate source of change to the rules comes from the fact that "institutions are fraught with tensions because they inevitably raise resource considerations and invariably have distributional consequences" (Mahoney & Thelen, 2010: 8). While nearly all the focus on distributional consequences is on intragenerational winners and losers, a potential source of tension is from intergenerational change. For example, what has been referred to as "displacement" and "conversion" can occur from intergenerational conflicts. As forms of institutional change, displacement occurs from institutional incoherence, and conversion from "soft spots" and gaps between rules and enactment (Mahoney & Thelen, 2010: 14). Both be understood from changes in how different generations make sense of existing institutions and what they expect them to do. As Wolfgang Streeck has argued, these forms of institutional change can be understood as part of "'dialectical' tendencies in social institutions undermin-ing themselves in the course of their normal operation" (Streeck, 2009: 15). Differences in what generations want and expect from institutions will lead to new coalitions or broad agreements on how to reap the benefits from the current institutional configuration now, even if it comes at a cost to later generations. Work in comparative capitalisms on national institutional com-petitiveness would suggest that greater funding support for institutions (from the public or private sector) and mechanisms for consensus building between institutions is crucial if society is to regenerate itself. This is sensibly linked to the presence of formal institutions for welfare provision (Esping-Andersen, 1990), the stability of employer–employee relationships (Hall & Soskice, 2001), as well as provision of education and health to the population. Such aspects are fundamental to understandings of socioeconomic regeneration in the work on institutional change and comparative capitalisms.

All of these themes are addressed primarily through an *intragenerational* lens. The emphasis within much of the work is on incremental change, with "reproduction by adaptation" a process that favours continuity, while also pointing out that a lack of theoretical and conceptual innovation has led work on the welfare state and varieties of capitalism to "understate the magnitude and significance of current changes" (Streeck & Thelen, 2005: 5, 9). One way to address this issue is to think through the role of intergenerational dynamics as well as intragenerational distributional games.

Intergenerational equity concerns are central to socioeconomic regeneration and represent a significant source of national institutional competitiveness.

As discussed below, what determines a "generation" can differ, but the important element here in discussing intergenerational equity is that actors who belong to a generation (by cohort or experience) engage in sensemaking processes to express how their view of how the economy should work differs from other generations. This is interesting for studies of sensemaking because it necessarily engages a process of "maintaining a consistent, positive self-conception" (Weick, 1995: 23) through identification with a group and who that group differs from. Such identification will differ among societies, depending on social attitudes and their interaction with the institutions present within the system, and whether or not they demonstrate a high degree of complementarity. In this sense, belonging to a generation invokes what Norbert Elias refers to as "double-edged" norms that "bind people to each other and at the same time turn people so bound against others" (Elias, 1996: 159–60). In cases of high intergenerational equity we can predict that groups will not divide along generational lines and may reflect national identities, while in cases where there is a great deal of intergenerational conflict, being old or young—or stuck in the middle—may inform many preferences and choices in social and economic life (Seabrooke, 2011). This line of thinking fits with a sensemaking framework because sensemaking stresses what is plausible rather than factually accurate (Weick, 1995). Where generational conflicts and fractures exist agents will extract cues to form plausible narratives on who is getting what and who is missing out that are linked to broader social concepts such as national economic competitiveness. I suggest that such cues are typically derived from areas of everyday concern, such as access to housing finance, as highlighted here and in other work (Seabrooke, 2010; 2012). Importantly, attitudes that reflect intergenerational conflict need not be objectively rational. If the material well-being of a birth cohort is objectively substantially better than their parents, this may not, by itself, reduce conflict between generations if perceptions about one's life chances and the stresses of maintaining an expected lifestyle lead to an idea of inequity or unfairness.

In essence, generational change is about the "existence of biological rhythm in human existence—the factors of life and death, a limited span of life, and ageing" (Mannheim, 1952: 290; Simirenko, 1966). Many generational changes are related to demography and the relationship between institutional complementarities and demographic change. In advanced industrial economies, societies are getting older and fewer children are being born from the extant population. There is increased disparity between "age-gapped" families, where there are longer lengths of time between generations, and "age-condensed" families, where grandparents, children, and grandchildren are born close together. Such differences correlate closely with socioeconomic classes, with richer "beanpole" families with many years between the grandparents, parents, and children, and with few cousins, contrasting with more horizontal families with shorter periods of time between parents and more cousins (Kohli et al., 2010). The most obvious matter is that in societies that have lowered welfare provision and have failed to address problems with low fertility, there will not be a sufficient supply of young taxpayers to pay for old retirees. These low fertility societies also happen to be the ones that are normally seen as having highly skilled, productive, and efficient economies (such as Germany and Japan, see Seabrooke & Tsingou, 2014a). Interestingly, they are also the very countries that are commonly identified in the comparative capitalisms literature for their institutional complementarities that assist the development of human capital through skills training (Thelen, 2004).

7.3 SENSEMAKING AND GENERATIONAL CHANGE

Scholarship on intergenerational mobility during the last century tended to focus on occupational attainment, primarily if the son is able to replicate or succeed the position of the father. The key findings in this literature are that socioeconomic status determines the prospects of sons becoming like fathers, that property relationships lead to greater immobility (children stay to inherit the farm, for example), and that access to education is more important than the father's occupation, and position in society, for mobility (Ganzeboom, Treiman, & Ultee, 1991).

A "generation" is commonly understood in four different ways, of which three are relevant for our discussion. The first is to understand generation as kinship, from the grandparent to the parent to the child. This is the most common way of talking about generations when discussing genealogy. For our purposes this understanding of generations is useful in locating chains of belonging, but is not useful in helping us to understand intergenerational equity or conflict. The second is to understand generations identified by birth cohorts (Ryder, 1965), which is how generations are typically studied by demographers and economists. The approach here is to package the population by sets of five, ten, and fifteen years and then assume a life cycle with preferences in regular patterns (puberty, marriage, first house, etc.). This understanding of generation as cohort permits us to infer social meanings from assumptions about age and linked preferences (teenagers will rebel against their parents more than 40-year-olds). A third understanding is to understand generations by historic events that are not tightly age-dependent, but matched to cohorts. The 1968 generation is the most obvious example because of the benefit of retrospect and nostalgia (Edmunds & Turner 2002), but we could also refer to East Germans who experienced the fall of the Berlin Wall in their teens or twenties and then quickly were aware of new life chances as a historic generation in this sense. East Germans who then adopt West

German norms, including demonstrating less family solidarity and transfers of wealth from parents to children, may attribute this change to the historical event and following "necessary" adaptation (Kohli et al., 2000). A fourth understanding that borrows from Karl Mannheim (1928) and, much more recently, the work of Louis Chauvel (2006; 2010) is the concept of a "social generation." A social generation is understood as a combination of the demographic and historical understanding of generations, with the stress on deriving hypotheses from the demographic data and then applying more inductive sociological methods to establish how meanings are given.

But can we understand generations as a group? Understanding group emergence is a common problem for political economy and sociology. Groups are generally understood to arise around a shared identity and interest, from which point on they fight with other groups as they anchor their identities or take flight and switch between networks and domains (or "netdoms," White, 2008; Seabrooke, 2014). The "Germans" or the "Danes," etc., are a group based on a national identity that follows a political settlement. "Workers," "managers," and "owners" are groups based on an assumed shared preferences, that workers want more pay, managers want control, and owners want profit (Gourevitch & Shinn, 2005). In political economy the common understanding of preference formation and institutional change follows this basic equilibrium understanding of emergence—that there was a settlement, it was disturbed, a new settlement was then created, and the group identity and their interests follow from that settlement (Seabrooke, 2007). This explanation of group emergence and preference formation is a foundation of studies in comparative political economy as it allows us to locate interests across time and space, and also to form a common analytic shorthand with which to understand case variation.

The usefulness of this shorthand can be disputed if the groups we attribute with power and predetermined preferences are not those that are key to explaining institutional realignment. The work on "everyday politics," among other bodies of literature on social and economic change has questioned the assumption that coalitions or interest groups are the drivers of change rather than reacting to what can be legitimately changed with the broader consent of the population (Hobson & Seabrooke, 2007; Kerkvliet, 2009). Such is the case also with generational change. To rely on the assumption that corporate structure within LMEs or CMEs has remained fixed over the previous few decades as the "Varieties of Capitalism" literature is commonly interpreted (Hall & Soskice, 2001), ignores the importance of changing social attitudes and demographic changes; not to mention changing trends in corporate structure that are obscured by the static analysis (neatly captured in Mark Blyth's borrowed Talking Heads phrase, "same as it never was," Blyth, 2003). Such analyses are also static in the sense that they do not permit us to identify how existing structures may place more stress on particular generations in a population and not others. To use an example, if we have an average age for a first-time homeowner, then the Australian cohort who bought in 1985 has been economically fortunate compared with those in 2005. But chronology is not sufficient for a sociological understanding on the variance in fortunes. We should also consider if the experience of financial hardship matters for these homeowners. Interweaving changes among cohorts, to generalize, with narratives of experience, to specify changes in attitudes and habits, is how we can best identify intergenerational conflicts.

The key problem in thinking through these matters is defining what is considered to be a generation and if that term should be understood demographically, historically, or sociologically, as already discussed. An analysis of how much individuals have been able to acquire from the welfare state is one way of doing so—and this can be seen in the literature on "intergenerational accounting" (Becker, 2000). More persuasive solutions can be found from those who advocate that taxation of the population should reflect intergenerational concerns, such as proposals for incomes for the working population and retirees to adopt a "fixed relative position" so that income is steady and smoothed between the generations rather than unbalanced (Musgrave, 1986; Esping-Andersen, 2009: 154–7). Such notions on changing income and welfare through taxation recognize that the:

> welfare state edifice that we know today was created in response to a profile of risks and needs that prevailed in the age of our grandparents, parents, and those of us who came to maturity in the post-war decades. Today's young workers face a very different risk profile, and this needs to be factored into our retirement projections for the mid-century (Esping-Andersen, 2009: 160).

Another innovative idea that could also address intergenerational concerns comes from Bob Goodin and colleagues (2008), who suggest that "discretionary time" is the best index of freedom and that in post-industrial societies actors may actively choose to forfeit income to improve life and time quality.[1] Such a change may reflect shifts in generational attitudes and expectations about how to live, including the move to a more post-industrial or post-productivist society with greater stress on work-life balance that would allow parents to spend more time with their children (Esping-Andersen, 1999; Goodin, 2001; 2011).

To study generations we need a better understanding of the intersection between age, period, and cohort. Socialization processes are typically understood during transition periods or "establishment phases" from which family

---

[1] This measure is particularly interesting in that it transforms the common logic of more welfare and wages are better. In Goodin et al.'s study the Dutch fare better than the Swedes, and the Americans do better than the Australians on the grounds that the Swedes and the Australians have much higher "time poverty," or less time at their discretion.

and educational background become more settled positions for one's life course (Gulbrandsen & Langsether, 2000). Polarization among a cohort can lead to what Mannheim called "generational units" that can be deeply socialized and have an effect on the new generation (Mannheim, 1928). Mannheim's conception sees generations as a social category akin to class in that belonging to a generation provides a range of modes of behavior, feelings, and thought, and that when a cohort is able to demarcate its "historical-social consciousness", then it becomes a true generation (Pilcher, 1994: 490).

Generally, the work on generations stresses that the experience of new forms of socialization by cohorts in a transition phase may have pronounced effects on social change. For example, new everyday attitudes towards careers, leisure, and housing during an economic downturn in England in the 1920s had an impact on the development of Keynesian economics and arguably paved the way for its legitimacy in the 1930s (Seabrooke, 2007). Chauvel argues, among others, that periods of welfare state expansion are most likely to accelerate and compound social change among generations, while the opposite is also true. Chauvel suggests that with welfare state retrenchment younger generations will experience "scarring effects" as the divergence between expected outcomes and income, and the actual experience of welfare decline bites upon them (Chauvel, 2010). In the French case, where his analysis is primarily located, we can indeed talk of the withdrawal of the welfare state compared to the Anglophone and the Nordic states (see Hay, 2006), which contributes to the scarring effect Chauvel notes.

Chauvel's argument is that, in the French case, the youth have been isolated from political power and are facing a "general dismemberment of the 'new' middle class," that they are better educated and worse paid than the middle class of their parents' generation, while also knowing that, even if full participants in the tax system, pension benefits will be far less than their parents' and grandparents'. The same then applies for healthcare, education, and state family benefits (Chauvel, 2010: 91–2). For Chauvel, the anomic rioting by French youth is early evidence of scarring effects, rioting from a perception of "missing out" rather than directed at any particular political purpose. The London riots of 2011 can be seen in the same light as expressions of intergenerational conflict, and certainly much more so than conscious class conflict. From a sensemaking perspective the "anomic riots" are a consequence of plausible accounts and narratives of how the rich and older generations have diminished the range of life chances, as access to housing and credit has become harder, the chance of job satisfaction less likely, and so on. Some have argued that the London riots reflected a transformation over three decades from "social corporatist" to "neoliberal" riots where social cohesion has given way to individualism (Gilroy, 2013). Others have suggested that the rioters had a lack of social identity and actively sought to acquire a strong sense of identity through consumerism by force, or looting (Aiello & Pariante, 2013). From an individual perspective the riots make little sense, but from a generational sensemaking perspective, including in the basic organization of the riots, the threat of a further lowering of expectations allows us to speculate as to the motivations of those involved.

Beyond the London riots it is also clear that prospective replication-based sensemaking leading to frustration and guilt is not found simply among the urban poor associated with the looters of 2011. For example, Liam Stanley's (2014) recent work, from conducting focus groups in Birmingham on the theme of austerity, has found that those under significant financial pressure to access credit for housing, due to high-speed financialization in Britain, also experienced feelings of guilt and shame about their indebtedness. Such sense-making expressions show how individuals are not simply following their rational interests in their national economy, but bouncing off intergenerational social norms on what is appropriate while the institutional composition of the economy is transforming in, from the viewpoint of one generation, often perverse ways. Take for example, a moaning article written by an unemployed graduate that was published in *The Observer* in January 2010. Writing on intergenerational equity, he outlined that he understood that his grandmother shopped around for the best value meat to cook for dinner to save money, and that his mother took it from the aisle in the local supermarket. These choices, however, differed from his choice to buy steak in a restaurant and spend his meagre income that way. In his view, a view that extends to late 1920s and 1930s Britons, he is not squandering his cash, but compensating for a perceived decline in career recognition compared with educational achievement, an increase in financial stresses, and the knowledge that the state may not be there to help him later on because the old are voting away benefits they have enjoyed. He ended the piece with the words:

> No doubt the older generation will have a good time with their free bus passes and villas in Spain. They'll enjoy the pensions and property. Shame about the smashed unions that might have got us decent wages and pensions. Shame about houses only being affordable to trust-funders. Shame about the abandonment of industry and its replacement with . . . coffee? Shoes? Credit? We're just cheap labour, here to fund a bit more wealth. We know that now. And don't worry, we'll pay off the debt. Have a nice life.[2]

---

[2] "How graduates are picking up the tab for their parents' lives," *The Observer*, Sunday 31, January 2010, <www.guardian.co.uk/money/2010/jan/31/unemployed-graduates-credit-crunch-andrew-hankinson>.

7.4 PROSPECTIVE REPLICATION, SOCIOECONOMIC, REGENERATION, AND HOUSING MARKETS

What can intergenerational change tell us about prospective replication-based sensemaking processes and how they are linked to institutional changes that have influence on the national economy? A focus on socioeconomic regeneration and generational change calls us to take a broader view of the structural factors affecting relations between generations, while a sensemaking perspective asks us to narrow in on the pressures and opportunities that force prospective replication-based sensemaking.

On the broader picture, a recent study from the Bertelsmann Stiftung (2013) provides a cross-national comparison of intergenerational justice in twenty-nine OECD countries and much food for thought on the macro conditions for prospective replication-based sensemaking. The basic results from the report are presented in Table 7.1. Those ranked higher ("1") are dealing better with intergenerational issues, with those ranked lower ("29") ignoring or not handling these issues well. Issues featured here include environmental sustainability assessed by ecological footprints, child poverty, child debt (assessed by total government debt divided by persons between 0 and 14 years) and a new elderly-bias indicator of social spending (Effective Behavioral and Instructional Support Systems—EBISS), developed by Pieter Vanhuysse (Vanhuysse, 2012; Vanhuysse & Goerres, 2012; Bertelsmann Stiftung, 2013). This new indicator assesses elderly spending as pensions and other cash benefits related to old age, disability pensions, survivors' benefits in cash, occupational injury and disease-related pensions, and early retirement for labor market reasons. Non-elderly spending includes family benefits in cash (family allowances and parental leave) and in kind (day care and like benefits), active labor market programs, income maintenance cash benefits, unemployment compensation and severance pay, and education spending from primary school to university. Importantly, EBISS does not include public health expenditure and is therefore on the conservative side in its estimates.

Comparing the results against the typical frameworks used in Comparative Political Economy provides much food for thought on long-term aspects of socioeconomic regeneration. The Netherlands' eco-friendly post-productivist regime is thrown into doubt, just as it is for Denmark. The elderly-bias in social spending combined with high levels of public debt in the German, Italian, and Japanese cases also raises alarms about the long-term capacity for fiscal sustainability as well as investment in younger generations, such as in apprenticeships. The differences present between the liberal Anglophone regimes are also notable, pointing to different institutions within these societies to mediate these long-term challenges.

Table 7.1 Bertelsmann Stiftung Intergenerational Justice Indicators (IJIs)

	Ecological footprint	Child poverty	Debt per child	Elderly bias in social spending	IJI i (overall)
Australia	26	22	8	12	15
Austria	20	6	20	21	19
Belgium	27	13	26	4	14
Canada	25	24	24	11	21
Czech Republic	19	9	5	24	23
Denmark	29	1	14	7	13
Estonia	12	17	1	5	1
Finland	22	2	12	14	8
France	15	10	18	18	17
Germany	8	8	25	15	11
Greece	16	20	27	28	26
Hungary	1	7	7	19	9
Ireland	23	16	19	2	10
Israel	3	27	10	17	5
Italy	7	25	28	27	25
Japan	5	23	29	25	29
Netherlands	24	12	17	6	20
New Zealand	6	18	6	3	3
Norway	14	3	23	9	4
Poland	2	21	3	29	27
Portugal	4	28	15	23	24
Slovakia	10	15	4	26	22
Slovenia	18	4	9	22	18
South Korea	9	14	2	1	2
Spain	13	26	13	16	16
Sweden	21	5	11	10	6
Switzerland	17	11	22	13	12
United Kingdom	11	19	16	8	7
United States	28	29	21	20	28

Source: Compiled from Bertelsmann Stiftung (2013) based on the study by Pieter Vanhuysse. Ecological footprint data from <http://www.footprintnetwork.org>, data extracted June 1, 2012. Data for government debt data from IMF World Economic Outlook April 2012. Population data from World Bank Develpoment Indicators online database. Data for child poverty and social spending from OECD (2011b).

Such research has also been linked to surveys that examine intergenerational solidarity and spending. Much of the literature here suggests that intergenerational links provide a source of security when times are tough (Inglehart, 2008: 131–2), and that over time political differences between parents and children wear off through fatigue and socialization (Demartini, 1985). This often suggests that the youth have not simply confronted enough economic realities to bend them into shape (Abramson & Inglehart, 1992: 200). Recent research has also shown that older people are more likely to support public childcare when more engaged with their grandchildren, and in contexts where either very few women work, or where there is a cultural expectation that men and women are equal in the workplace (Goerres & Tepe, 2010). Research shows also that there is intergenerational solidarity among older people in most OECD societies, but that support between the young and the old is highly dependent on cultural, normative, and welfare institutions. A recent survey of university students in eight democracies found that youth (18–35 years) in social democratic economies such as Norway and Sweden are most likely to support, in principle, welfare transfers to the elderly (65+ years). "Radical" or "Antipodean" societies such as Australia and New Zealand, which maintain high equality but low social security, also have lower perceptions of injustice among the youth. Liberal societies such as the United States and United Kingdom have higher perceptions of inequality, perhaps reflecting high income inequalities. Surprisingly, conservative societies, such as France, Italy, and Germany, have the highest levels of perceptions of economic injustice among the youth *and* the highest perceptions of economic justice among the elderly (Sabbagh & Vanhuysse, 2010), suggesting widely diverging views on how the economy should work. Of course these general attitudes can vary among different groups in societies, including what we could identify as a social generation (Andress & Hein, 2001). Such research provides the structural context for prospective replication-based sensemaking and links it up to socioeconomic regeneration, as well as environmental sustainability.

Another way to look at prospective repetition-based sensemaking and intergenerational change is to locate it in one of the key pressures for younger generations (again, this may be by experience or cohort) seen through the lens of housing access and financing. Figure 7.1 presents the basic "varieties of residential capitalism" from Schwartz and Seabrooke (2008; 2009). This growing literature speaks to established debates in Comparative Political Economy and studies of welfare regimes in addressing questions of "welfare trade-offs" made by individuals and families in societies, through the lens of housing ownership (Kemeny, 1980; 2005; Castles, 1998). By assessing owner-occupation rates and levels of mortgage debt to gross domestic product (GDP), the "varieties of residential capitalism" identify four types that are important in socioeconomic regeneration. These four types are liberal-market, corporatist-market, statist-developmental, and familial systems of residential capitalism (Schwartz & Seabrooke, 2008: 243–8). The liberal type relies heavily on mortgage securitization recycling and low deposit to loan ratios, including an element of "sub-prime" lending blamed for the recent financial crisis (Schwartz, 2009; Seabrooke, 2010). This type also suggests lower provisions of welfare, and more reluctance to pay taxes, given that the population invests in housing as a means to create wealth in the future. The corporatist-market model is reliant on less of the population actually being owner-occupiers, but with those who do so holding very high levels of debt. In such systems, such as in Denmark and the Netherlands, there are high levels of social rental housings and these systems also have non-recycling mortgage securitization.

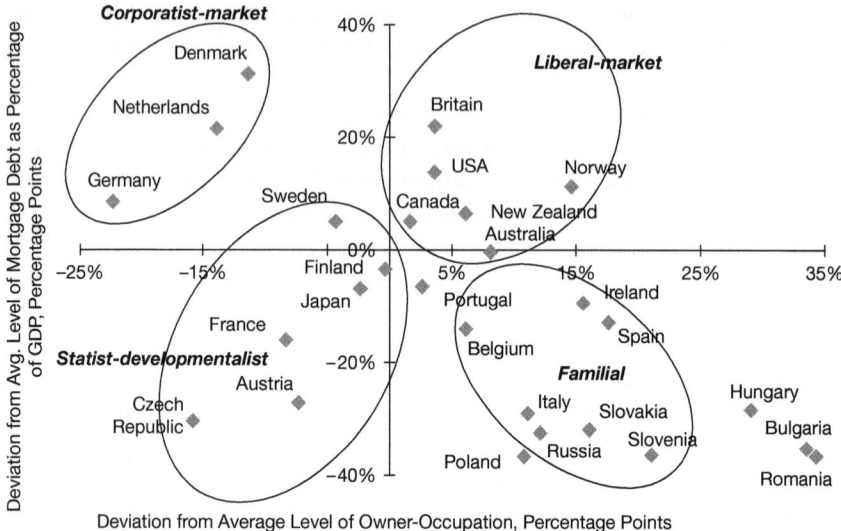

Figure 7.1 Relative deviation from average OECD levels of mortgage debt to GDP and owner-occupation prevailing 1992–2002 (percentage points)
Source: Schwartz and Seabrooke, 2008.

In this system significant tax breaks go to those who can afford to buy huge amounts of debt. The statist-development form is reliant on the state to support access to housing, where access to housing credit is tight, and where private institutions hold a great deal of housing stock. The familial model relies very heavily on the family to transfer property between parents and children, or with parents assisting children to acquire property given very high deposit to loan ratios. This type is less commodified than in the liberal-market and corporatist-market types, and the transfer of property is more likely to follow personal networks than the more open market of the liberal-market type (for an excellent example, see Zavisca, 2008).

The "varieties of residential capitalism" approach has been criticized for failing to recognize that there are "uneven benefits of homeownership to different cohorts of homeowners" (Fung & Forrest, 2011: 1235). While this approach explicitly contrasts conflicts between societal groups who view housing as a social right or a means to wealth, this criticism can be addressed through a focus on intergenerational change and conflict. The approach does recognize that access to housing resources is essentially about conflict, be it between generations, classes, genders, or along racial and ethnic lines (Roberts, 2013). The approach can be linked up to what some have called "housing poverty" that affects those who often are not income poor, but have less access to housing resources, which then increases the chance of income poverty in the future (Stephens & van Steen, 2011). Furthermore, introducing interge-nerational considerations to this approach brings into frame intergenerational and intragenerational conflicts over issues such as family formation. On this note, access to housing is also extremely important for family formation, with recent research demonstrating that choosing to have a second child is often constrained by access to housing in the statist and corporatist systems, such as in Italy, Austria, and France—the same countries identified above as conser-vative with widely diverging views on intergenerational economic justice among the young and the elderly (Flynn, 2013). Housing is also deeply involved in the reproduction of social inequalities harming socioeconomic regeneration in societies known for their equality, such as Norway (Tranøy, 2008) and Sweden (Christophers, 2013). Part of this story about change among the Nordics is that social cohesion on issues of belonging— retrospective replication-based sensemaking—is combined with a strategic sense of atomized individualism on many issues (Newman, 2008: 664–5).

We can locate some of these issues through a brief comparison of the intergenerational politics involved with housing in the Australian and Danish cases. These cases provide an example of different types of societies and economies in the standard literature in Comparative Political Economy lit-erature. Australia is an LME, a liberal welfare regime, a liberal-market type of residential capitalism, and also "radical" in view of economic justice between the young and the elderly. Denmark is a CME, a social democratic welfare regime, a corporatist-market type of residential capitalism, and also a harmo-nious social democratic view of economic justice between the young and the elderly. We should note that in the intergenerational justice indicators (EBISS), Australia scored 13 out of 29 and Denmark 15, so both are dealing with significant, if not severe, intergenerational pressures. My aim here is to provide vignettes on the conditions under which prospective replication-based sensemaking is occurring in these two countries, highlighted by the intersec-tion between housing politics and intergenerational change. I also emphasize how rational strategic decision-making is better understood as sensemaking given that choices are heavily informed by cultural norms, which strongly color what cues to take from changing conditions.

In Australia the cultural norm is to be an owner-occupier, with those who fail to achieve this by the time they hit their forties considered to have lost out in the game of life. Between 1985 and 2005 the average cost of the average home compared with the average salary increased sixfold, placing extraor-dinary pressure on first-time homeowners (Mortensen & Seabrooke, 2008). Intergenerational issues in the Australian context revolve around institutional structures for taxation and for access to housing credit. While many OECD countries provide tax breaks for those who have mortgages on homes in which they reside—a system to maintain the middle classes—the Australian system instead provides tax incentives to landlords who can "negatively gear" the difference between imputed rent from a tenant and the cost of the mortgage to the landlord (Gruis & Nieboer, 2007). The difference can be deducted from their taxable income, as are expenses on home improvements, making petty investor-landlordship a stable and often lucrative form of investment. As a consequence there is a strong incentive for what is known elsewhere as "buy to let" property in Australia (Leyshon & French, 2009). This has been compounded by reductions in capital gains tax in the early 2000s, as well as permissions to access pension funds for property investment post-55 years of age as part of a "Transition-to-Retirement" scheme from 2005. As a consequence investor-landlords are not simply from the upper income brackets, but firmly within the middle classes, with half of those claiming deductions receiving around median income in the mid-2000s. The taxation system, following political maneuvering from a conservative government, was distorted in favor of Baby Boomers, doubling the number of investor-landlord property purchases between the early 1990s and the 2000s. Significant financial innovations, including interest-only loans, fuelled this market in the 2000s and the early 2010s. These changes placed intense pressure on first-time buyers and owner-occupation in Australia fell during the 2000s. While in 1996 a household needed five times its disposable income to afford a home, this had increased to seven times by 2006 (NATSEM, 2008: 7, 12). After 2001 younger Australians had a declining share of owner-occupation and were much more engaged in rental markets, with wealth disparities becoming ever more related to income from housing assets (Yates, Kendig, & Phillips, 2008). In 2007 the Australian Labor Party based part of its campaign in a national election on the "'crisis' of housing affordability," and after winning power introduced a range of schemes to assist first-time homeowners. These had a modest effect and boosted those only just able to afford property, while not addressing the taxation system that is a source of intergenerational conflict.

By 2010 owner-occupation among 35–44 year olds was 4.5 percent lower than in 2001 as a consequence of rising housing prices. In the same year 31 percent of Australian households were using nearly all their disposable income on housing, and 14 percent were under "major financial and wellbeing pressures" (Burke, Stone, and Ralston, 2011: 18). Such stresses are a likely source of intergenerational conflict. In urban Australia changes in housing have led to children being much more dependent on parents for deposits to afford housing loans (even given the very low thresholds for deposits in this liberal-market system). While this may, in theory, bring some families together, there is both a generation by cohort and also by experience in Australia that feel significant pressures that are a consequence of institutional design to make a particular cohort, the Baby Boomers, more "competitive." The now widespread self-identification as the "Battlers" for ordinary families trying to make their way through these stresses is one result and a reflection of the ongoing desire for owner-occupation despite potentially more rational uses of capital (e.g. renting and investing in the stock market). These are the conditions under which younger Australians engage in prospective replication-based sensemaking in a liberal market variety of residential capitalism—trapped by a norm of ownership and also by an institutional complex that distributes tax benefits to a particular generation of current political significance.

In the Danish case we have a more subtle story, yet no less potent for future intergenerational conflicts. A covered bond market that provides a significant amount of stability to housing finance supports the Danish housing system. The system is also supported by tax breaks in the form of deductions on interest paid on mortgages, especially for those who owned homes prior to 1998 when the rates were reduced (now 35 percent) (Green-Pedersen, 2002: 127). Danes who own property have extremely high debt and in general Danes have the most household debt in the world. Those who are not owners of freehold property live in social or private rental housing, or in housing cooperatives (*andelsboligforeninger*) in the major urban centers like Copenhagen and Aarhus. During the 1980s and 1990s housing finance was deregulated, partially from European pressure to provide more competition (Seabrooke, 2012). A government-induced housing crisis in the late 1980s deliberately burst a property bubble to prevent over-exuberance in housing prices and the significant tax drain from mortgage deductions. During the 2000s the opening up of the interest-only loan market led to a significant change in investment in housing in Denmark, with young owner-occupiers choosing to take on these loans at a significant scale after 2005 and during a property boom. This shift signaled a normative shift from viewing housing as a social right to a means to wealth, more like the liberal-market style of residential capitalism than the corporatist-market type (Mortensen & Seabrooke, 2009). Signaling this shift also for the older Danes has been widespread political support for a freeze on property tax based on arguments that increases would hurt the elderly. On top of these changes the conservative government in 2001 liberalized the housing cooperative market, which led prices for those apartments to triple within five years in Copenhagen. With a combination of increased financialization and a political consensus against increasing taxation there was mounting financial and well-being pressure on younger Danes seeking to own property.

As with the Australian case, this can lead to intergenerational tensions, especially in a system where the sense of economic injustice between generations is low. One source of tension comes from a growing trend for *forældrekøb* or "parents-buy" in urban centers, where parents buy, typically, an apartment for their child. One estimate following the property crash in Denmark in 2008 was that *forældrekøb* made up 60 to 70 percent in 2005, during the boom period (Mortensen & Seabrooke, 2009). Such a change in the system places pressure on younger owner-occupiers, given that the parents obviously have greater resources to purchase property and can therefore drive up prices. In 2012 it was estimated that half the property owners between 30 and 40 years of age were technically insolvent due to high loans and falling property prices.[3] Financial and well-being pressures can also be seen on younger owner-occupiers, with a recent study finding that Denmark has seen the highest collapse in the younger cohort (<35 years of age) in Europe, with 7.6 percent less owner-occupation between 2007 and 2011 (Lennartz, Arundel, & Ronald, 2014: 13). Even in a society where intergenerational equity is thought to be high, the conditions for prospective replication-based sense-making have changed rapidly as different generations benefit differentially from the liberalization of housing finance and the declaration of increased taxation as a no-go zone. Such changes are having an effect in Denmark with more couples staying in properties they own in urban centers rather than moving out to houses in the suburbs they can no longer afford. One knock-on effect of such changes is increased pressure on childcare systems, linking us back to the relationship between housing and family formation. Lastly, in a case of rotten luck, international pressures on the Danish system of housing finance, primarily from international scrutiny of economies with high private housing debt following the "subprime" crisis, threatens to make conditions worse for Danes not already on the housing ladder (Kjar & Seabrooke, 2014).

7.5 CONCLUSION

This chapter suggests that institutional competitiveness is essentially about socioeconomic replication and that intergenerational change is an important aspect of this. Such matters are important for prospective replication-based sensemaking because they inform the life chances, or conditions of possibility, observed by different generations as they seek to make sense of their lives. Importantly, the conditions of socioeconomic regeneration can also be seen in what institutions benefit what generations and if institutional complementarities provide intragenerational and/or intergenerational benefits. I have discussed how these issues can be seen within OECD countries over the long term, and in the cases of institutional change in housing access in the Australian and Danish cases. In closing, my plea here is simple: thinking through the topic of generations, be they understood as by cohorts or by experience, is important when considering the conditions for socioeconomic regeneration and the sources of national institutional competitiveness.

---

[3] "Realkreditlån bliver dyre og uigennemskuelige," Forbrugerrådet Tænk, March 9, 2012, available at <http://taenk.dk/presse/realkreditlaan-bliver-dyre-og-uigennemskuelige>.

8

How Institutional Competitiveness Emerged from Complementarities between Nordic Welfare and Innovation Systems

Robert Boyer

8.1 INTRODUCTION

Since their emergence as modern societies, the Nordic capitalisms have puzzled many foreign analysts and social scientists. This "third way" between capitalism and socialism was severely analyzed by Friedrich von Hayek (1944) who anticipated the collapse of the social constructivism typical of the Swedish way out of the interwar crisis. After the Second World War, the outstanding macroeconomic and social performance of the Swedish and Nordic economies was perceived as defining the core of a common social democratic form of capitalism. In the early 1970s it became the institutional configuration that quite any government—either conservative or left wing—wanted to emulate. Nevertheless, whereas outsiders admired this model, insiders were prone to detect that the very success of a vigorous state intervention and extended redistribution via a universal welfare state was triggering adverse trends and a crisis that required a redesign of some basic institutions, for instance the "solidaristic" wage formation. With globalization, the rise of financial capitalism, and the process of Europeanization, these Nordic capitalisms have been submitted to the vagaries of the world economy and the strong competition from a new productive paradigm associated with Information and Communication Technologies (ICT) and more generally the transition toward a Knowledge-based Economy (KBE). Therefore, the specialists of Nordic welfare do stress that the typical Nordic model is under pressure in order to respond both to new social demands (Goodin, 2001) and to overcome the internal disequilibria observed in the diverse components of welfare (Kvist & Greve, 2011).

But the turmoil in the transformations of other brands of capitalism is still more dramatic. Consequently, both specialists of international comparisons and international organizations do find that the social democratic capitalisms fare far better than finance-led capitalisms such as US and UK or even state-governed capitalisms, as observed in continental and southern Europe. Implicitly at least, the so-called Lisbon Strategy (Rodrigues, 2002; 2009) took as a benchmark most of the typical features of Nordic economies, such as life-long learning, high-quality education, and security in the transition from one job to another. One chief economist of a French investment bank has tried to detect what the national economies are that perform better after the Lehman Brothers collapse and the quite uncertain redeployment of the world economy (Artus, 2009). The findings are quite surprising compared with the pessimism of insiders of these Nordic economies.

The Nordic countries are known to be shaped by an extended welfare state able to provide a generous safety net and limit the widening of social and income inequalities associated with internationalization and financialization. Standard economic theory predicts poor economic performance compared with liberal capitalisms, but the empirical evidence contradicts this suggested opposition between economic efficiency and social justice. The Scandinavian welfare state, associated with active employment policy, is a fat bumblebee that can fly in spite of very large social transfers (Madsen, 2008). These economies are also among the more dynamic in terms of technological and organizational innovations. Finland, Sweden, and Denmark benefit from the higher density of researchers. They are very efficient since the number of patents per inhabitant scores among the highest among the Organisation for Economic Co-operation and Development (OECD) countries. Furthermore, the Nordic countries spend a large fraction of gross domestic product (GDP) on education and display a pattern quite similar to that of the most innovative economies, such as Korea and the US. In contemporary economies, a large fraction of innovativeness derives from tertiary education: again Sweden, Denmark, and Finland score among the best performances. Many experts forecast that the next productive paradigm will be energy saving and again Finland, Denmark, and Sweden are the best equipped in the production of renewable energy. It is then no surprise if the intensity of research and development expenditure is among the highest in these countries. Are these performances paid by a deterioration of the well-being of Nordic citizens? Quite on the contrary; the young fraction of the population expresses the most optimistic expectation about their futures in contrast with the deep pessimism of the European Union and especially in southern Europe.

The objective of this chapter is to explain some of the factors that have shaped the long-term historical process that has generated these Nordic-specific configurations of welfare and to derive some common patterns in the mix of society-wide values, economic evolutions, capital/labor conflicts and political intermediation (section 8.2). It comes out that the fact that a periodic redesign of welfare states has generated a largely unintended complementarity between dynamic innovation and social solidarity, but ex post sensemaking has helped actors to manage and eventually reform both national innovation and welfare systems in order to cope with a permanently evolving environment (section 8.3). Finally, in section 8.4, I consider whether the understanding of the sources of past performance is a sufficient foundation for the long-term resilience of Nordic welfare capitalisms.

8.2 LESSONS FROM THE HISTORY OF NORDIC WELFARE

Synthesizing the three trajectories (Boyer, 2012: 2–3; 25–9) helps in deriving some common features in the complex process of welfare emergence and maturation, both at the analytical level and concerning the nature of welfare.

8.2.1 The Progressive Building of a Modern Welfare System

The naive use of neoclassical economic theory is challenged by this brief survey of its history: the contemporary welfare systems do not result from choices made by actors who would design an optimal architecture from scratch, but from the adaptation of a complex configuration inherited from the past in the context of conflicting demands. Each generation has tried to cope with insecurity and develop collective devices to address particular challenges to social ties and society cohesion for their time. The present configuration is the outcome of this pragmatic process, including key periods when actors try to make sense of the past and design reforms in order to adjust the welfare system to the social demands and economic opportunity of the epoch. No one in the enlightened Denmark of the eighteenth century could anticipate the contemporary flexicurity model, itself challenged by the severity of the world crisis.

In rural feudal economies survival during famines and wars is the main objective. With the first industrial revolution, a new form of urban poverty emerges as a key social and political issue; whereas with the second, the recognition of workers' rights is shaping a new path where the breakthrough concerns industrial accident insurance, union recognition, and unemployment compensation. Each new epoch uses the previous source of legitimacy and mobilizes private organizations and political institutions in order to build new components of welfare. As time elapses, these adjustments may deliver a quite new configuration: path dependency does not mean a given structure of

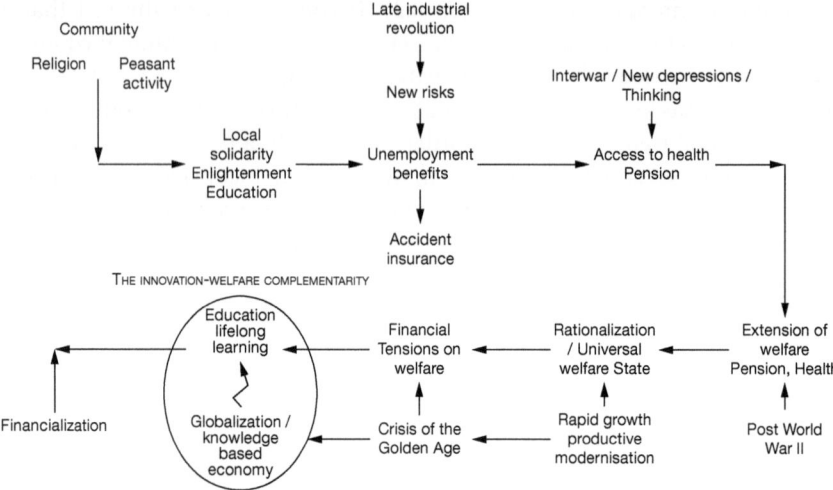

Figure 8.1 The long-run co-evolution of solidarity, ideas, economy, and welfare

welfare is locked in, but it implies that the direction of institutional change is informed by the past achievements and possibly the persistence of an explicit or implicit national style that relies on community, state, or markets.

Looking at the mapping of this hypothesis (Figure 8.1), it is tempting to characterize the related changes according to the three major mechanisms put forward by comparative historical institutionalism (Thelen, 2004; Streeck & Thelen, 2005a; Mahoney & Thelen, 2010).

The concept of *layering* fits quite well with the multiplicity of risks covered by welfare and their superposition: they might be compatible, complementary, or partially conflicting one with another. If so one component can be adapted and converted by changing the precise arrangement or even the objectives: *conversion* reconciles some continuity with novelty. For instance, sick benefit societies shift under a unified regulatory system, various pension regimes are unified within the same entity, or the school is transformed according to the demand of polity and/or economy.

Finally, *recombination* becomes necessary when some concerns decline whereas others take the ascendency, therefore some links are severed and new ones are formed. When this mechanism is repeated from period to period, a qualitatively new configuration may emerge and display features— good or bad, and sometimes unexpected even for the better informed actors. For instance, in Denmark the traditional concept of school as the instrument for learning provided to each member of the community can be mobilized when the productive paradigm shifts from mass production to information technologies and finally innovation-led growth.

Thus, the historical and comparative institutionalism can usefully be associated with an evolutionary approach of economic dynamics and sustains the core argument of this chapter: the Nordic welfare and their national system of innovation have become complementary, since a large part of the education, training, and welfare arrangements facilitate adaptation to technological and economic change; and, conversely, the success of innovation fosters the ability to pay for a quite extensive welfare and tax system. This virtuous circle can first be detected by analysts and social scientists, but after a period the actors involved can perceive the logic of this configuration and adapt their strategies accordingly. Hence, *sensemaking becomes a powerful coordinating mechanism*, consciously used by social partners and civil servants in order to monitor the permanent adjustment to a changing international environment (Pedersen, 2011).

8.2.2 The Interplay of a Complex Web of Factors

Looking back at the history briefly mentioned (Boyer, 2012) one can propose some key determinants of their evolutions.

First of all, *moral values and society-wide conceptions* do play a role in the emergence of collective organizations that could cope with insecurity. For instance, solidarity at the local level is rarely the consequence of the pure and rational defence of self-interest, but the expression of beliefs quite outside the domain of the economy. Once welfare institutions have been constructed rational calculus may or may not sustain it, but their creation remains a mystery for methodological individualism in spite of quite interesting but unsuccessful attempts (Greif, 2006). For instance, the creation of a workers' union supposes altruistic or idealistic leaders, since no rational *homo oeconomicus* would undertake such a project (Corneo, 1995).

Secondly, the impulse of new components of welfare basically comes from society and rarely from an endogenous pressure from the managers or/and civil servants themselves, but the survival of a given regime is dependent on its compatibility with the evolution of the economic and political environment. *Reactivity to new social risks* is therefore a major factor of innovation in the welfare system, but also in the management of an aging regime: conversion (i.e. keeping the same objective, but reforming the tools to fulfil it; or, alternatively, using the experience of the organization to aim at new but related objectives) is a recurring feature of welfare evolution.

Nevertheless, some adjustments are marginal, but operate continuously, unnoticed, whereas major *economic and financial crises* abruptly destabilize the whole institutional architecture, including the welfare state: its financing becomes more difficult at odds with the surge of the volume of interventions and pressing new demands. Economic historians have shown that the Great Depression of the 1930s has triggered in Sweden a drastic reorientation of economic policy and institution building under the aegis of a new political alliance. An equivalent change took place in Finland and Denmark, but the effective implementation of a whole set of new institutions, including an extensive welfare state, was only observed after the Second World War. De facto dramatic *war episodes* also reconstitute the feeling of national identity and solidarity, a key ingredient in welfare building (Campbell et al., 2008; Kaspersen, 2008). During the reconstruction period, catching up on growth allows for easy financing and a virtuous circle may warrant the sustainability of large transfers from individual to socialized income. Statistical analyses confirm this timing, namely the bifurcation generated or associated with wars, at least for most advanced economies.

A fourth trend characterizes the Nordic countries: the embryos of welfare appear at the local/community level, inspired by religion, and could appeal to reciprocity in order to balance the benefits and costs. Princes and kings have interest in organizing under their ruling this search for security and enlightenment, and when nation-state building took off, the construction of welfare appeared as a trump card in acquiring legitimacy, both in order to alleviate social unrest at home and to respond to permanent external threats. Generally, during the twentieth century, welfare has moved from a largely decentralized configuration toward a remarkable *trend toward centralization*: many analysts conclude that Nordic economies are welfare capitalisms (Fellman et al., 2008). Even when Swedish authorities drastically cut the size of state and welfare expenditures, they retain control of the rules that govern decentralization and privatization of the services contributing to that welfare.

The multiplication of welfare regimes (health, unemployment benefit, family allowance, pension, disability, training, and, by extension, general education) makes the whole system *intrinsically more and more complex, and quite demanding in terms of public finance and social contributions*. At its origin, welfare was internalizing some of the externalities emanating from the private sector (unemployment and social unrest, the negative impact of epidemics on the population, a lack of incentive for firms to invest in general education, and the retraining of workers), but as the layering is pursued from period to period, the logic of each sub-regime might become counterproductive given the changing general context and some instruments of welfare become contradictory, one with another. The generosity of welfare may put a brake on mobility and increase the tax burden on employees and employers; early retirement can facilitate industrial structuring and reduce the number of the unemployed, but at the cost of worsening the public pension regime. Consequently, since the 1990s, the welfare has been torn by such dilemmas: should welfare benefits be reduced or taxes and social contributions augmented? How should the cost of unemployment between young and old workers, insiders and outsiders be balanced? In a period of permanent flux of job destruction and creation, where should priority investment be made: upgrading the requirement of general education (learning to learn) or pushing lifelong learning? Actually, the negative externalities are now also within the public sector and welfare; quite a paradox indeed. Given their size and extreme complexity, some *negative externalities* now run from the public to the private sector.

A last noteworthy feature of the Nordic countries is that, along with the Netherlands (Visser & Hemerijck, 1997), they have been among the first to exert *reflexivity* upon the logic of their welfare states and their contribution not only to the well-being of the population, but also to the ability of the economy to sustain a high/better standard of living (i.e. the definition of competitiveness). The *intelligibility* of such imbricated systems becomes crucial for deciding and monitoring the periodic resynchronization of each subregime with an evolving domestic and international context. This is a definite plus compared with societies that delegate to the market their strategic choices or rely too much on state voluntarism.

A deepening of this process occurs when this intelligibility is not restricted to experts, some civil servants, and politicians, but is shared by a large fraction of the actors who, on a daily basis, use a common understanding to decide their strategy, bargain, and coordinate their expectations. It is a shift *from intelligibility to sensemaking*, understood as the cognitive and interpretative process through which agents of change attribute meaning and define their interactions with each other and with the institutional set-up (see also editors' introduction to this volume). This is a powerful coordinating mechanism that permeates, explicitly or implicitly, the society since it is "providing a narrative to continuity, reasons for institutional change, rallying points to generate consensus, and justifications to those who are affected by institutional transformation" (Borrás and Seabrooke, this volume). Such a common understanding is a requisite starting point for social partners to agree upon successive reforms of welfare, education, or even tax system. In a sense, the organization of welfare and the redesign of public services are the core of this negotiated form of capitalism (Pedersen, 2006a; 2011; Greve, 2009).

The issue is then, where does sensemaking come from? Can the process observed in Nordic countries be extended to other contemporary societies with different political and social histories? How is sensemaking related to the extent and depth of democracy?

8.3 FROM REPLICATION TO ABSTRACTION: USING THE WELFARE-INNOVATION COMPLEMENTARITY FOR COMPETITIVENESS ENHANCEMENT

From an analytical standpoint, an important turning point has been the *aggiornamento* that took place in the Netherlands after the tripartite Wassenaar Accord in 1982, which paved the way for the recovery of the Dutch economy.

8.3.1 The Theoretical Synergy between Social Justice and Dynamic Efficiency

It turns out that some public interventions and components of welfare could enhance structural competitiveness. Whereas in most liberal capitalist and state-led economies welfare is considered a cost that hinders the macroeconomic performance of the economy, researchers put forward the idea that some of the related expenditures were also an investment in a social capital via education, training, consensus formation via collective negotiation, less absenteeism, and better health. Even the provision of a minimum income via direct wage or welfare allocation could alleviate the resistance to productive restructuring and act as stabilizers of demand during recessions, thus minimizing the erosion of competences associated with long-run unemployment as soon as active employment policies complement unemployment benefit. Ex post the success of the polder model legitimized a new vision of welfare (Visser & Hemerijck, 1997): while aiming at more social justice, some configurations of welfare promote dynamic efficiency and thus they can be complementary with the search of competitiveness (Figure 8.2).

8.3.2 The Key Role of Social Conflicts Intermediated by Polity: the Flexicurity Model Revisited

The pattern of Nordic welfare and innovation systems identified above can be found in the contemporary system through emergence of the flexicurity model in Denmark. Academic research has been theorizing the compromise negotiated by social partners in response to the dramatic economic situation of the early 1990s: high unemployment, tension on public finance, and poor macroeconomic performance. The annual reports of the OECD were quite alarming indeed and they blamed the excessive rigidity of Danish labor market institutions. It took several years to understand the source of the spectacular recovery of Denmark, to provide a convincing narrative and diffuse it at the European level, and inspire part of the implementation and revision of the Lisbon agenda in the direction of a (rather mythical) European Social Model (Jørgensen & Konghøj, 2007).

A review of the evidence suggests that there are both factors of continuity and innovation in the early 1990s (Boyer, 2006). The continuity dates back to 1899, a year when entrepreneurs and workers after a severe labor conflict reached a compromise about the future organization of industrial relations: unions recognized the legitimacy of firms in searching for survival via adoption of techniques and adaptation of employment; and, conversely, the business association granted the right to unions to defend workers in their search for better

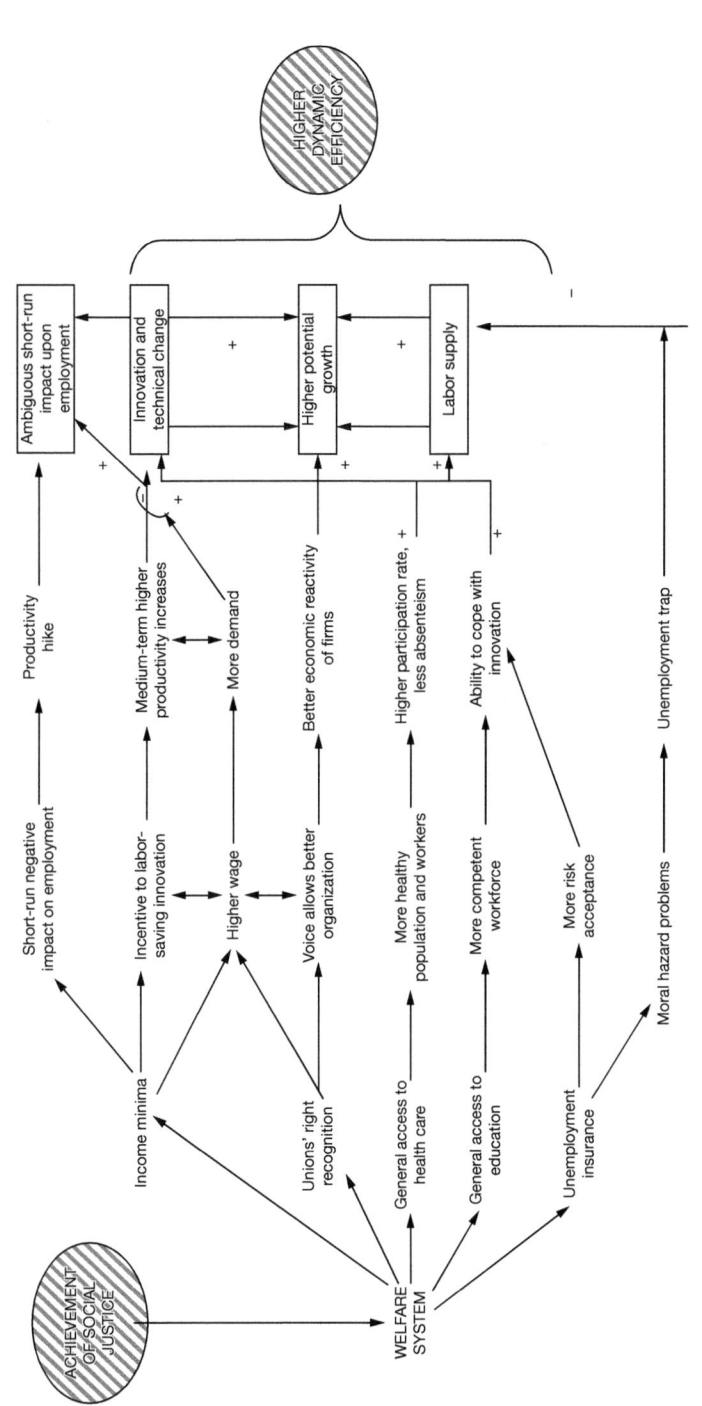

Figure 8.2 How some welfare systems enhance dynamic efficiency

standards of living and security. In the 1990s the novelty comes from the initial frontal opposition between the will of firms to redeploy jobs in response to stiff foreign competition and the strong resistance of employees who refuse a drastic reduction of quite generous unemployment benefit, which is supposed to be hindering competitive adjustment. The way out of the dead end was to call for a third component that could reconcile the contradictory demands of both sides: officials proposed to monitor the flow of job redeployment by an active employment policy mixing retraining of workers with incentives to search for a new job. The triangle of flexicurity turned out to be performing quite well and satisfied the objectives of the three partners. My reading of the literature is that the complementarity between this reconfiguration of the welfare with dynamic efficiency and forward-looking innovation was largely an ex post discovery, since that which was assumed to be a short-term correction to previous unbalances has proven to define a new institutional pattern for Denmark (Figure 8.3).

The concept of *serendipity* captures the flavor of this discovery that results in a genuine growth regime. Creative destruction is recognized as a fact of life in capitalist economies that can only be blocked at the expense of lower standards of living in the long run. The name of the game is then to accept job destruction in firms that cannot create a sufficient level of value added per employee, given the evolution of the world economy and productive paradigms. It is detrimental to follow the low value added, low wage path, and thus generous replacement ratio for the unemployed is a good incentive that partially blocks the downward adjustment of wages. The retraining of wage

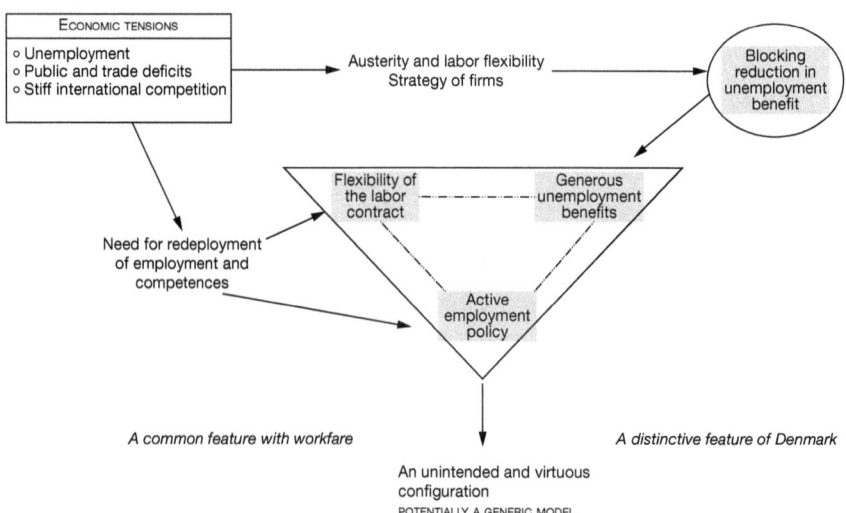

Figure 8.3 The flexicurity Danish model: the unintended consequence of an unemployment crisis and the conflict of opposite interests and rationales

earners becomes crucial in order to prevent the formation of a dual labor market with a large low-skills and low-wage sector. In a sense, the policymakers in Nordic countries adopt a dynamic vision of the process of technological and organizational change in capitalism. In this context, there exists a form of *competition state* where the mobilization of productive factors, including labor through employment policies, are a core task for the public sector, along with the constant effort to do so in the most cost efficient ways with the general purpose of creating institutional comparative advantage for the private sector, both the export-oriented and the private service sector (Pedersen, 2006b; 2011).

Such a configuration can also be labelled as a neo-Schumpeterian welfare based on a key objective: to try to redesign the welfare and all the components of economic policy in order to foster technological and organizational innovations that could sustain high and possibly increasing standards of living. In such new welfare systems (Jessop, 2002), intense public transfers are compatible with the dynamism of innovation. The Nordic countries, such as Finland, Denmark, and Sweden, have been the more advanced in intensifying research and development expenditures and improving total factor productivity by mobilizing ICT (Bassanini, Scarpetta, & Visco, 2000: 27). The bumblebee can fly smartly and this falsifies the predictions of conventional neoclassical theory that only considers static efficiency in a world dominated by price competition on standardized goods without permanent and endogenous innovation in order to capture oligopolistic rents.

From an analytical point of view, the figure above gives an intuitive representation of the concept of institutional complementarity. The group of Nordic countries combines, during the 1990s, an acceleration of total factor productivity, an increase in employment, and the most extended welfare state. This means that their welfare systems are enhancing the implementation and benefits of the KBE, at odds with the conventional neoclassical prediction about the inescapable trade-off between social solidarity and economic dynamic efficiency. But of course, some conditions have to be fulfilled (Andersen, 2009). The general interpretation provided by Figure 8.2 is therefore given some empirical evidence. One of them is the small size of these economies, which entitles an easier political intermediation and the building of a national identity in response to the evolution of world markets (Katzenstein, 1985; 2008).

The representation of the economy is shared by the majority of the actors—firms, wage earners, citizens, high civil servants, and politicians—and thus it plays an active role in their coordination in everyday decisions. There is a qualitative gap between the abstract representation by researchers of the potential merits of a welfare economy and a specific national embeddedness of only some of the positive feedback linking welfare and innovation systems. This is all the difference between a set of heterogeneous *individual ideas* and *sensemaking*, as a collective and shared representation delivered by a past *institutionalized compromise*.

8.3.3 How Conflicting Interests and Ideas have to Compromise to Generate Sensemaking

In this approach, interests and ideas are intertwined and nested, and only their confrontation delivers a higher level of comprehension of the functioning of the economic system, transformed by the accord of collective actors. Here comes sensemaking after a social compromise or the emergence of a new political alliance. The uncertainty generated by a crisis favours such institutional and/or political innovations. The emergence of the "Swedish Model" seems to follow the same general pattern. In a context of great economic uncertainly like the Great Depression of the 1930s, the Swedish Social Democratic Party successfully managed to put forward ideas based on the need to provide universalistic protection to individuals (regardless of their class) against the excesses of market forces. The party was able to build a new political consensus across the aisle, which was simultaneously redistributive and pro-market. Such environments compel actors to resort to "repertoires of action that resonate with their core identities and transform their conceptions of self and others' interest" (Blyth, 2002; 2006).

Let us contrast this analytical framework with two other approaches of institutional change.

Rational choice theory would imply that institutional change could happen at any time, as soon as actors realize that it is in their mutual interest to shift smoothly from one configuration to another. This neglects the fact that collective action is involved, that the flexicurity was not on the cognitive maps of the actors involved and that radical innovations tend to cluster during crises.

Conventional political economy puts forward the asymmetry of power that allows a collective actor, be it capital or state, to impose a new order (Swenson, 1991). Such a configuration might exist (e.g. Bismarck's welfare initiative), but it does not fit with the Nordic experience, where many components of welfare have emerged out of compromises between conflicting but not totally unbalanced interests.

The present framework that derives from an extension of *regulation* theory encounters an echo in the research of some political scientists that look for explanations of political change. "Viewing politics as situated in multiple and not necessarily equilibrated order suggests a way of synthesizing institutional and ideational approaches and developing more convincing accounts of political change. In this view, change arises out of *'friction' among mismatched institutional and ideational patterns*" (Lieberman, 2002: 697).

Seen in the historical and comparative perspective, institutional changes in Sweden, Finland, and Denmark displayed differences over time but converged in the 1990s (Mjøset, 2000; 2001) and today share the specificity of a clear innovation-welfare system complementarity. Broadly speaking, they have in common a strong social democratic legacy, interpreted as the accepted principle of a negotiation of the realignment of the institutional forms that govern their brand of capitalism. A variant of the mechanisms described for Denmark are operating in Sweden and Finland.

8.3.4 Intelligibility of Nordic Welfares does not Imply Sensemaking Elsewhere

This competition state (Pedersen, 2011) does not seem to have found the configuration of interests, representations of society, and economic ideas elsewhere (Campbell, 2002; Campbell & Pedersen, 2014) that would sustain an equivalent virtuous circle. The US trajectory is quite interesting in this respect (Levine, 1978; Somers & Block, 2005). The agrarian interests do nurture more individualism than the solidarity typical in traditional European rural communities. Unions are difficult to establish given the recurring flows of immigrants, the large-scale regional mobility, and the very ideology of the Founding Fathers and the representation of the New Continent as a land of opportunity, far away from the legacy of feudalism of Europe. The constitution has been designed for preventing the initiatives of a strong federal state, at odds with the close link between society and government, welfare and state in Nordic countries. Self-regulation is seen as the ideal and this does not favour the kind of constructivism that is required for a fully fledged welfare system. The general vision points to the fact that labor regulations and welfare are intrinsically bad for entrepreneurial dynamism, innovation, and growth. Even a large fraction of citizens think that a compulsory welfare would be an infringement on their constitutional rights about freedom of choice. The idea that market rewards talents, pushes toward a residual welfare, built as a safety net for the deserving poor population. Ideology and dominant interests shape quite an idiosyncratic North American trajectory (Table 8.1).

Thus, an economist or social scientist could well conclude a careful comparison of the US and Denmark by pointing the Pareto superiority of the innovation-welfare complementarity, but it is highly unlikely that they would convince a majority of citizens and politicians to adopt this "model." Sensemaking is a localized and idiosyncratic process.

But there are more than two configurations for the relations between welfare and capitalism, as demonstrated by the earlier comparative analyses of welfare systems (Esping-Andersen, 1996; Manow, 2008), innovation systems (Amable & et al., 1997; Boyer, 2001), and more recent taxonomy of capitalisms (Amable, 2004b) and growth regimes (Boyer, 2004). In this respect the French trajectory is emblematic (Boyer, 2000). Quite conflicting industrial relations, the choice of a Bismarckian welfare financed by social contributions of

Table 8.1 Welfare as a part of a social and ideational long-run history: Denmark versus the US

1880–1933	Denmark	US
Labor	Relative immobility makes possible local solidarity	High expectation of mobility mutes political conflicts
Institutional legacy	Guilds transformed into trade unions	Difficult construction of unions out of successive immigration waves
Conceptions of state/government-society relations	Quasi-fusion between "society" and "government" Institutional pragmatism Grundtvig enlightenment	Liberty and democracy have to be defended against the expansion of government Social nationalism, self-regulating system, Lockean liberalism
Political configuration	Social Democrat as third way between Left and Right, Socialism and Liberalism	Socialism was never an option, nor a legitimate challenge
Economic argument for/against welfare	An extension of community "help to self-help" at the national level	Welfare reserved to "worthy poor." The cost of welfare may hinder economic dynamism
General concept of welfare	Continuation and updating of widely recognized principles	A threat to individual liberty and founding principles
Conclusion	Welfare is a part of a long tradition of mutual responsibility	Welfare may undermine personal responsibility

Source: Freely inspired from Daniel Levine (1978); Tom Knudsen, Bo Rothstein (1994); Ove Korsgaard (2000); Robert Henri Cox (2001); Margaret Somers and Fred Block (2005).

employees and employers, and a strong polarization of elites frequently selected by a very selective education system, all shape a quite specific welfare system and make problematic the typical French approach: badly designed institutional reforms from above. Furthermore, a state-driven innovation system once governed via *Grands Programmes* has not been renovated to cope with the transformations of competition, productive paradigms, European integration, and emerging industrial giants.

This coalescence of interests, asymmetry of bargaining powers, and economic representations has generated a long-lasting vicious circle. Lagging and difficult reforms, due to the polarization of antagonist interests and behaviours, have been unable, until now, to interrupt this process. During the 2000s, alternatively, the Danish flexicurity strategy and the German "model" have been invoked as a target for economic policy, but the road has been blocked because it did *not make sense* within French society.

8.4 DEEP TRANSFORMATIONS OF NORDIC WELFARE CAPITALISMS WITH RESILIENT MACROECONOMIC PERFORMANCE

A recurring theme of this chapter is the permanent evolving nature of capitalism and welfare, either via the accumulation of seemingly marginal transformations, or during dramatic episodes such as wars and major economic crises. Does it help in assessing the viability of the welfare-innovation complementarity to look at the specificity of Nordic societies in response to the present crisis? A first answer comes from a comparative empirical analysis of the distribution of a significant sample of European, North American, and East Asian economies, using quantitative data that try to capture the degree of competition, labor market institutions, education, welfare, degree of opening, and extent of financialization (Harada & Tohyama, 2011). Clustering analysis concludes that Finland, Sweden, and Denmark belong to the same group, characterized by an acute competition on the product market and high social security, that is, two of the components of the welfare-innovation complementarity configuration. But they also have a large financial opening, a risky feature indeed, given the pervasiveness and severity of the subprime crisis. Nordic economies belong to the same cluster as the Netherlands—this is coherent with the argument developed earlier—but also Switzerland, Germany, and Austria, which are usually ranked under the continental European model (Amable, 2004b). The macroeconomic performance of this group has proven to be better than average for the sample, proving its resilience and reflecting how *small states* continue to fare not so badly in the world economy.

8.4.1 Societies in Flux; Contrasted Diagnosis

The challenge is simultaneously theoretical (what are the criteria for assessing that a complex system has changed?) and empirical (how to conclude if contrasted evolutions occur in the various sub-regimes of welfare?). A very brief survey suggests that the jury is still out, because opposite prognoses coexist given the diversity of methodologies involved. If characterized by centralized wage bargaining, the genuine Swedish model is passé (Iversen, 1996). Others stress that changes have been endogenously generated and that new complementarities have emerged in ways that account for the persistence of some of the main features of the post-war Swedish model (Schnyder, 2012). Political scientists find that the division between insiders and outsiders, and the inclusion of outsiders, has become an important issue for the strategy and electoral success of the parties in Sweden (Lindvall & Rueda, 2012). Political economists stress the abrasive role of the diffusion of market mechanisms on the viability of more solidarity in social democratic societies (Amable, 2004a).

Another analysis on Denmark concludes: "The Nordic model of welfare is still distinct, but less so than it was...concerning health care and pensions...social citizenship is split between a universal coverage of basic entitlements, and a coverage supplemented by contributory and purely market-based provision and service" (Abrahamson, 2008). In both cases, dualization is a threat for social democratic parties and thus the viability of the Nordic model. Still another research on Denmark concludes," The coverage is still universal in core welfare state areas...but the nation has been transformed into a multi-tiered welfare state that is more dualistic and individualistic." (Kvist & Greve, 2011). In any case, a new form of the state is probably emerging (Rojas, 2005).

If we compare the distribution of the same sample of economies in the 1990s and 2000s, it turns out that the shift of Nordic countries has been relatively marginal; especially compared with the fast transformation of East Asian economies that moved in the direction of liberal capitalisms (Harada & Tohyama, 2011). Nevertheless, they are far from being absorbed within this group: this means that their institutional architecture remains original.

8.4.2 Three Neglected Assets for the Resilience of Social Democratic Societies

Adverse forces clearly play against the permanence of the Nordic model. The vagaries of the world economy, the radical uncertainty about the future of the international financial system, and the pressure borne by the present policies of the European Union bring major external risks. Domestically, the rise of individualism, the difficult integration of the recent wave of immigrants, the limit of the tax system, the aging population, and the rise of xenophobic parties and their challenge over an inclusive welfare state, put the former model under pressure. Some anticipate that the forces of the market and finance will finally wipe out the post-World War Two Nordic model (Notermans, 2000; Amable, 2004a).

These threats are real, but Nordic countries enjoy some precious competitive advantages. First, it can be argued that Beveridgian Welfare configurations, when articulated in a highly democratic political system, are much more resilient than those based upon the solidarity among wage earners or pure market mechanisms, and an exclusion of the underprivileged from the political process, as observed in liberal capitalisms (Boyer, 2008). Paradoxically, an industrial democracy or at least a negotiated capitalism does reinforce the bargaining power of workers and makes more resilient their ability to defend the security provided by the welfare system (Figure 8.4).

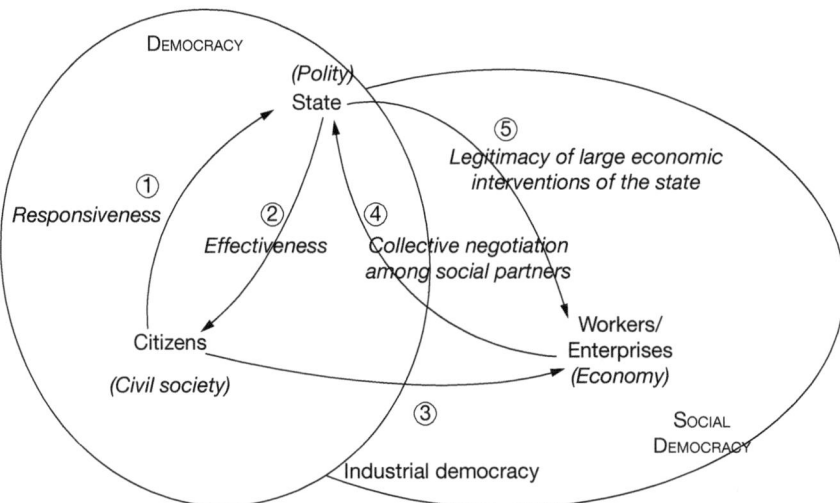

Figure 8.4 Social democratic citizenship protects the rights of wage earners, hence dynamic efficiency

The second asset is the persisting contribution of the quality of an inclusive education to the nurturing of the competences necessary to cope with a fast technical change and the abstraction of labor. One has to remember that the best pupils of the new economy have been Denmark, Finland, and Sweden. Furthermore, societies that have based their education system on the process of "learning to learn" (Lundvall, 2011) are in good position to compete internationally by innovation, quality of the goods and services, and versatility of the production due to labor mobility and the dynamism of small and medium-sized enterprises, in Denmark especially (Kristensen & Lilja, 2011). This asset is embedded into the organization of work within and among firms, at odds with the legacy of Taylorist and even lean production in other economies.

Last but not least, few societies have a well-developed understanding of the source of their growth and competitiveness, as a starting point for the negotiation of new organizations and institutions. Sensemaking about the logic and reform of Nordic welfare capitalisms is a definite competitive advantage compared with the ideologies that affect liberal market economies and state-led capitalisms.

8.5 CONCLUSION

The present analyses have related the role of welfare in the construction and resilience of the institutional competitive advantage of Nordic economies. Here are some provisional conclusions to be confirmed by further research.

The literature usually characterizes these economies by the complementarity of an extended universal welfare, institutionalized and coordinated wage formation, and a high-quality and inclusive education system. The present survey suggests that the remarkable social and economic performances of Nordic countries are due to the *synergy between the security provided by the welfare and the dynamism of innovation*, itself fostered by the high value attributed to education, from the primary to the tertiary levels. The collapse of solidaristic wage policy, observed for instance in Sweden, is not necessarily evidence for the end of the social democratic model.

Rational choice approaches and the functionalist visions are unable to explain *the primacy of identity building* as an unintended precondition for the progressive construction of a universal welfare system. Only the rich history of community formation, guild practises, religion, and enlightened successive monarchs and governments have created the *repertoire of sensemaking* shared ideas that have allowed a pragmatic adjustment to structural domestic and international crises and social conflicts. Nordic social capitalisms are deeply embedded into a rich web of social interactions and values that cannot be easily reiterated or imported by quite different societies, such as in North America.

Contrary to the recurring prognosis made by conventional economists about the irrevocable vanishing of social democratic capitalisms, the recognition of *extended citizenship rights*, quite distinct from the socioeconomic status, strengthens the *bargaining power of wage earners*, even when confronted with rising unemployment. Consequently, tax-based welfare systems are much more resilient than those built upon the contribution of employees and employers, and the institutionalization of sharing growth dividends and the risk of internationalization make easier the reforms required by a changing environment. But, of course, new generations have to understand and accept high taxation, which could be eroded by the growth of a more atomized form of individualism.

Sensemaking is a definite and *precious catalyst* in this *complex process* of periodic institutional change and reform; but ideas do not fall from the sky, they are always space-and time-related. 'Pure' ideas and 'perfect' organizations or institutions cannot be imported as such, since they usually do not fit with the repertoire of legitimized values, concepts, or institutions inherited from past social and political struggles. The recurring dead end for many *institutional reforms* elsewhere is a good illustration of this difficult transposition of sensemaking from one society to another.

A first and rough historical analysis suggests that *sensemaking may come after the negotiation of an innovative compromise* among a priori totally incompatible interests and visions of the world. Retrospectively, the actors have to build a common understanding of their interactions; but this enlightenment comes afterwards as a rationalization. Then, external and distant observers might conclude that this provisional and new configuration defines a stable and universal model, but when they try to sell it to their governments they are quite disappointed by the final outcome, which is generally negative. It is too easy to blame the incompetence of decision-makers and the irrationality of economic actors. Frequently, the principle of obliquity delivers superior outcomes than substantive rationality (Kay, 2010). Furthermore, the real reason for the failure of most reforms is nothing less than their *systemic incompatibility* with the prevailing core societal paradigm. Who can imagine a US government successfully implementing a Nordic welfare state, in complete opposition to the highly individualistic values that have been the founding block of American democracy?

Systemic crisis periods—the interwar and the present—make explicit the weaknesses of previous institutional configurations and they are generating a *radical uncertainty* that makes sensemaking and strategic decisions quite crucial. Nevertheless, the synergy between universal welfare and institutional competitiveness seems limited to the small, open economy that enjoys a long tradition in the art of *mixing cooperation and competition*. Such a process is quite difficult to engineer within medium or large societies that have been unable to elaborate a concept of citizenship that could counteract the corrosive individualistic ethos and habitus typical of liberal capitalism. This asymmetry between the proponents of economic liberalism and those of social democracy might constitute the main danger for the stability of the world economy and ultimately the viability of social democratic capitalisms themselves.

9

Conclusion

Sensemaking, Politics, Ideas, and Discourses in Institutional Change

Susana Borrás, Leonard Seabrooke, and Vivien Schmidt

9.1 INTRODUCTION

This volume provides an ambitious framework for understanding the role of sensemaking in institutional change. The contributors provide a range of cases demonstrating how sensemaking processes influence institutional competitiveness, moving from traditional areas of investigation in the work on comparative capitalisms, such as employment, welfare, firms, and public management regimes, as well as new areas such as knowledge regimes, conflicts over housing access, and regional innovation policies. The "take home" message from the framework and cases is that sensemaking is a source of institutional competitiveness, since sensemaking processes bring agents together to articulate narratives and strategies for socioeconomic success, or to talk and think through attributions tied to existing successes or failures. As such, this volume adds a relational framework to the work on comparative capitalisms. As opposed to more objective or rational views on why institutions are configured in a certain manner (Hall & Soskice, 2001) or types of institutional change assessed from a fixed point over time (Mahoney & Thelen, 2010), the sensemaking as institutional change approach locates how agents make sense of their institutions in relation to concerns with identity, normative intentions, and strategy.

This book contributes not only to the comparative capitalisms literature, but also brings in a macro perspective to the sensemaking scholarship in organization studies that concentrates on micro intra-organizational processes (Weick, 1995), joining calls for situating sensemaking within broader institutional frames (Weber & Glynn, 2006). Importantly, the sensemaking in institutional change approach provides a boon to existing scholarship on reasoning and discourse formation in the work on comparative capitalisms (Blyth, 2002; Culpepper, 2003; Schmidt, 2003; Campbell & Pedersen, 2001; Seabrooke, 2006), which we reflect on in this concluding chapter.

The contributors to this volume have provided cases of sensemaking in the four dimensions outlined by the editors in their introduction, with combinations of prospective and retrospective perceptions of time, and replication and abstraction forms of experience. From these combinations one can locate: (1) how sensemaking about expectations changes behavior among social groups, (2) why conceptions of belonging can be particularly sticky in periods of institutional change, (3) why agents design search systems to gather information as a resource for sensemaking, and (4) how the search for explanations in sensemaking leads to narratives about causes. These four types are also linked to three dimensions of how agents draw upon identities, normative intentions, and strategies when engaging in sensemaking processes (Figure 1.1 in the editors' introduction). The three dimensions and four types comprise the analytical framework to study processes of sensemaking in institutional change.

The sensemaking in institutional change framework provides unique insights into how national economies are being transformed and how institutional competitiveness is being articulated by a range of actors. It focuses on how actors are agents who determine their own goals when responding to uncertainty by creating new meanings and narratives on what happened and what is happening. However, the richness of the preceding chapters cannot be captured only by the sensemaking framework and there are a series of advances and reflections to be made. The chapters provide indications on how to move forward in the sensemaking approach to further ways of thinking about the interaction between sensemaking and narrative formation, the role of different ideas in this process, and the power of certain discourses in governing institutional change. The purpose of this concluding chapter is to theorize further about sensemaking in institutional change, to interrogate the framework in order to augment it. We discuss potential biases in the cases presented and consider how sensemaking is a micro-foundation of discourse and idea formation. In particular, this chapter focuses on three interrelated issues: the role of politics and power interactions in the sensemaking process; the processes of sensemaking and the formation/diffusion of specific sets of ideas (i.e. neoliberal ideas in advanced welfare states); and lastly, and most relevant, the role of sensemaking processes as a micro-foundation for discursive institutionalism. The last section of this chapter identifies future research avenues.

9.2 POLITICS AND SENSEMAKING IN INSTITUTIONAL CHANGE

The cases in this volume demonstrate that sensemaking processes are important for institutional change within national economies, as well as for inter-action between national, regional, and international economies. From the empirics in the preceding chapters one could summarize the "output" of sensemaking as narratives on what has happened (belonging), why it happens (causal analysis), how to cope (expectations), and how to find information to deal with it in the future (search systems). The determination of institutional competitiveness through sensemaking processes leads to concrete institutional changes. This relates to specific agents of change, how they perceive the nature of the problem at stake, and how they aim at controlling their environment.

In the conventional literature on sensemaking the focus is on how organizations act as systems of shared meaning and how those engaged in sense-making must "extract cues" from the context to see what is relevant and appropriate (Weick, 1995; Brown et al., 2008). The emphasis here is on giving meaning to experience. As seen in many of the preceding chapters, sensemaking constructs specific narratives and broader ideas about how to understand what is happening. Sensemaking can be seen as a process that is initiated by "disruptive ambiguity." Such ambiguity mobilizes the agents of change (or no-change) to extract cues through a process of sensemaking that can be based on abstraction or replication and in prospective or retrospective processes. From these contexts agents formulate plausible narratives (Weick, 2005: 413). They might also engage in the creation of new ideas about how things have worked and why they should operate differently. We see narratives as the direct outcomes of the process of sensemaking, a process that is based on expect-ations, search systems, causal analysis, or belonging. For this perspective, ideas emerge from the articulation of specific sets of narratives and give shape to broader accounts of action-oriented explanations and visions. This is where politics enters the scene. These narrative-based ideas are obviously not neutral in political terms. They are, in fact, politically laden with assumptions of what is good or bad (sensemaking invokes normative propositions), with specific understandings of who is "us"—ultimately the beneficiary of action (sense-making conforms to specific identities), and with broad yet feasible courses of possible action (sensemaking involves strategy). From this, it follows that sensemaking processes are intrinsically political processes. The politics of sensemaking has been underplayed in the organizational studies literature on the concept, which has focused more on problem-solving. We also suggest that sensemaking helps us to understand the politics of change within other-wise static conceptions of varieties of capitalism (Hall & Soskice, 2001). This operates at both abstraction and replication levels of experience and learning.

Abstraction-based forms of sensemaking create search systems and make it possible to narrate about causes and prepare for change and evolution (Crouch, 2005; Streeck, 2009). With replication, sensemaking about expectations and identities assists in spotting how institutional configuration can be "same as it never was" (Blyth, 2003), and how conceptions of belonging and expectations differ from established ideal types. All four sensemaking processes are political in creating frictions between groups and their conceptions of whom institutional competitiveness should benefit. The likely political cleavages here can be seen in the chapters in this volume—between employers and employees, firms, trade unions and governments, think tanks and political parties, experts and policymakers, and between generations. Generally speaking, we see sensemaking as a crucial phase in a larger and far more complex process of idea formation and discourse coordination/communication in institutional change. In particular, we suggest that this sensemaking framework can be extended into the study of how agents take advantage of ambiguity and uncertainty to shape sets of narratives that might ultimately be related to the push for new ideas.

The studies in this book provide rich examples of how this idea formation takes place, and how this is highly related to politics and to power-seeking more generally. For those looking at sensemaking as abstraction, the link between sensemaking and politics is immediate and obvious. For example, Peer Hull Kristensen's chapter on prospective abstraction-based sensemaking clearly demonstrates that the development of tools for monitoring, diagnosing, and reporting in firms and school systems (such as the Finnish case) requires an ideational shift in the identification of how to achieve self-determined notions of institutional competitiveness. This is not formed simply from the extraction of cues and the creation of a plausible narrative, but also from a reconceptualization of more general and new ideas regarding how to treat workers and students (c.f. Andersson, 2009). Politics can also be left more implicit in some specific contexts. Susana Borrás's chapter on prospective abstraction-based sensemaking deals with a policy area that has traditionally been quite technocratic, namely science, technology, and innovation. The low political saliency of this policy area in terms of public attention means that processes of sensemaking have tended to be confined to the stakeholders. The specialized and technical nature of the concrete topics discussed means that the articulation of narratives into ideas has a relatively low political echo in the society. In this situation, the dimension of identity tends to be less relevant in this process (except when it relates to changes in stakeholders' own senses of identity), whereas strategy and normative dimensions become more important.

John L. Campbell and Ove Kaj Pedersen's chapter on retrospective abstraction-based sensemaking reveals that competition or cooperation interaction among policy research organizations shapes how causes are located and policies developed. Taking the cases of Denmark and the US they find that the competition-based American knowledge regime favors open competition and generates politically divergent policy recommendations for institutional change. The sensemaking process was quite divergent and, in this context, very much embedded in political party contestation, with think tanks seeking to establish non-politicized causes from which superior policies can be created. For Campbell and Pedersen the Danish case is quite different. The cooperative organization of the knowledge regime, with different policy advice organizations collaborating across the aisle, generated a sensemaking process that was more homogeneous. The narratives for institutional change were not so divergent, and political contestation was mainly occupying the center of the political spectrum, with causes agreed upon by the main agents involved.

In most cases the sets of narratives upon which ideas are based establish what is accepted and what is not, and the selection of cues in the sensemaking process is often implicitly political, ushering in moments of challenge and crisis. This is particular the case for replication forms of sensemaking. As Carsten Greve demonstrates in his chapter, sensemaking processes led to a direct challenge from the *Opgavekommission* on the power and authority of the Copenhagen local government. Greve shows how the liberal-conservative government in power at the time successfully managed to engage the trade unions to support a narrative around the reform. Other crucial organizations and stakeholders were also involved in the preliminary discussions about the reform, in a collective process of sensemaking on the need to improve the quality of public administration to boost economic growth and competitiveness. This not only illustrates the consensus-based political culture in Denmark, but also shows how retrospective replication sensemaking processes, based on belonging, can mobilize a wide set of agents. The agents of change succeeded in promoting the need for public management reform by referring to retrospective issues about plausible yet unfinished business (yet to be completed reforms from the 1980s) and using replication-based learning to mobilize agents (learning from experience on the basis of replicating past success without providing a causal understanding). This sensemaking process is what we have labeled "belonging." This case study shows that in some circumstances this process is able to produce politically powerful narratives and ideas for major institutional change, a change that is largely path dependent to previous reform processes. We suggest that this understanding of the role of sensemaking in belonging creates forms of agency that are implied in other explanations of institutional change, which rely more on aggregating agency into structural shifts, such as drift, conversion, layering, and displacement (Streeck & Thelen, 2005; Mahoney & Thelen, 2010).

Differently, Leonard Seabrooke's chapter on generational change and housing points to how sensemaking about expectations ushers in political struggles between generations or against political parties that fail to provide the institutional conditions for expectation to be met. This includes the deepening of dependence between parents and children in economies where housing credit is harder to obtain, leading to social changes such as delayed family formation. In economies where housing credit is easier to obtain there has been much greater financial stress on the young compared to the old, leading to fluctuations in support for what are considered to be established institutions for welfare and economic competitiveness. The general story here is that prospective replication-based sensemaking alters institutions through everyday behavior and especially through changing ideas about how the economy should work (Seabrooke, 2006). This then informs discourses about obligations between citizens and the state, and whether broadly held social contracts between generations are being upheld or broken. Such changes have important implications for the normal range of institutions included in institutional competitiveness, especially for informing changes to education, employment, finance, and taxation.

9.3 SENSEMAKING, IDEAS, AND INSTITUTIONAL CHANGE

The chapters in this volume compare different cases of sensemaking processes in institutional change, paying particular attention to Denmark while comparing it to other countries. The distinctiveness of the Danish welfare state, public management tradition, and economic/industrial structure is an important issue to take into account when examining processes of sensemaking in institutional change. These distinctive features are especially important when considering the particular content of the narratives and ideas that result from that sensemaking process. "Content" refers here to the specific narratives and ideas about what institutional changes should occur, and how. Discussing the concrete content of ideas relates to the recent scholarly discussions about the resiliency of neoliberalism during the past decade (Schmidt & Thatcher, 2013), and to the nature of the institutional change during this period. We examine these two issues, namely the role of distinctive features in varieties of capitalism in processes of sensemaking and their outcomes, and the resiliency of neoliberal ideas during the past decade's context of socioeconomic crisis. The starting point for this will be the empirical cases in the chapters of this book, as they explore the way in which the processes of sensemaking are relevant for understanding the specific content of the ideas that ultimately result in institutional change.

Following the literature on varieties of capitalism, there is a growing understanding that the Nordics represent a sort of third model, a "hybrid" model which, even having some features similar to coordinated market economy (CME), has a substantial amount of features from the liberal market economy (LME) model (Campbell & Pedersen, 2007). The argument is that the blending of CME and LME features has generated institutional complementarities that helped improve their socioeconomic performance during the past two decades. There are some differences within this third/hybrid model, as each of the Nordic countries has certain idiosyncrasies shaped by their historical and socioeconomic particularities (Kristensen & Lilja, 2011). Nonetheless, their commonalities are visible in the multiple performance rankings and comparative indicators of socioeconomic development, which show them in very similar venues (world economic competitiveness, etc.). This hybridity has implications for processes of sensemaking and, particularly, for the outcomes of these processes in terms of narratives and ideas for institutional change. The self-understanding of how particularly devised national institutions affect the competitive position of the economy, and the equality and adaptability of the society to rapid transformations at the global level, forms part and parcel of the sensemaking process. In the Nordic countries, and in Denmark in particular, the sensemaking takes it starting point from a deepseated understanding that there is no necessary trade-off between levels of social welfare and equality, and economic competitive position. Generous social welfare is seen to perform a function of adaptability and societal accommodation for a rapidly changing economic context, while some crucial issues (like flexibility of labor force) are left to a market-based form of interactions. Below we will come back to this issue with examples provided by the chapters of Andersen and Boyer in this volume. What is worth noting at this stage is the fact that the macro-level context of social organization influences micro-level actors in their processes of meaning construction. This issue has been relatively underexplored by the literature on sensemaking, which has traditionally tended to look mainly at intra-organizational processes. Sensemaking is a process of constructing meaning with (not in spite of) institutions understood as these macro-level contexts (Weber & Glynn, 2006).

One general situation where the interactions between the macro-level context and the micro-level sensemaking processes are clearly reflected is in the resiliency of neoliberal ideas over the past two decades. As Vivien Schmidt and Mark Thatcher (2013) rightly point out, neoliberal ideas have continued to dominate policy debates in Europe, even in times of crisis. Generally speaking, neoliberalism is based on the belief in competitive markets through free trade, promoting labor flexibility and limiting the state while commodifying the provision of public goods. There are many national variants of neoliberalism, and the Nordic version is one that enhances the importance of market competition, free trade, and labor flexibility. In the Danish case, however, the state's role is not diminished but reconceptualized and re-tooled. This re-conceptualization of the state, as a state that provides an institutional basis for adaptability and competitiveness is known as "the competition state" (Pedersen, 2011). The distinctiveness of the Nordic model is that it has been able to retain and maintain the fundamental values, while it has absorbed some neoliberal ideas, particularly in relation to the role of the state as an enabler of economic competitiveness. As the cases in this volume show, sensemaking processes produce narratives and ideas about institutional change in Denmark are engrained in broader neoliberal approaches to the state and the role of the individual in society. For example, Leonard Seabrooke demonstrates in his chapter that Danish homeowners have engaged in flexible forms of housing credit and reforms to housing systems with great gusto because of perceived financial rewards, even when they impose costs on future generations. Yet, even if Danish sensemaking processes have generally resulted in a major modernization and institutional change, it has retained social welfare as a core characteristic of Danish identity.

Robert Boyer's chapter makes an additional point here. He argues, via a longer historical approach from 1880s until today, that three crucial issues have made the Nordic model continue to be successful even in times of crisis, and even when introducing some neoliberal elements. These three crucial issues are: (1) the combination of Beveridgian welfare configurations with an advanced form of democratic system, which avoids the dynamics of political exclusion; (2) the quality of an inclusive education system that nurtures the necessary competences to cope with fast technical change; and (3) a particularly well-developed understanding in society of the country's sources of competitiveness. This latter issue is a key background in the processes of sensemaking.

Not all our contributors, however, show the same general trends. Søren Kaj Andersen's chapter deals with the issue of change and non-change in employment policies during the current economic crisis. Germany introduced short-term work schemes by which working hours and payment were reduced as an alternative to lay-offs. This was not introduced in the United Kingdom or Denmark. The former is not a surprise, given their lack of tradition for these types of schemes. But Denmark is a surprise, because this scheme did already exist in the country, and the decision was made not to extend it by using it as an alternative to lay-offs. Andersen argues that part of the reason for the Danish non-change, and continued liberal features of its labor market, was the way in which the political and socioeconomic groups made sense of the crisis. The shared understanding was that the crisis was to be a relatively short-term problem, and that levels of employment were to be restored quickly after a short period. Besides, the low costs of lay-offs did not economically force the issue of finding cheaper alternatives through short-time work schemes. This case indicates that the liberal features of the Danish system—a hybrid form of varieties of capitalism—showed some signs of resilience even in highly pressured situations.

9.4 SENSEMAKING AND DISCURSIVE
INSTITUTIONALISM

The sensemaking perspective brings about the process of meaning creation in contexts of institutional change. It incorporates an approach typically developed in the context of micro-level analysis (intra-organizational dynamics) into a wider context of institutional change. We see sensemaking as a crucial element in a larger and more complex process of idea formation and discourse coordination/communication in situations of institutional change. To be sure, we have seen in this book how sensemaking is the process by which agents create meaning by shaping a series of narratives. They do so in a context of ambiguity and uncertainty, and with differing outlooks towards the future or the past, and with different modes of reflection and interaction through abstraction and replication. The outputs of sensemaking processes are narratives that are articulated around specific sets of content-laden ideas, which ultimately become discourses of institutional change.

It follows that sensemaking is about the dynamics of meaning construction. It is anchored at the level of the agents who construct that meaning, those who use ambiguity and uncertainty. This implies that the sensemaking process is not about the dynamics of collective communication of that meaning, but that coordination corresponds to discourses in the political process of institutional change (Schmidt, 2003). Having said that, we need to look more precisely now at how the process of sensemaking is the micro-foundation of discursive institutionalism. In order to do that, we first revert to the theory of discursive institutionalism and look at the coordination and communication dimensions of discourses. After that we examine how sensemaking processes fit into that analytical framework in processes of top-down or bottom-up sensemaking and their effects on discourses. And, last but not least, we develop the argument that the process of institutional change does not follow a linear model, but a recursive one between sensemaking and the coordination/communication of discourses.

The recent ideational turn in institutionalist theories has put forward the overall view that ideas and discourses are an inescapable dimension of institutional change (Schmidt, 2002; Blyth, 2002). Discursive institutionalism covers a vast range of works in political science and sociology, which place emphasis on the substantive content of ideas and their interactive processes in the study of institutional change in society and politics (Schmidt, 2010). Core to the understanding of discursive institutionalism is the view that discourses have two interrelated dimensions: a coordinative dimension and a communicative dimension (Schmidt, 2003; 2008). In the coordinative dimension, policy ideas are constructed by a wide range of actors, such as "epistemic communities" (Haas, 1992), or "advocacy coalitions" (Sabatier & Jenkins-

Smith, 1999). In the communicative dimension, discourses are used by a wide range of actors to bring ideas to the public for deliberation and legitimation, in "policy forums" of "informed publics" (Schön & Rein, 1994) or wider public debates.

The process of sensemaking is intrinsically related to discursive institutionalism in that it provides the micro-foundation for the understanding of the construction of meaning. By using abstraction or replication, and by looking retrospectively or prospectively, actors engage in a process of constructing meaning out of their ambiguous context and own ambiguous experience. When looking at the agents who are engaged in the sensemaking process, our chapters provide different views. Some are top-down and elite-based sensemaking processes, whereas others are bottom-up lay-people/citizens/ workers-based processes. This is important from the point of view of understanding how sensemaking processes are related to the political coordination and communication of discourses (Schmidt, 2006, 2007). The empirical evidence in the chapters of this book tells us how.

Campbell and Pedersen's chapter provides an example of how sensemaking processes inside and across policy research organizations in a country shape the political discourse of institutional change differently. In their study, sensemaking is a process taking place in a top-down fashion, meaning that it's run by political elites, who use the sensemaking outcomes in order to coordinate the creation of ideas and discourses of change. The coordinative discourse around sensemaking from those seeking to shape how causes are articulated concentrates on a narrative of partisan impartiality through abstraction-based retrospection. Data-sharing among think tanks, for example, is a practice that seeks to provide cues for abstraction-based sensemaking during periods of uncertainty. For Campbell and Pedersen there is a clear shift in communicative discourses, between policy elites and the public, with a shift to replication as those doing the communicating seek to construct meaning in terms of expectations and notions of belonging. Another case of a top-down elite-run process feeding into coordination of discourse-formation is to be found in Borrás's chapter. In this case, small groups of expert civil servants make sense of their respective countries' science, technology, and innovation policies and their systems' strengths and weaknesses in an explicit effort (through the "open method of coordination") to coordinate the formation of ideas and discourses for a synchronized effort of simultaneous national institutional changes and policy reforms. Here the coordinative discourse is strong because of agreement on how to identify cues and create narratives about how to foster innovation, while the communicative discourse is downplayed because the public are not paying so much attention.

The chapters by Greve, Boyer, and Andersen present three different cases of sensemaking processes that are top-down. However, they contrast with the previous two cases in that they are less concerned with coordination and more with communicative discourses. This is particularly clear in Greve's study of public management reform in Denmark during the past few years. The strong path dependency that he finds in the public justification of the reforms is a strong indication that the communicative dimension of the pro-reform discourse was strongly related to a sensemaking process based in "belonging," namely based in retrospective and replication-based sensemaking about the need for reform. Moreover, for Greve, this sense of belonging is not "spin" from the policymakers in trying to convince the public of the necessity of completing reforms, but also a key element of the identity of those involved in the coordinative discourse. Boyer's chapter looks at the wider historical picture of the institutional competitiveness of the Nordic countries. Here the particularly well-developed consensus culture on democratic politics is the backbone for a process of sensemaking that binds the advancement and reform of the welfare state with the technology and innovation system. The successful communication of this narrative to the society in a well-articulated discourse is key to an understanding of the continuous adaptability of the Nordic societies and economies, and ultimately of their institutional competitiveness. In contrast with this, the communication of a discourse of non-change is a relevant counterbalance story here. Andersen's chapter is an example of a sensemaking process that feeds into the communicative discourse of non-change in the context of high unemployment levels in the current crisis.

Bottom-up processes of sensemaking by citizens, lay-people, or workers are brought forward by Seabrooke's and Kristensen's chapters. By looking at intergenerational issues of house credit, the sensemaking processes during the housing bubble were based on expectations (replication and prospective) about getting into the housing market and the role of the state in supporting institutions that provide housing. Seabrooke demonstrates how expectations differ among countries according to ease of access to credit and familial relations, which then provide an insight into generational conflicts and tensions in societies. Expectations about likely changes in policy and the market also inform coordinative discourses about how to ease tensions and not lose electorally. Kristensen's case of the prospective abstraction-based sensemaking shows how bottom-up processes of sensemaking among workers and employees induced a coordinated discourse of change that fostered an experimental reorganization of production in multinational firms. Here the notion of phantom communities (very different from Athens' original case material) provided a grounding for sensemaking among those developing search systems in a manner that fostered a narrative about how institutional change occurs through recursive learning.

Having seen the findings of these empirical cases of sensemaking, and communicative and coordinative discourses, we might need to re-examine one of the key aspects of our current analytical framework. In our framework, sensemaking is the process of meaning construction that results in a series of narratives, which in turn constitutes the backbone of idea and discourse formation. In a way this view tends to suggest a kind of a linear move from sensemaking to discourse formation, and to discourse coordination and communication. This might be a bit problematic, as it implies a very direct organization of time and location of sensemaking in a sequence that goes invariably from one to the next. However, the scholars of institutional change in comparative political economy have extensively shown that sometimes that timeline is not entirely evident. Discourses of institutional change are politically communicated and sensemaking narratives justify changes that are defined ex-post. We might not expect a systematic linear-time process between sensemaking and discourse coordination/communication. The same happens with the location of agency promoting (or preventing) institutional change. We cannot assume that the sensemaking and discourse for change is initiated at the top of a society (from the socio-political and economic elites) and its discourse is communicated and coordinated to the society thereafter. Several case studies indicate that the agents of change might be making sense of their institutional competitiveness from their own position, giving rise to potential for "everyday politics" to matter (Hobson & Seabrooke, 2007). Of course, sometimes narratives that are successfully conveyed into coordinated and communicated discourses of political action require agents to have their own organizational capacities (Borrás, 2011). In other words, a strong civil society, requires resourceful leaders and citizens who are able to advance institutional change by making sense of their own situations.

9.5 THE FUTURE RESEARCH AGENDA

This volume suggests that sensemaking is the micro-foundation for the formation of ideas and discourses, and their (successful) political coordination and communication in contexts of institutional change. Sensemaking is invariably embedded in the ambiguity of the agents' own past experience and of the particular institutional context where those agents are embedded. We have also argued that sensemaking is essentially a process by which agents of change construct meaning around the competitive advantage (or lack thereof) of some specific national institutions. Seen this way, sensemaking is a process creating meaning by identifying the sources of national/regional/local institutional competitiveness. This concluding chapter has examined how this analytical approach to sensemaking links with three wider theoretical contexts, namely to theories of institutional change and ideas in a general sense, to the politics of certain content ideas (such as neoliberalism), and to the theoretical framework of discursive institutionalism in particular. There are, however, a series of items for a future research agenda in this field. Two specific items seem to surface in this regard. First is the role of agency in theories of institutional change and, in particular, theories of discursive institutionalism. Second are the possible relationships between our four ideal types of sense-making and how they can be linked to other theoretical axioms of governance and politics.

The sensemaking approach aims at bringing to the foreground the role of agency in discursive institutionalism and other epistemic-based theories of political and social change. We can identify the top-down or bottom-up dynamics of sensemaking, according to how power is distributed among agents and who has claims to authority within coordinative and communicative discourses. This top-down and bottom-up view is useful to identify whether the agents who are making sense are socio-political and economic elites, or whether they are lay citizens, workers, or families. This separation might be useful to identify the origin of the agency that drives institutional change, but may also be a bit too simplistic a distinction given the multilayer and complex nature of our advanced capitalist societies. Other agencies such as professionals, experts, activists, or trade union representatives might be difficult to classify, and/or might be taking part in elite and lay-citizens' processes at once. The agenda for future research in this area might consider a careful examination of who can make claims to "know well" and have superior knowledge and ideas in sensemaking processes, as well as the dynamics of cross-group sensemaking processes cutting across analytically relevant distinctions (Seabrooke & Tsingou, 2014b). Such an agenda will not only serve to fine-tune the theoretical assumptions regarding the agency of change, but also to conduct solid cross-national comparative empirical analysis determining the origins of agency in different contexts. Such comparative studies might help identifying generalizable patterns in sensemaking and how various combinations of abstraction and replication, and prospective and retrospective orientations vary in different societies. These future studies might serve to provide answers to questions such as: under what conditions are top-down patterns of sensemaking in processes of institutional change successful? When and how are top-down and bottom-up sensemaking reinforcing each other in sensemaking processes prior/during/after substantive institutional change?

The second open issue for a future research agenda has to do with the theoretical connections between each of our four sensemaking ideal types and existing theories in the areas of sociology and political sciences more generally, and beyond institutionalism. Our search systems' ideal type of sensemaking that is prospective and abstraction-based can be strongly related to the literature on "governance," particularly the one related to new modes of governance (Borrás & Radaelli, 2014) and to views on experimentalism (Sabel & Zeitlin, 2008). For its part, our ideal model of sensemaking by "expectations" (which is prospective and replication-based) can be strongly linked to current theoretical work on "everyday politics" that cuts across political economy and economic sociology (Hobson & Seabrooke, 2007). Likewise, the ideal type of sensemaking by "belonging" (retrospective and replication-based) is strongly related to studies of path dependence in institutional change, particularly those focusing on ideational content of that path dependency (Pierson, 2000). Last but not least, "causal analysis" as our fourth ideal type of sensemaking (retrospective and abstraction-based) can be associated with the literature on policy learning (Dunlop & Radaelli, 2013).

A new research agenda focusing on how agents of change engage in sensemaking, the politics of ideas, and how they are placed in coordinative and communicative discourses will tell us a great deal more about the sources of national institutional competitiveness. It will tell us, in particular, about institutional replication and regeneration in institutional change rather than focus on continuity. This is particularly relevant in the current context of deep socioeconomic crisis in Europe and the US. The ability to understand when and how institutional change happens is a key element in our need to decipher the trends and dynamics of our societies. We hope the analytical framework developed in this book, together with the rich and detailed cases examined in the empirical chapters, makes a step forward in this endeavor.

Bibliography

Aagaard, K. & Mejlgaard, N. (eds) (2012) *Dansk forskningspolitik efter årtusindskiftet*. Aarhus: Aarhus Universitetsforlag.

Aagaard, K. & Ravn, T. (2012) Forskningsrådssystemet: Tilføjelser og forskydninger. In Aagaard, K. & Mejlgaard, N. (eds). *Dansk forskningspolitik efter årtusindskiftet*. Aarhus: Aarhus Universitetsforlag. pp. 159–93.

Abrahamson, P. (2008) Welfare Reform: Renewal or Deviation. In Campbell, J. L., et al. (eds). *National Identity and the Varieties of Capitalism. The Danish Experience*. Copenhagen: DJØF. pp. 356–74.

Abramson, P. R. & Inglehart, R. (1992) Generational Replacement and Value Change in Eight West European Societies. *British Journal of Political Science*. 22 (2). pp. 183–228.

Academie des Sciences (2010) *Rapport du groupe de travail sur la loi 99–587 du 12 julliet 1999 innovation et recherche*. Paris: Academie des sciences.

ACAS (2010) "Riding Out the Storm: Managing Conflict in Recession and Beyond", ACAS Policy Discussion Papers, London, March 10.

Aiello, G. & Pariante, C. M. (2013) Citizen, Interrupted: The 2011 English Riots from the Psychosocial Perspective. *Epidemiology and Psychiatric Sciences*. 22 (1). pp. 75–9.

Amable, B. (2004a) Reforming Europe: Is the Third Way the Only Way? *Prisme 3*. Paris: Centre cournot pour l'economie.

Amable, B. (2004b) *The Diversity of Modern Capitalisms*. Oxford: Oxford University Press.

Andersson, J. (2009) *The Library and the Workshop*. Palo Alto: Stanford University Press.

Andress, H. J. C. & Hein, T. (2001) Four Worlds of Welfare State Attitudes? A Comparison of Germany, Norway and the United States. *European Sociological Review*. 17 (4). pp. 337–56.

Andrews, M. (2010) Good Government Means Different Things in Different Countries. *Governance*. 23 (1). pp. 7–35.

Ansell, C. K. (2011) *Pragmatist Democracy. Evolutionary Learning as Public Philosophy*. Oxford: Oxford University Press.

Artus, P. (2009) Emprunt d'Etat Français: priorités stratégiques & opportunités d'investissement. *Flash Economie*. 549, 16 décembre. Paris: Natixis.

Athens, L. (2007) Radical Interactionism: Going Beyond Mead. *Journal for the Theory of Social Behavior*. 37 (2). pp. 137–65.

Barzelay, M. (2001) *The New Public Management*. Berkeley: University of California Press.

Barzelay, M. & Gallego, R. (2006) From New Institutionalism to Institutional Processualism: Advancing Knowledge about Public Management. *Governance*. 19 (4). pp. 531–57.

Barzelay, M. & Gallego, R. (eds) (2010) Symposium on the Comparative Historical Analysis of Public Management Policy Cycles in France, Italy and Spain: Symposium Conclusion. *Governance.* 23 (2). pp. 297–307.

Bassanini, A., Scarpetta, S., & Visco, I. (2000) Knowledge, Technology and Economic Growth: Recent Evidence from OECD Countries. Mimeograph OECD Economic Department. Prepared for the 150th Anniversary of the National Bank of Belgium How to Promote Economic Growth in the Euro Area. Brussels, May 11–12.

Becker, H. (2000) Discontinuous Change and Generational Contracts. In Arber, S. & Attias-donfut, C. (eds) (2000) *The Myth of Generation Conflict.* London: Routledge. pp. 114–32.

Berger, S. & Dore, R. (1996) *National Diversity and Global Capitalism.* Ithaca: Cornell University Press.

Bertelsmann Stiftung (2013) *Intergenerational Justice in Ageing Societies: A Cross-National Comparison of 29 OECD Countries.* Gütersloh. Bertelsmann Stiftung.

Bendix, R. (1984) *Force, Fate and Freedom.* London: University of California Press.

Bentzon, K-H. (ed.) (1988) *Fra vækst til omstilling.* Copenhagen: Nyt fra samfundsvidenskaberne.

Bitard, P., Edquist, C., et al. (2008) Reconsidering the Paradox of High R&D Input and Low Innovation: Sweden. In Edquist, C. & Hommen, L. (eds). *Small Country Innovation Systems. Globalization, Change and Policy in Asia and Europe.* Cheltenham: Edward Elgar. pp. 237–80.

Blyth, M. (2002) *Great Transformations: Economic Ideas and Institutional Change in the Twentieth Century.* Cambridge: Cambridge University Press.

Blyth, M. (2003) Same as it Never was? Typology and Temporality in the Varieties of Capitalism. *Comparative European Politics.* 1 (2). pp. 215–25.

Blyth, M. (2006) Great Punctuations: Prediction, Randomness, and the Evolution of comparative political science. *American Political Science Review.* 100 (4). pp. 493–8.

Borrás, S. (2009a) The Politics of the Lisbon Strategy: The Changing Role of the Commission. *West European Politics.* 32 (1). pp. 97–118.

Borrás, S. (2009b) The Widening and Deepening of Innovation Policy: What Conditions Provide for Effective Governance? *CIRCLE Electronic Working Paper Series.* Lund: CIRCLE, Lund University. 2. p. 28.

Borrás, S. (2011) Policy Learning and Organizational Capacities in Innovation Policies. *Science and Public Policy.* 38 (9). pp. 725–34.

Borrás, S. & Radaelli, C. M. (2011) The Politics of Governance Architectures: Creation, Change and Effects of the EU Lisbon Strategy. *Journal of European Public Policy.* 18 (4). pp. 461–82.

Borrás, S. & Radaelli, C. M. (2014) The Transformation of EU Governance, The Open Method of Coordination, and the Economic Crisis. In Rodrigues, M. J. (ed.). *The Eurozone Crisis and the Transformations of EU Governance.* Aldershot: Ashgate.

Boudon, R. (2001) *The Origins of Values.* Somerset: Transaction.

Bourdieu, P. (1990) *In Other Words: Towards a Reflexive Sociology.* Stanford: Stanford University Press.

Boyer, R. (2000) The French Welfare: An Institutional and Historical Analysis in European Perspective. *Couverture Orange CEPREMAP* 2000–7.

Boyer, R. (2001) The Diversity and Future of Capitalisms: A régulationnist Analysis. In Hodgson, G. M., Itoh, M., & Yokokawa, N. (eds). *Capitalism in Evolution: Global Contentions—East and West.* Cheltenham: Edward Elgar. pp. 100–21.

Boyer, R. (2004) New Growth Regimes, but Still Institutional Diversity. *Socio-Economic Review.* 2 (1). pp. 1–32.

Boyer, R. (2006) La flexicurité danoise: quels enseignements pour la France? *Opuscule Cepremap 2—May.*

Boyer, R. (2008) Democracy and Social Democracy facing Contemporary Capitalism: A "régulationist" Approach. *WP-PSE 2008-36.*

Boyer, R. (2012) The Welfare-Innovation Institutional Complementarity: Making Sense of Scandinavian History. *Mimepograph Institut des Amériques.*

Bresser-Pereira, L. C. (2004) *Democracy and Public Management Reform.* Oxford: Oxford University Press.

Brown, A. D., Stacey, P., & Nandhakumar, J. (2008) Making Sense of Sensemaking Narratives. *Human Relations.* 61 (8). pp. 1035–62.

Burke, T., Stone, M., & Ralston, L. (2011) The Residual Income Method: a New Lens on Housing Affordability and Market Behaviour. AHURI Final Report no. 176, Australian Housing and Urban Research Institute.

Campbell, J. L. (2002) Ideas, Politics and Public Policy. *Annual Review of Sociology.* 28 (1). pp. 21–38.

Campbell, J. L. (2004) *Institutional Change and Globalization.* Princeton: Princeton University Press.

Campbell, J. L. & Hall, J. A. (2009) National Identity and the Political Economy of Small States. *Review of International Political Economy.* 16 (4). pp. 547–72.

Campbell, J. L., Hall, J., & Pedersen, O. K. (2008) *National Identity and the Varieties of Capitalism. The Danish Experience.* Copenhagen: DJØF.

Campbell, J. L. & Pedersen, O. K. (eds) (2001) *The Rise of Neoliberalism and Institutional Analysis.* Princeton: Princeton University Press.

Campbell, J. L. & Pedersen, O. K. (2007) The Varieties of Capitalism and Hybrid Success: Denmark in the Global Economy. *Comparative Political Studies.* 40 (3). pp. 307–33.

Campbell, J. L. & Pedersen, O. K. (2014) *The National Origins of Policy Ideas: Knowledge Regimes in the United States, France, Germany, and Denmark.* Princeton: Princeton University Press.

Campbell, J. L., Quincy, C., Osserman, J., & Pedersen, O. K. (2013) Coding In-Depth Semi-Structured Interviews: Problems of Unitization and Inter-Coder Reliability and Agreement. *Sociological Methods Research.* 42 (3). pp. 294–320.

Carr, D. (1986) *Time, Narrative and History.* Bloomington: Indiana University Press.

Castles, F. G. (1998) The Really Big Trade-off: Home Ownership and the Welfare State in the New World and the Old. *Acta Politica.* 33 (1). pp. 5–19.

Chauvel, L. (2006) Social Generations, Life Chances and Welfare Regime Sustainability. In Culpepper, P. D., Hall, P. A., & Palier, B. (eds). *Changing France: The Politics that Markets Make.* New York: Palgrave Macmillan. pp. 150–75.

Chauvel, L. (2010) The Long-Term Destabilization of Youth, Scarring Effects, and the Future of the Welfare Regime in Post-Trente Glorieuses France. *French Politics, Culture & Society.* 28 (3). pp. 74–96.

Christensen, T. & Lægreid, P. (eds) (2011) *The Ashgate Research Companion to New Public Management.* Aldershot: Ashgate.

Christiansen, P. M. & Baggesen Klitgaard, M. (2008) *Den utænkelige reform.* Odense: Syddansk Universitetsforlag.

Christophers, B. (2013) A Monstrous Hybrid: The Political Economy of Housing in Early Twenty-First Sweden. *New Political Economy.* 18 (6). pp. 885–911.

Coglianese, G. (2009) The Transparent President? The Obama Administration and Open Government. *Governance.* 22 (4). pp. 529–44.

Corneo, G. (1995) Social Custom, Management Opposition and Trade Union Membership. *European Economic Review.* 39 (2). pp. 275–92.

Cox, R. (2001) The Social Construction of an Imperative. Why Welfare Reform Happened in Denmark and the Netherlands but Not in Germany. *World Politics.* 53 (3). pp. 463–98.

Crouch, C. (2005) *Capitalist Diversity and Change.* Oxford: Oxford University Press.

Crouch, C. & Farrell, H. (2004) Breaking the Path of Institutional Development? Alternatives to the New Determinism. *Rationality and Society.* 16 (1). pp. 5–43.

Crozier, M. (1964) *The Bureaucratic Phenomenon.* Chicago: University of Chicago Press.

Culpepper, P. D. (2003) *Creating Cooperation: How States Develop Human Capital in Europe.* Ithaca: Cornell University Press.

Czarniawska, B. (2008) *A Theory of Organizing.* Cheltenham: Edward Elgar.

Davis, G. F. (2009) *Managed by the Markets: How Finance Re-shaped America.* Oxford: Oxford University Press.

Delmestri, G. (1998) Do All Roads Lead to Rome . . . or Berlin? The Ecolution of Intra- and Inter-organizational Routines in the Machine Building Industry. *Organization Studies.* 19 (4). pp. 630–65.

Demartini, J. R. (1985) Change Agents and Generational Relationships: A Reevaluation of Mannheim's Problem of Generations. *Social Forces.* 64 (1). pp. 1–16.

Denham, A. & Stone, D. (eds) (2004) *Think Tank Traditions,* Manchester: Manchester University Press.

Dimaggio, P. & Powell, W. W. (1983) The Iron Cage Revisited: Institutional Isomorphism and Collective Rationality in Organizational Fields. *American Sociological Review.* 48 (2). pp. 147–60.

Dimaggio, P. & Powell, W. W. (1991) *The New Institutionalism in Organizational Analysis.* Chicago: University of Chicago Press.

Due, J., Madsen, J. S., Jensen, C. S., & Petersen, L. K. (1994) *The Survival of the Danish Model: A Historical Sociological Analysis of the Danish System of Collective Bargaining.* Copenhagen: DJØF.

Dunleavy, P., et al. (2006) New Public Management Is Dead. Long Live Digital Era Governance. *Journal of Public Administration Research and Theory.* 16 (3). pp. 467–97.

Dunlop, C. A. & Radaelli, C. M. (2013) Systematising Policy Learning: From Monolith to Dimensions. *Political Studies.* 61 (3). pp. 599–619.

Edmunds, J. & Turner, B. S. (2002) *Generations, Culture and Society.* Buckingham: Open University Press.

Ejersbo, N. & Greve, C. (2005) *Moderniseringen af den offentlige sector*. Copenhagen: DJØF.

Elias, N. (1996) *The Germans: Power Struggles and the Development of Habitus in the Nineteenth and Twentieth Centuries*. New York: Columbia University Press.

ERAC Expert Group (2012) *Peer-Review of the Danish Research and Innovation System: Strengthening Innovation Performance Brussels*. ERAC: European Commission.

Ergas, H. (1987) The Importance of Technology Policy. In Dasgupta, P. & Stoneman, P. (eds). *Economic Policy and Technological Performance*. Cambridge: Cambridge University Press. pp. 51–96.

Esping-Andersen, G. (1990) *The Three Worlds of Welfare Capitalism*. Princeton: Princeton University Press.

Esping-Andersen, G. (1996) *Welfare States in Transition. Social Security in the New Global Economy*. London: Sage.

Esping-Andersen, G. (1999) *Social Foundations of Postindustrial Economies*. Oxford: Oxford University Press.

Esping-Andersen, G. (2009) *The Incomplete Revolution: Adapting to Women's New Roles*. Oxford: Oxford University Press.

European Commission (2010) Short Time Working Arrangements as Response to Cyclical Fluctuations. A joint paper, prepared in collaboration by Directorate-General for Economic and Financial Affairs and Directorate-General for Employment, Social Affairs and Equal Opportunities. Brussels: European Commission.

European Foundation for the Improvement of living and Working Conditions (2007) *Fourth European Working Conditions Survey*. Dublin: European Foundation for the Improvement of Living and Working Conditions.

European Foundation for the Improvement of Living and Working Conditions (2009) *Europe in Recession: Employment Initiatives at Company and Member State Level*. Dublin: European Foundation for the Improvement of Living and Working Conditions.

European Foundation for the Improvement of Living and Working Conditions (2010) *Extending Flexicurity—The Potential of Short-time Working Schemes*. Dublin: European Foundation for the Improvement of Living and Working Conditions.

Eurostat (2010a) Newsrelease, Euroindicators. 162/2010. November 29, 2010.

Eurostat (2010b) *Newsrelease, Euroindicators*. 180/2010. November 30, 2010.

Fellman, S., Iversen, J. M., Sjögren H., & Thrue, L. (eds) (2008) *Creating Nordic Capitalism. The Business History of A Competitive Periphery*. New York: Palgrave Macmillan.

Flynn, L. (2013) Housing Costs and Family Formation: Empirical Evidence. *LIS Working Paper Series*. No. 585, Luxembourg Income Study.

Follett, M. P. (1951) *Creative Experience*. New York: Peter Smith.

Foucault, M. (1970) *The Order of Things. An Archaeology of the Human Sciences*. New York: Random House.

Frietsch, R. & Schubert, T. (2012) Public Research in Germany: Continuity and Change. In KoschAtzky, K. (ed.). *Innovation System Revisited. Experiences from 40 years of Fraunhofer ISI Research*. Karlsruhe: Fraunhofer Verlag. pp. 65–84.

Fung, K. K. & Forrest, R. (2011) Securitization, the Global Financial Crisis and Residential Capitalisms in an East Asian Context. *Housing Studies*. 26 (7–8). pp. 1231–49.

Ganzeboom, H. B. G., Treiman, D. J., & Ultee, W. C. (1991) Comparative Intergenerational Stratification Research: Three Generations and Beyond. *Annual Review of Sociology.* 17. pp. 277–302.

Gilroy, P. (2013) 1981 and 2011: From Social Democratic to Neoliberal Rioting. *South Atlantic Quarterly.* 112 (3). pp. 550–8.

Goerres, A. & Tepe, M. (2010) Age-based Self-interest, Intergenerational Solidarity and the Welfare State: A Comparative Analysis of Older People's Attitudes Towards Public Childcare in 12 OECD countries. *European Journal of Political Research.* 49 (6). pp. 818–51.

Goldfinch, S. & Wallis, J. (eds) (2009) *International Handbook of Public Management Reform.* Cheltenham: Edward Elgar.

Goodin, R. (2001) Work and Welfare: Towards a Post-Productivist Welfare Regime. *British Journal of Political Science.* 31 (1). pp. 13–39.

Goodin, R. (2011) The New Social Question: Rethinking the Welfare State. *Economics and Philosophy.* 17 (1). pp. 121–45.

Goodin, R. E., Rice, J. M., Antti Parpo, L. R. (2008) *Discretionary Time: A New Measure of Freedom.* Cambridge: Cambridge University Press.

Gornitzka, Å. (2005) *Coordinating Policies for a "Europe of Knowledge"—Emerging Practices of the "Open Method of Coordination" in Education and Research.* Oslo: ARENA.

Gourevitch, P. & Shinn, J. (2005) *Political Power and Corporate Control.* Princeton: Princeton University Press.

Green-Pedersen, C. (2002) *The Politics of Justification.* Amsterdam: Amsterdam University Press.

Greif, A. (2006) *Institutions and the Path to the Modern Economy: Lessons from Medieval Trade.* Cambridge: Cambridge University Press.

Greve, C. (2012) *Reformanalyse. Hvordan den offentlige sektor blev forandret grundlæggende i 00'erne.* Copenhagen: DJØF.

Grindle, M. S. (2011) Governance Reform. The New Analytics of Next Steps. *Governance.* 24 (3). pp. 415–18.

Gruis, V. & Nieboer, N. (2007) Government Regulation and Market Orientation in the Management of Social Housing Assets: Limitations and Opportunities for European and Australian Landlords. *European Journal of Housing Policy.* 7 (1). pp. 45–62.

Gulbrandsen, L. & Langsether, Å. (2000) Wealth Distribution Between Generations: A Source of Conflict or Cohesion? In Arber, S. & Attias-Donfut, C. (eds). *The Myth of Generation Conflict.* London: Routledge. pp. 69–87.

Gwiazda, A. (2011) The Europeanization of Flexicurity: the Lisbon Strategy's Impact on Employment Policies in Italy and Poland. *Journal of European Public Policy.* 18 (4). pp. 546–65.

Haas, P. (1992) Introduction: Epistemic Communities and International Policy Co-ordination. *International Organization.* 49 (1). pp. 1–35.

Hall, P. A. (1993) Policy Paradigms, Social Learning, and the State: The Case of Economic Policy Making in Britain. *Comparative Politics,* 25 (3). pp. 275–96.

Hall, P. A. & Soskice, D. (eds) (2001) *Varieties of Capitalism: The Institutional Foundations of Comparative Advantage.* New York: Oxford University Press.

Harada, Y. & Tohyama, H. (2011) Asian Capitalisms: Institutional Configurations and Firm Heterogeneity. In Boyer, R., Uemura, H., & Isogai, A. (eds). *Diversity and Transformations of Asian Capitalisms*. London: Routledge. pp. 243–63.

Hartley, J. (2011) Public Value through Innovation and Improvement. In Bennington, J. & Moore, M. H. (eds). *Public Value: Theory and Practice*. London: Palgrave Macmillan. pp. 171–84.

Hay, C. (2006) What's Globalization Got to Do with It? Economic Interdependence and the Future of European Welfare States. *Government and Opposition*. 41(1). pp. 1–22.

Hayek, F. (1944) *The Road to Serfdom*. London: Routledge Press.

Herrigel, G. (2010) *Manufacturing Possibilities. Creative Recomposition in the United States, Germany and Japan*. Oxford: Oxford University Press.

Herrigel, G. & Wittke, V. (2005) Varieties of Vertical Disintegration: the Global Trend toward Heterogeneous Supply Relations and the Reproduction of Difference in US and German Manufacturing. In Morgan, G., et al. (eds). *Changing Capitalisms? Internationalisation, Institutional Change and Systems of Economic Organization*. Oxford: Oxford University Press. pp. 312–51.

Heyes, J., Lewis, P., & Clark, I. (2012) Varieties of Capitalism: The State, Financialization and the Economic Crisis of 2007–? *Industrial Relations Journal*. 43 (2). pp. 222–41.

Hobson, J. M. (1997) *The Wealth of States*. Cambridge: Cambridge University Press.

Hobson, J. M. & Seabrooke, L. (eds) (2007) *Everyday Politics of the World Economy*. Cambridge: Cambridge University Press.

Hollingsworth, J. R. & Boyer, R. (1997) Coordination of Economic Actors and Social Systems of Production. In Hollingsworth, J. R. & Boyer, R. (eds). *Contemporary Capitalism: The Embeddedness of Institutions*. Cambridge: Cambridge University Press. pp. 1–48.

Hood, C. (1991) A Public Management of All Seasons? *Public Administration*. 69 (1). pp. 3–19.

Hollingsworth, J. R. & Boyer, R. (eds) *Contemporary Capitalism*. Cambridge: Cambridge University Press.

Höpner, M. & Schäfer, A. (2010) A New Phase of European Integration: Organized Capitalisms in Post-Ricardian Europe. *West European Politics*. 33 (2). pp. 344–68.

Hotho, J. J. & Pedersen, T. (2012) Institutions and International Business Research: Three Institutional Approaches and Recommendations for Future Research. In Van Tulder, R., Verbeke, A., Voinea, L. (eds). *New Policy Challenges for European Multinationals (Progress In International Business Research, Volume 7)*. Bingley: Emerald Group Publishing Limited. pp. 135–52.

Inglehart, R. (2008) Changing Values among Western Publics from 1970 to 2006. *West European Politics*. 31 (1–2). pp. 130–46.

Iversen, T. (1996) Power, Flexibility, and the Breakdown of Centralized Wage Bargaining. Denmark and Sweden in Comparative Perspective. *Comparative Politics*. 28 (4). pp. 339–436.

Jacobsen, J. K. (1995) Much Ado about Ideas: The Cognitive Factor in Economic Policy. *World Politics*. 47 (2). 283–310.

Jessop, B. (2002) *The Future of the Capitalist State*. Cambridge: Polity.

Jordana, J. & Levi-Faur, D. (2004) *The Politics of Regulation in the Age of Governance. The Politics of Regulation: Institutions and Regulatory Reforms for the Age of Governance.* London: Routledge.

Jørgensen, H. & Kongshøj, P. M. (eds) (2007) *Flexicurity and Beyond.* Copenhagen: DJØF.

Kaiser, R. & Prange, H. (2005) Missing the Lisbon Target? Multi-Level Innovation and EU Policy Coordination. *Journal of Public Policy.* 25 (2). pp. 241–63.

Karnøe, P., Kristensen, P. H., & Andersen, P. H. (eds) (1999) *Mobilizing Resources and Generating Competences.* Copenhagen: Copenhagen Business School Press.

Kaspersen, L. B. (2008) The Formation and Development of the Welfare State. In Campbell, J. L., et al. (eds). *National Identity and the Varieties of Capitalism. The Danish Experience.* Copenhagen: DJØF. pp. 99–132.

Katzenstein, P. (1985) *Small States in World Markets: Industrial Policy in Europe.* Ithaca: Cornell University Press.

Katzenstein, P. (2008) Denmark and Small States. In Campbell, J. L., et al. (eds). *National Identity and the Varieties of Capitalism. The Danish Experience.* Copenhagen: DJØF. pp. 431–40.

Kay, J. (2010) *Obliquity. Why our Goals are Best Achieved Indirectly.* London: Profile Books Ltd.

Kemeny, J. (1980) Home Ownership and Privatisation. *International Journal of Urban and Regional Research.* 4 (3). pp. 372–88.

Kemeny, J. (2005) "The Really Big Trade-Off" between Home Ownership and Welfare: Castles' Evaluation of the 1980 Thesis, and a Reformulation 25 Years on. *Housing, Theory, and Society.* 22 (2). pp. 59–75.

Kenworthy, L. (2004) *Egalitarian Capitalism.* New York: Russell Sage Foundation.

Kerkvliet, B. J. T. (2009) Everyday Politics in Peasant Societies (and Ours). *Journal of Peasant Studies.* 36 (1). pp. 227–43.

Kettl, D. F. (2005) *The Global Public Management Revolution.* Washington, DC: Brookings.

Kettl, D. F. (2009) *The Next Government of the United States. How Our Institutions Fail Us and How to Fix Them.* New York: W. W. Norton.

Kitschelt, H., Lange, P., Marks, G., & Stephens, J. D. (eds) (1999) *Continuity and Change in Contemporary Capitalism.* Cambridge: Cambridge University Press.

Kjar, I. & Seabrooke, L. (2014) Rotten Luck in International Financial Governance: Financial Corporatism in Post-crisis Banking Regimes. Mimeo: Department of Business and Politics, Copenhagen Business School.

Knudsen, T. & Rothstein, B. (1994) State Building in Scandinavia. *Comparative Politics.* 26 (2). pp. 203–20.

Kohli, M., et al. (2000) Families Apart? Intergenerational Transfers in East and West Germany. In Arber, S. & Attias-donfut, C. (eds). *The Myth of Generation Conflict.* London: Routledge. pp. 88–99.

Kohli, M., Albertini, M., & Künemund, H. (2010) How European Families Transfer Resources across Generations. Conference on Healthy Ageing and Retirement, Brussels, July 3, 2007.

Korsgaard, O. (2000) Learning and the Changing Concept of Enlightenment: Danish Adult Education over Five Centuries. *International Review of Education*. 46 (4). pp. 305–25.

Kristensen, P. H. (1989) Denmark: an Experimental Laboratory for New Industrial Models. *Entrepreneurship & Regional Development*. 1 (3). pp. 245–55.

Kristensen, P. H. (1999) Towards a New Sociology of Business Firms. *International Studies of Management & Organization*. 20 (2). pp. 94–112.

Kristensen, P. H. (2006) Business Systems in the Age of the New Economy: Denmark Facing the Challenge. In Campbell, J. L., Hall, A., & Pedersen, O. K. (eds). *National Identity and the Varieties of Capitalism. The Danish Experience*. Montreal: McGill & Queens University Press. pp. 295–320.

Kristensen, P. H. & Lilja, K. (eds) (2011) *Nordic Capitalisms and Globalization. New Forms of Economic Organization and Welfare Institutions*. Oxford: Oxford University Press.

Kristensen, P. H. & Lotz, M. (2011) Taking Teams Seriously in the Co-creation of Firms and Economic Agency. *Organization Studies*. 32 (11). pp. 1465–85.

Kristensen, P. H., Lotz, M., & Rocha, R. (2011) Denmark: Tailoring Flexicurity for Changing Roles in Global Games. In Kristensen, P. H. & Lilja, K. (eds). *Nordic Capitalisms and Globalization. New Forms of Economic Organization and Welfare Institutions*. Oxford: Oxford University Press. pp. 86–140.

Kristensen, P. H. & Morgan, G. (2012) From Institutional Change to Experimentalist Institutions. *Industrial Relations*. 51 (S1). pp. 413–37.

Kristensen, P. H. & Zeitlin, J. (2005) *Local Players in Global Games: On the Strategic Constitution of a Multinational Corporation*. Oxford: Oxford University Press.

Kvist, J. & Greve, B. (2011) Has the Nordic Welfare Model been Transformed? *Social Policy and Administration*. 45 (2). pp. 146–60.

Laperche, B. & Uzunidis, D. (2011) The Impacts of Reforms on Research and Innovation in France: Direction, Planning and Co-ordination. *Higher Education and Policy—OECD*. 23 (2). pp. 1–18.

Lennartz, C., Arundel, R., & Ronald, R. (2014) Young People and Homeownership in Europe through the Global Financial Crisis. *Working Paper Series* No. 03, Centre for Urban Studies, University of Amsterdam.

Lepori, B., van den Besselaar, P., et al. (2007) Comparing the Evolution of National Research Policies: What Patterns of Change? *Science and Public Policy*. 34 (6). pp. 372–88.

Levine, D. (1978) Conservatism and Tradition in Danish Social Welfare Legislation, 1890–1933: a Comparative View. *Comparative Studies in Society and History*. 20 (1). pp. 54–69.

Leyshon, A. & French, S. (2009) "We All Live in a Robbie Fowler House": The Geographies of the Buy to Let Market in the UK. *British Journal of Politics and International Relations*. 11 (3). pp. 438–60.

Lieberman, R. (2002) Ideas, Institutions, and Political Order: Explaining Political Change. *American Political Science Review*. 96 (4). pp. 696–712.

Lindgaard Christensen, J., Gregersen, B., et al. (2008) An NSI in Transition? Denmark. In Edquist, C. & Hommen, L. (eds). *Small Country Innovation Systems. Globalization, Change and Policy in Asia and Europe*. Cheltenham: Edward Elgar. pp. 403–41.

Lindvall, J. & Rueda, D. (2012) Insider-outsider Politics. Party Strategies and Political Behaviour in Sweden. In Emmeneger, P., et al. (eds). *The Age of Dualization.* Oxford: Oxford University Press. pp. 277–303.

Lissoni, F., Lotz, P., et al. (2009) Academic Patenting and the Professor's Privilege: Evidence on Denmark from the KEINS Database. *Science and Public Policy.* 36 (8). pp. 595–607.

Llerena, P., Matt, M., et al. (2003) The Evolution of French Research Policies and the Impacts on the Universities and Public Research Organizations. In Geuna, A., Salter, A. J., & Steinmueller, E. W. (eds). *Science and Innovation. Rethinking the Rationales for Funding and Governance.* Cheltenham: Edward Elgar. pp. 147–68.

Lorenz, E. & Valeyre, A. (2003) Organizational Change in Europe: National Models or the Diffusion of a New "One best Way"? Paper prepared for the 15th Annual Meeting on Socio-Economics LEST, Aix-en-Provence, June 26–28.

Lundvall, B. Å. (2008) *A Note on Characteristics of and Recent Trends in National Innovation Policy Strategies in Denmark, Finland and Sweden.* Aalborg: Kunnskapsdugnaden.

Lundvall, B. Å. (2011) The Changing Global Knowledge Landscape and the Financial Crisis. Presentation at the Pufendorf Institute, Lund.

Madsen, P. K. (2004) The Danish Model of "Flexicurity": Experiences and Lessons. *Transfer.* 2 (4). pp. 187–207.

Madsen, P. K. (2008) How Can it Fly? The Paradox of a Dynamic Labour Market in a Nordic Welfare State. In Campbell, J. L., Hall, P., & Pedersen, O. K. (eds). *National Identity and the Varieties of Capitalism. The Danish Experience.* Copenhagen: DJØF. pp. 321–55.

Magnusson, M., McKelvey, M., et al. (2009) The Forgotten Individuals: Attitudes and Skills in Academic Commercialization in Sweden. In McKelvey, M. & Holmén, M. (eds). *Learning to Compete in European Universities. From Social Institution to Knowledge Business.* Cheltenham: Edward Elgar. pp. 219–50.

Mahoney, J. & Thelen, K. (2010) A Theory of Gradual Institutional Change. In Mahoney, J. & Thelen, K. (eds). *Explaining Institutional Change. Ambiguity, Agency and Power.* Cambridge: Cambridge University Press. pp. 1–37.

Mailand, M. (2010) The Common European Flexicurity Principles: How a Fragile Consensus was Reached. *European Journal of Industrial Relations.* 16 (3). pp. 241–57.

Mann, M. (1986) *The Sources of Social Power, Volume 1.* Cambridge: Cambridge University Press.

Mannheim, K. (1952) The Problem of Generations. In Kecskemeni, P. (ed) *Essays on the Sociology of Knowledge.* New York: Oxford University Press, pp. 276–322.

Manow, P. (2008) Electoral Rules, Class Coalitions and Welfare State Regimes, or How to Explain Esping-Andersen with Stein Rokkan. *Socio-economic Review.* 7 (1). pp. 101–21.

March, J. (2010) *The Ambiguities of Experience.* Ithaca: Cornell University Press.

March, J. G. & Olsen, J. P. (1989) *Rediscovering Institutions: The Organizational Basis of Politics.* New York: Free Press.

Marginson, P. & Sisson, K. (2004) *European Integration and Industrial Relations— Multi-level Governance in the Making.* New York: Palgrave Macmillan.

Maurice, M., Sellier, F., & Silvestre, J- J. (1986) *The Social Foundation of Industrial Power*. Cambridge: MIT Press.

McNamara, K. R. (1998) *The Currency of Ideas: Monetary Politics in the European Union*. Ithaca: Cornell University Press.

McNutt, K. & Pal, L. (2011) Modernising Government: Mapping Global Public Policy Networks. *Governance*. 24 (3). pp. 419–38.

Mead, G. H. (1934) *Mind, Self and Society*. Chicago: The University of Chicago Press.

Mjøset, L. (2000) The Nordic Economies 1945–1980. *ARENA Working Paper*.

Mjøset, L. (2001) The Nordic Countries: a régulation Perspective on Small Countries. In Boyer, R. & Saillard, Y. (eds). *Regulation Theory. The State of Art*. London: Routledge. pp. 254–9.

Morano-Foadi, S. (2008) The Missing Piece of the Lisbon Jigsaw: Is the Open Method of Coordination Effective in Relation to the European Research Area? *European Law Journal*. 14 (5). pp. 635–54.

Morgan, G., Whitley, R., & Moen, E. (eds) (2005) *Changing Capitalisms? Internationalisation, Institutional Change and Systems of Economic Organization*. Oxford: Oxford University Press.

Mortensen, J. L. & Seabrooke, L. (2008) Housing as Social Right or Means to Wealth? Comparing the Politics of Property Booms in Australia and Denmark. *Comparative European Politics*. 6 (3). pp. 305–24.

Mortensen, J. L. & Seabrooke, L. (2009) Framing Egalitarian Politics in Property Booms and Busts: Housing as Social Right or Means to Wealth in Australia and Denmark. In Schwartz, H. M. & Seabrooke, L. (eds). *The Politics of Housing Booms and Busts*. Basingstoke: Palgrave. pp. 121–45.

Moschella, M. & Tsingou, E. (eds) (2013) *Great Expectations, Slow Transformations*. Colchester: ECPR Press.

Muller, E., Zenker, A., & Hèraud, J. -A. (2009) France: Innovation System and Innovation Policy. Fraunhofer ISI Discussion Paper No. 18,, Innovation Systems and Policy Analysis. Karlsruhe: Fraunhofer ISI.

Musgrave, R. (1986) *Public Finance in a Democratic Society. Vol II: Fiscal Doctrine, Growth and Institutions*. New York: New York University Press.

NATSEM (2008) Wherever I Lay My Debt, That's My Home: Trends in Housing Affordability and Housing Stress, 1995–96 to 2005–06. AMP/NATSEM Income and Wealth Report, 19. NATSEM, University of Canberra.

Newman, K. S. (2008) Ties that Bind: Cultural Interpretations of Delayed Adulthood in Western Europe and Japan. *Sociological Forum*. 23 (4). pp. 645–69.

North, D. C. (2005) *Understanding the Process of Economic Change*. Princeton: Princeton University Press.

Notermans, T. (2000) *Money, Markets and the State: Social Democratic Policies since 1918*. Cambridge: Cambridge University Press.

OECD (2005) *Modernising Government*. Paris: OECD.

OECD (2009) *OECD World Economic Outlook*. Paris: OECD.

OECD (2010) *Value for Money: Public Administration after "New Public Management"*. Paris: OECD.

OECD (2011a) *Open Government*. Paris: OECD.

OECD (2011b) *Society at a Glance*. Paris: OECD.

OECD (2012) *OECD Reviews of Innovation Policy: Sweden.* Paris: OECD.

Parsons, C. (2003) *A Certain Idea of Europe.* Ithaca: Cornell University Press.

Peck, J. (2001) *Workfare States.* New York: The Guilford Press.

Pedersen, O. K. (2006a) Corporatism and Beyond: The Negotiated Economy. In Campbell, J. L., Hall, J. A., & Pedersen, O. K. (eds). *National Identity and the Varieties of Capitalism. The Danish Experiment.* Montreal: McGill & Queens University Press. pp. 245–70.

Pedersen, O. K. (2006b) Denmark: An Ongoing Experiment. In Campbell, J. L., Hall, J. A., & Pedersen, O. K. (eds). *National Identity and the Varieties of Capitalism. The Danish Experiment.* Montreal: McGill & Queens University Press. pp. 453–69.

Pedersen, O. K. (2010) Institutional Competitiveness: How Nations Came to Compete. In Morgan G., Campbell, J. L., Crouch, C., Pedersen, O. K., & Whitley, R. (eds). *The Oxford Handbook of Comparative Institutional Analysis.* New York: Oxford University Press. pp. 625–58.

Pedersen, O. K. (2011) *Konkurrencestaten.* Copenhagen: Hans Reitzels Forlag.

Pedersen, O. K. & Lægreid, P. (1994) *Forvaltningspolitik i Norden.* Copenhagen: DJØF.

Peters, B. G. (2005) *Institutional Theory in Political Science: The "New Institutionalism".* London: Continuum.

Pierson, P. (2000) Increasing Returns, Path Dependence, and the Study of Politics. *The American Political Science Review.* 94 (2). pp. 251–67.

Pierson, P. (2004) *Politics in Time.* Princeton: Princeton University Press.

Pilcher, J. (1994) Mannheim's Sociology of Generations: An Undervalued Legacy. *The British Journal of Sociology.* 45 (3). pp. 481–95.

Pollitt, C. & Dan, S. (2013) Searching for Impacts in Performance-Oriented Management Reform: A Review of the European Literature. *Public Performance and Management Review* 37 (1). pp. 7–32.

Pollitt, C. & Bouckaert, G. (2011) *Public Management Reform. A Comparative Analysis: New Public Management, Governance and the Neo-Weberian State.* Oxford: Oxford University Press.

Porter, M. (1990) *The Competitive Advantage of Nations.* New York: Free Press.

Radaelli, C. M. (2000) Whither Europeanization? Concept Stretching and Substantive Change. *European Integration Online Papers.* 4 (8).

Radin, B. (2006) *Challenging the Performance Management Movement.* Washington DC: CQ Press.

Ragin, C. C. (1987) *The Comparative Method. Moving Beyond Qualitative and Quantitative Strategies.* Berkeley: University of California Press.

Ricci, D. (1993) *The Transformation of American Politics.* New Haven: Yale University Press.

Rich, A. (2004) *Think Tanks, Public Policy, and the Politics of Expertise.* New York: Cambridge University Press.

Roberts, A. (2010) *The Logic of Discipline.* Oxford: Oxford University Press.

Roberts, A. (2013) Financing Social Reproduction: The Gendered Relations of Debt and Mortgage Finance in Twenty-first-century America. *New Political Economy.* 18 (1). pp. 21–42.

Robin, S. & Schubert, T. (2012) Cooperation with Public Research Institutions and Success in Innovation: Evidence from France and Germany. *Research Policy* 42 (1). pp. 149–166.

Rodrigues, M. J. (ed.) (2009) *Europe, Globalization and the Lisbon Agenda.* Cheltenham: Edward Elgar.

Rodrigues, M. J. (ed.) (2002) *The New Knowledge Economy in Europe, A Strategy for International Competitiveness and Social Cohesion.* Cheltenham: Edward Elgar.

Rojas, M. (2005) *Sweden after the Swedish Model. From the Tutorial State to the Enabling State.* Stockholm: Timbo.

Ryder, N. B. (1965) The Cohort as a Concept in the Study of Social Change. *American Sociological Review.* 30. pp. 843–61.

Sabatier, P. A. & Jenkins-Smith, H. (1999) *The Advocacy Coalition Framework: An Assessment. Theories of the Policy Process.* Boulder: Westview Press.

Sabbagh, C. & Vanhuysse, P. (2010) Intergenerational Justice Perceptions and the Role of Welfare Regimes: A Comparative Analysis of University Students. *Administration & Society.* 42 (6). pp. 638–67.

Sabel, C. F. (1982) *Work and Politics.* Cambridge: Cambridge University Press.

Sabel, C. F. (1994) Learning by Monitoring: The Institutions of Economic Development. In Smelser, N. & Swedberg, R. (eds) *Handbook of Economic Sociology.* Princeton: Princeton University Press. pp. 231–76.

Sabel, C. F. & Zeitlin, J. (2008) Learning from Difference: The New Architecture of Experimentalist Governance in the EU. *European Law Journal.* 14 (3). pp. 271–327.

Sabel, C., Saxenian, A., Miettinen, R., Kristensen, P. H., & Hautamäki, J. (2011) Individualized Service Provision in the New Welfare State: Lessons from Special Education in Finland. *Sitra Studies.* 62.

Sachverständigenrat (2010) Chancen für einen stabilen Aufschwung. *Jahresgutachten.* 2010/11.

Schäfer, A. (2006) A New Form of Governance? Comparing the Open Method of Co-ordination to Multilateral Surveillance by the IMF and the OECD. *Journal of European Public Policy.* 13 (1). pp. 70–88.

Scharpf, F. (1999) *Governing in Europe. Effective and Democratic?* Oxford: Oxford University Press.

Schmidt, V. A. (2002) *The Futures of European Capitalism.* Oxford: Oxford University Press.

Schmidt, V. A. (2003) How, Where, and When does Discourse Matter in Small States' Welfare State Adjustment? *New Political Economy.* 8 (1). pp. 127–46.

Schmidt, V. A. (2006) *Democracy in Europe.* Oxford: Oxford University Press.

Schmidt, V. A. (2007) Trapped by their Ideas: French Élites' Discourses of European Integration and Globalization. *Journal of European Public Policy.* 14 (7). pp. 992–1009.

Schmidt, V. A. (2008) Discursive Institutionalism: the Explanatory Power of Ideas and Discourse. *Annual Review of Political Science.* 11. pp. 303–26.

Schmidt, V. A. (2010) Taking Ideas and Discourse Seriously: Explaining Change through Discursive Institutionalism as the Fourth New Institutionalism? *European Political Science Review.* 2 (1). pp. 1–25.

Schmidt, V. A. & Thatcher, M. (eds) (2013) *Resilient Liberalism in Europe's Political Economy.* Cambridge: Cambridge University Press.

Schnyder, G. (2012) Like a Phoenix from the Ashes? Reassessing the Transformation of the Swedish Political Economy Since the 1970s. *Journal of European Public Policy* 19 (8). pp. 1126–45.

Schön, D. A. & Rein, M. A. (1994) *Frame Reflection.* New York: Basic Books.

Schwartz, H. M. (2009) *Subprime Nation: American Power, Global Capital, and the Housing Bubble.* Ithaca: Cornell University Press.

Schwartz, H. M. & Seabrooke, L. (2008) Varieties of Residential Capitalism in the International Political Economy: Old Welfare States and the New Politics of Housing. *Comparative European Politics.* 6 (3). pp. 237–61.

Schwartz, H. M. & Seabrooke, L. (eds) (2009) *The Politics of Housing Booms and Busts.* Basingstoke: Palgrave.

Seabrooke, L. (2001) *U. S. Power in International Finance.* Basingstoke: Palgrave Macmillan.

Seabrooke, L. (2006) *The Social Sources of Financial Power.* Ithaca: Cornell University Press.

Seabrooke, L. (2007a) The Everyday Social Sources of Economic Crises: From "Great Frustrations" to "Great Revelations" in Interwar Britain. *International Studies Quarterly.* 51 (4). pp. 795–810.

Seabrooke, L. (2007b) Varieties of Economic Constructivism in Political Economy: Uncertain Times Call for Disparate Measures. *Review of International Political Economy.* 14 (2). pp. 371–85.

Seabrooke, L. (2010) What Do I Get? The Everyday Politics of Expectations and the Subprime Crisis. *New Political Economy.* 15 (1). pp. 49–68.

Seabrooke, L. (2011) Everyday Politics and Generational Conflicts in the World Economy. *International Political Sociology.* 5 (4). pp. 456–9.

Seabrooke, L. (2012) The Everyday Politics of Homespun Capital: Economic Patriotism in Housing Credit Systems. *Journal of European Public Policy.* 19 (3). pp. 358–72.

Seabrooke, L. (2014) Identity Switching from Transnational Professionals, *International Political Sociology.* 8 (3). pp. 334–6.

Seabrooke, L. & Tsingou, E. (2014a) Professional Emergence on Transnational Issues: Linked Ecologies on Demographic Change. *Journal of Professions and Organization* 1 doi: 10.1093/jpo/jou006.

Seabrooke, L. & Tsingou, E.(2014b) Distinctions, Affiliations, and Professional Knowledge in Financial Reform Expert Groups. *Journal of European Public Policy* 21 (3). pp. 389–407.

Selznick, P. (1957) *Leadership in Administration. A Sociological Interpretation.* Berkeley: University of California Press.

Shaw, C. & Laffan, B. (2007) *Policy Memorandum on Evaluation of OMC in Research Policy. EU Integrated Project New Modes of Governance.* Project CIT1-CT-2004–506392. European Commission, Sixth Framework Programme.

Simirenko, A. (1966) Mannheim's Generational Analysis and Acculturation. *The British Journal of Sociology.* 17 (3). pp. 292–9.

Skocpol, T. (1979) *States and Social Revolutions.* Cambridge: Cambridge University Press.

Skogstad, G. (2011) Conclusion. In Skogstad, G. (ed.). *Policy Paradigms, Transnationalism and Domestic Politics.* Toronto: University of Toronto Press.

Smith, J. A. (1991) *The Idea Brokers.* New York: Free Press. pp. 237–54.

Somers, M. & Block, F. (2005) From Poverty to Perversity: Ideas, Markets, and over 200 years of Welfare Debate. *American Sociology Review.* 70. (2). pp. 260–87.

Stanley, L. (2014) "We're Reaping what we Sowed": Everyday Crisis Narratives and Acquiescence to the Age of Austerity. *New Political Economy.* 19 (6). pp. 895–917.

Steinmo, S., Thelen, K., & Longstreth, F. (1992) (eds) *Structuring Politics.* Cambridge: Cambridge University Press.

Stephens, M. & van Steen, G. (2011) Housing Poverty and Income Poverty in England and the Netherlands. *Housing Studies.* 26 (7–8). pp. 1035–57.

Strange, S. (1998) Who are EU? Ambiguities in the Concept of Competitiveness. *Journal of Common Market Studies.* 36 (1). pp. 101–14.

Strauss, L. A. (2008) *Continual Permutations of Action.* New Brunswick: Aldine Transaction.

Streeck, W. (2009) *Re-forming Capitalism. Institutional Change in the German Economy.* Oxford: Oxford University Press.

Streeck, W. & Thelen, K. (eds) (2005a) *Beyond Continuity.* Oxford: Oxford University Press.

Streeck, W. & Thelen, K. (2005b) Introduction: Institutional Change in Advanced Political Economies. In Streeck, W. & Thelen, K. (eds). *Beyond Continuity: Institutional Change in Advanced Political Economies.* Oxford: Oxford University Press. pp. 4–39.

Sum, N.-L. & Jessop, B. (2013) *Towards a Cultural Political Economy: Putting Culture in its Place in Political Economy.* Cheltenham, UK: Edward Elgar.

Swenson, P. (1991) Bringing Capital Back in, or Social Democracy Reconsidered. *World Politics.* 43 (4). pp. 513–44.

Thelen, K. (1999) 'Historical Institutionalism in Comparative Politics', *Annual Review of Political Science* 2 (1). pp. 369–404.

Thelen, K. (2004) *How Institutions Evolve: The Political Economy of Skills in Germany, Britain, the United States and Japan.* New York: Cambridge University Press.

Thelen, K. (2009) Institutional Change in Advanced Political Economies. *British Journal of Industrial Relations.* 47 (3). pp. 471–98.

Thèves, J., Lepori, B., et al. (2007) Changing Patterns of Public Research Funding in France. *Science and Public Policy.* 34 (6). pp. 389–99.

Thorslund Granat, J., Elg, L., et al. (2005) The End of an Era? Governance of Swedish Innovation Policy. In *Governance of Innovation Systems.* Vol. 2. Case Studies in Innovation Policy. Paris: OECD. pp. 245–83.

Tranøy, B. S. (2008) Bubble, Bust and More Boom: The Political Economy of Housing in Norway. *Comparative European Politics.* 6 (3). pp. 325–45.

Traxler, F. (1995) Farewell to Labour Market Associations? Organized versus Disorganized Decentralisation as a Map for Industrial Relations. In Crouch, C. & Traxler, F. (eds). *Organized Industrial Relations in Europe: What Future?* Avebury: Aldershot. pp. 3–19.

Van der Walle, S. (2009) International Comparisons of Public Sector Performance: How to move ahead? *Public Management Review.* 11 (1). pp. 39–56.

Vanhuysse, P. (2012) Does Population Aging Drive Up Pro-Elderly Social Spending? *European Social Observatory (OSE) Research Paper Series*, No. 7, February.

Vanhuysse, P. & Goerres, A. (eds) (2012) *Ageing Populations in Post-Industrial Democracies: Comparative Studies of Policies and Politics.* Abingdon: Routledge/ECPR Studies in European Political Science.

Visser, J. & Hemerijck, A. (1997) *"A Dutch Miracle"—Job Growth, Welfare Reform and Corporatism in the Netherlands.* Amsterdam: Amsterdam University Press.

von Ledebur, S., Buenstorf, G., et al. (2012) University Patenting in Germany Before and After 2002: What Role Did the Professors' Privilege Play? *Industry and Innovation.* 19 (1). pp. 23–44.

Weber, K. & Glynn, M. A. (2006) Making Sense with Institutions: Context, Thought and Action in Karl Weick's Theory. *Organization Studies.* 27 (11). pp. 1639–60.

Weick, K. E. (1995) *Sensemaking in Organizations.* Thousand Oaks: Sage.

Weick, K. E. (2001) *Making Sense of the Organization.* Oxford: Blackwell Publishers.

Weick, K. E. (2009) *Making Sense of the Organization, Volume 2: The Impermanent Organization.* Chichester: Wiley.

Weiss, L. (1998) *The Myth of the Powerless State.* Ithaca: Cornell University Press.

White, H. (2008) *Identity and Control.* Princeton: Princeton University Press.

Whitley, R. (2007) *Business Systems and Organizational Capabilities. The Institutional Structuring of Competitive Competences.* Oxford: Oxford University Press.

Whitley, R. (2010) Changing Competition Models in Market Economies: The Effect of Internationalization, Technological Innovations, and Academic Expansion on the Conditions Supporting Dominant Economic Logics. In Morgan, G., et al. (eds). *The Oxford Handbook of Comparative Institutional Analysis.* Oxford: Oxford University Press. pp. 363–97.

Whitley, R. & Kristensen, P. H. (eds) (1996) *The Changing European Firm: Limits to Convergence.* London: Routledge.

Wilthagen, T. & Tros, F. (2004) The Concept of "Flexicurity": a New Approach to Regulating Employment and Labour Markets. *Transfer* 2 (4). pp. 166–86.

World Economic Forum (2012) The Global Competitiveness Report, 2010–2012. Geneva: World Economic Forum.

Woywode, M. (2002) Global Management Concepts and Local Adaptions: Working Groups in the French and German Car Manufacturing Industry. *Organization Studies.* 23 (4). pp. 497–524.

Yates, J., Kendig, H., & Phillips, B. (2008) Sustaining Fair Shares: the Australian Housing System and Intergenerational Sustainability. AHURI Final Report no. 111, Australian Housing and Urban Research Institute.

Zavisca, J. (2008) Property without Markets: Housing Policy and Politics in Post-Soviet Russia, 1992–2007. *Comparative European Politics.* 6 (3). pp. 365–86.

Zeitlin, J. & Herrigel, G. (eds) (2000) *Americanization and its Limits. Reworking US Technology and Management in Post-war Europe and Japan.* Oxford: Oxford University Press.

Zysman, J. S. (1994) How Institutions Create Historically Rooted Trajectories of Growth. *Industrial and Corporate Change* 3 (1). pp. 243–83.

Index